# MASTER WORKS
# OF MEXICAN ART

*from pre-columbian times*
*to the present*

Los Angeles County Museum of Art

October 1963 - January 1964

The selection of the works, as well
as the writing and editing of all texts of
the catalog, was done by
Mr. Fernando Gamboa, director
of the exhibition.
The presentation and installation of
the exhibition was planned and
arranged by director Gamboa, in
collaboration with
director Richard F. Brown,
assisted by Emeterio Guadarrama
Romero, Emeterio Guadarrama
Guevara, Jorge Guadarrama Guevara,
Hanna van der Bruggen, and
the Los Angeles County Museum staff.
The photographs for the catalog
are by Arturo García Formentí, Armando
Salas Portugal, Hermanos Mayo,
Luís Limón, Walter Reuter, Hugo
Brehme, W. Drayer,
Robert Braunmüller, Lidia Kosova
Ivanova, E. Mandl, Nicolai
Belyaevim, Oscar Savio, and the
photographic departments of
the Ethnographical museum in Vienna
and of the Peabody
Museum at Cambridge, Mass., USA.
Enlargements by Mrs. María
Teresa Méndez. The translation of
the catalog was done
by Elsa Gress, M.A., and the
artist Clifford Wright.
The catalog and its jacket was designed
by Austin Grandjean.
© Copyright 1963 by Los Angeles County
Museum of Art, USA.
Printed by S. L. Møller's Bogtrykkeri,
Copenhagen.
Printed in Denmark.

EXHIBITION SPONSORED BY

Adolfo López Mateos
*president of the United States
of Mexico*

John F. Kennedy
*president of the United States
of America*

COMMITTEE OF HONOR

Manuel Tello, *Mexican Secretary of Foreign Affairs*
Jaime Torres Bodet, *Mexican Secretary of Education*
Antonio Carrillo Flores, *Mexican Ambassador to the USA*
Thomas C. Mann, *Ambassador of the United States to Mexico*

*Los Angeles County Board of Supervisors:* Warren M. Dorn, *Chairman*
Frank G. Bonelli, Burton W. Chace, Ernest E. Debs, Kenneth Hahn,
*Chief Administrative Officer,* Lindon S. Hollinger.

# COMMITTEE OF ORGANIZATION

## In Mexico

Prof. Fernando Gamboa, *Director of the Exhibition;* Dr. Leopoldo Zea,
*Director of Cultural Relations of the Foreign Ministry of Mexico;*
Dr. Eusebio Dávalos Hurtado, *Director of the Instituto Nacional de Antropología e
Historia;* Lic. Jorge Espinosa de los Reyes, *Head Secretary of Industry and Commerce;*
Celestino Gorostiza, *Director of the Instituto Nacional de Bellas Artes.*

## In The United States

*Board of Trustees of the Los Angeles County Museum of Art.*
Edward W. Carter, *President,* Howard F. Ahmanson, David E. Bright, Sidney F. Brody,
Richard F. Brown, Justin Dart, Charles E. Ducommun, C. V. Duff,
John Jewett Garland, Mrs. Freeman Gates, Ed N. Harrison, David W. Hearst,
Roger W. Jessup, Joseph B. Koepfli, Mrs. Rudolf Liebig,
Maurice A. Machris, Charles O. Matcham, Dr. Franklin D. Murphy,
John R. Pemberton, A. Raborn Phillips, Jr., Vincent Price,
John R. Rex, William T. Sesnon, Jr., William J. Sheffler, Norton Simon,
Mrs. Kellogg Spear, Maynard Toll, Dr. Rufus B. von Kleinsmid,
Mrs. Stuart E. Weaver, Jr., Dr. M. Norvel Young.

*Staff of the Art Museum*

Richard F. Brown, *Director,* James Elliott, *Director of Fine Arts,* Robert G. Tillotson,
*Director of Business Management,* John Van MacNair, *Director of Public Services,*
William Osmun, *Senior Curator,* Ebria Feinblatt, *Curator of Prints and
Drawings,* Stefania P. Holt, *Curator of Costumes and Textiles,* Eugene I. Holt, *Assistant
Curator of Costumes and Textiles,* Henry T. Hopkins,
*Head of Museum Education,* George Kuwayama, *Curator of Oriental Art,*
Gregor Norman-Wilcox, *Curator of Decorative Arts,*
Frieda Kay Fall, *Registrar,* Larry Curry, *Research Assistant.*

This exhibition has been promoted by the DEPARTMENT FOR CULTURAL RELATIONS OF THE
MEXICAN MINISTRY FOR FOREIGN AFFAIRS and by the LOS ANGELES COUNTY MUSEUM OF ART.

# Foreword

On a lovely summer morning in 1962, while strolling toward the Pont Alexandre, revelling in all the refined beauty that makes Paris "home" to every truly civilized man, I was suddenly stunned to encounter a six-ton Olmec head on the steps of the Petit Palais. The poster told me that inside was the great exhibition of Mexican art, about which I had heard so much during the previous four years while it had been touring the major capitals of Europe: London, Moscow, Leningrad, Stockholm, Berlin, Warsaw, Vienna, among the thirteen cultural centers it had visited.

Emerging breathless some hour later, I knew that this was the exhibition that *had* to be seen in Los Angeles. Consisting of over two-thousand magnificient objects, it would be the first big and truly *complete* survey of the arts of Mexico, covering all periods, ever seen in the United States. In addition to the supreme aesthetic quality of the material, the very comprehensiveness of the exhibition proved once again that art can be more than a delight to the senses or a singular human expression; the astonishing continuity of living forms, as well as the contrasts, displayed in three-and-a-half-thousand years of Mexican art revealed to me a whole people. In what New World capital of art, more than Los Angeles, could such an exhibition be shown with greater effect? Many reasons, of course, came to mind: geographic proximity; a larger population with direct Mexican heritage than any place in the world outside Mexico itself; centuries of common historical association between California and the nation just across our southern border; an awareness and a taste for all things Mexican unmatched elsewhere; numberless private collectors, large and small, who for long had enriched their homes and lives with the fruits of this culture; dealers who, for many years, had specialized in bringing Mexican art to Los Angeles.

In spite of all this, and largely because just such an exhibition had never been in Los Angeles, there were very few people indeed who had anything near a complete knowledge or accurate conception of Mexican art and its history. Its history was an enjoyable but misty legend based upon fragmentary experience or reading and vague ideas perpetuated at art "gatherings". This exhibition could bring the legend literally into reality, turn the vague ideas into more appreciable fact, and make what had been fragmentary a whole experience.

As the result of some "detective" work by one of our museum's trustees, Mr. Sidney F. Brody, it seemed, a few months later, that there might be a chance for the exhibition to be shown at one or two places in the United States before it went home after its long European tour. I began to write letters, making them as fervent as I dared. Mexicans like things fervent, and my spark kindled the imagination of Senor Fernando Gamboa, Director of the exhibition, who by now had taken it to Rome. Soon there was a meeting at the Mexican Embassy in Washington where the gracious cooperation and help of Ambassador Antonio Carrillo Flores was forthcoming, without which the project envisioned in Paris could not have been realized.

Shortly thereafter Senor Gamboa, distinguished art historian and ambassador extraordinary for his country, came to Los Angeles. He had already lent his help to the first Mexican exhibition of any importance in the United States, organized by René d'Harnoncourt and Miguel Covarrubias at the Museum of Modern Art in 1939. Later he worked with Daniel Catton Rich on a major Posada show called "Print maker of the Mexican People" for the Art Institute of Chicago in 1943. After organizing many other exhibitions in both his country and ours, he began the planning and direction of the present exhibition, the greatest of all. And, after five years fifteen major European museums, and nine-million visitors, we sat down together and very pleasantly worked out an agreement eminently satisfactory to us both to bring the exhibition to Los Angeles. It has been a personal as well as professional, experience of great satisfaction to be associated with a man of Mr. Gamboa's caliber in such a worthwhile undertaking. Without his vision, energy, imagination, knowledge, painstaking care and thoughtfulness for others, I would not have the happy occasion to write these words.

Mr. Gamboa took our agreement to his nation's ambassador in Washington who induced to sanction our proposals. We are deeply grateful to President Adolfo Lopez Mateos and the members of his administration, especially mr. Leopoldo Zea, Director of Cultural Relations, for making this exhibition available to us. It is my honor to express these sincere thanks to the Government of Mexico on behalf of the Board of Supervisors of Los Angeles County who are listed elsewhere in these pages.

On behalf of the staff of the art museum, and for the people of Los Angeles, I express deep appreciation to the Board of Supervisors for their approval and support of such a noble and beneficial venture. Also, these sentiments are due to Mr. Lindon S. Hollinger, Chief Administrative Officer, and his staff for cooperating so deligently for the success of the exhibition.

By spring of 1963 the exhibition was in Copenhagen, the last stop in Europe, and all the details of such a vast project were beginning to press upon us: translation of the catalog into English, printing and publication, packing, shipping and installation problems. In all of these matters, we cannot thank enough the extremely willing and efficient staff of the Louisiana Museum: especially Mr. Knud W. Jensen, Director and Mrs. Kirsten Strømstad, Assistant Director. We also greatly appreciate the deligence and care with which Mrs. Elsa Gress translated the text of the catalog from the original Spanish. A key to success in all these problems has been Miss Hanna van der Bruggen, secretary to Director Gamboa. And from this time forward, our pleasant association began with Senor Emeterio Guadarrama and his staff of technicians in charge of handling the priceless material in the show.

In addition to the hundreds upon hundreds of things lent by the National Anthropological Museum in Mexico City, the exhibition contains treasures from many provincial museums that most travellers seldom see, and from a number of private collections one never sees. We could not possibly overstate our gratitude for the generousity of all those who have deprived themselves so long of their precious objects. Together with Mr. Gamboa's catalog, which is not merely a record of the collection brought together, but a handbook and text of the entire history of Mexican art, we feel the exhibition will achieve the goals envisioned for it.

RICHARD F. BROWN

# Introduction

Pre-Hispanic art, art of New Spain, modern art, folk art — these designations are more than aesthetic terminology; the periods they refer to are also stages in the formation of our national existence. The collection of sculpture, paintings, ritual objects and domestic tools, toys and ornaments which is now offered the American public represents a vertical section of Mexican life since its first beginnings until our time. We want to show, not only a number of remarkable works and objects, but also a truthful and varied picture of "Mexican man", a picture in which the native and the European heritages merge. We wish to render the original character of the Mexican art, which in its various historical periods, throughout three millenia, has always been closely connected with life. In this sense one can affirm that art has been necessary, even in its most fantastic manifestations, to the Indian creators, to the baroque artists, and to the contemporary artists.

The presence of man on American soil, where he probably came from Asia, can be traced back about 25.000 years. The oldest material vestiges suggest a stage corresponding to the ethnic groups of the earlier stone age. In central Mexico fossil remains about 11,000 years old have been found. The first inhabitans of the country were mammoth hunters. But the populations that we have been able to obtain information about lived much later: about 1,500 B.C. It is still a source of much speculation among specialists that already fully constituted societies, whose immediate antecedents we are even now unable to define, appeared at the same time. In this period the division into two zones, which remained the same in all essentials till the Spanish Conquest, took place: the northern zone, mainly populated by nomads, and the southern zone of agriculture, political organization, the great religions and the great epochs of artistic style. The latter zone covered a territory, bordering on the 23rd parallel to the north, and including Costa Rica to the south. These two zones are designated by the term Mesoamerica.

In order to facilitate an understanding of the pre-Hispanic world we have preferred a disposition that emphasizes the interrelative connections of the various styles to a purely chronological or geographical one, without disrupting the continuity of the cultures.

The map of the cultures of old Mexico is, as a matter of fact, exceptionally rich. The sites where archeological finds have been made number at least 11,000. The oldest ones are those of the so-called pre-classic cultures. In each of those we distinguish three phases of development: the agricultural or lakedwelling period; the phase in which religion originating in magic was established, and the beginning of the political and sacerdotal organization took place; and finally the third phase, in which the urban centers and the architectural entities began to take form. As far as we know at this moment, it is in the Valley of Mexico where we must seek the oldest cultural sites in Mesoamerica: El Arbolillo, Tlatilco and Zacatenco. The remains we have from these are mainly jars and modelled figurines. Life for these groups of agriculturists was dominated by fertility cults and death rites.

This formative period was followed by the rise of the first great civilization of Mexico: the La Venta or Olmec civilization, south of the Gulf of Mexico. The oldest date in Mesoamerica was found in the Olmec site Tres Zapotes. The Olmecs developed a kind of hieroglyphic writing, an arithmetical system, and a calendar. They cut monoliths weighing over 30 tons and colossal heads, the proportions and features of which are truly gigantic. The maturity of the Olmec art, which reached its peak in La Venta, can be judged from its abundance of styles. One element, like the jaws of a jaguar, may appear in the most realistic fashion, as well as in a stylized form that amounts to abstraction. On the other hand the Olmecs have left strange portraits of monsters and dwarfs, rendered with a precision worthy of an anatomist.

The Olmec culture is recognized as the parent of all the great, classic cultures, and hardly any region in Mesoamerica has escaped its influence. The civilizations along the Pacific Coast appear in the pre-classic period and continue till the Conquest. Geographically they cover a zone, stretching from the State of Sinaloa to Guerrero, comprising Nayarit, Jalisco, Colima and Michoacán. Thanks to the custom of giving the dead numerous offerings in the tombs, we possess a wealth of small sculptures that allow us to reconstruct the life of this remote time, or at least of life in the last period of the pre-classic era. Strength, simplification, movement, psychological understanding, realism — an interpretative realism — all of which makes it possible to use the term expressionistic of the style of the Pacific Coast. The works that are considered the most perfect were created by the people of Colima and by the Tarascans in the region around the mountain lakes of Michoacán.

The so-called classic period finds expression in four great religious and artistic centers: on the plateau, Teotihuacán; on the Gulf-Coast, El Tajín; in the State of Oaxaca, Monte Albán; and towards the south, the Mayan towns. They have certain features in common: the cultivation of maize, the sacred calendar, the cosmogenic and religious principles, and finally, a theocratic system. Having reached their peak of development marked by the construction of large cultural centers, these cultures entered a period of decline, the cause of which is supposed to be a kind of petrification of the dominant theocracy.

The Teotihuacán civilization was centered in the large city that gave it its name. Its influence reached towards the north to the present State of Sinaloa, and towards the south to Guatemala. Architecture, sculpture and painting flourished here with true splendor. The urban concept of the sacred city still astonishes the spectator. Its very name says it: "The place where men became gods". Here we see the artistic expression moving between two extremes: a perfect economy of means conducive to a more elaborate stylization, and a love of the play between masses and empty spaces that gives an impression of majesty. It was probably also at Teotihuacán that a very complex theology evolved based on the cult of Tlaloc, the god of Rain, and of Quetzalcóatl, the "Plumed Serpent", which was to become the foundation of the religious concepts of later ages.

Continuity within the Zapotec civilization is unbroken from 400 B.C. til A.D. 1500. Its scene was the deep valleys of the State of Oaxaca. Already in the first period the Zapotecs represented their gods in the shape of clay urns, in which the ashes of the dead were kept. Later on, between the tenth and the sixteenth century, the Zapotecs came under the influence of the Mixtecs. The Mixtecs were the great goldsmiths of the pre-Hispanic world, and their refined precious art has left its stamp on the frescoes and mosaics in stone of Mitla. Their codices and mosaics made of turquoise are also remarkable.

The civilization along the Gulf of Mexico can be divided into three phases: La Venta (the Olmecs zone) that has already been mentioned, the Huaxtec, and the Totonac zone, which found its highest expression in the sacred city of El Tajín, famous both for its sculpture and its architecture. As sculptors the Totonacs excelled in imitations in stone of the ornaments for the pelote players. The pelote game was of a ritual character. It represented the fight of the Sun against darkness. In contrast to this severe art, the Tajín culture created figurines with smiling faces, representations of the deity of dance, poetry and music as well as of the new maize. It looks as if certain religious ideas and concepts that later were to spread all over Mesoamerica, e.g. the cult of Quetzalcóatl, had their origin in the Huaxtec zone in the northern part of the country. The dominant character of Huaxtec art is the tendency to reduce sculpture to two dimensions.

The Toltecs inherited the spirit of Teotihuacán. They also built grandiose cities like Tula. After an internal crisis, perhaps due to a religious conflict, they became the victims of an invasion of barbarians, the Chichimecs, who came from the north.

In the tenth century the Toltecs penetrated into the Maya region of Yucatán. Their artistic power was expressed in the so-called "Atlantean figures", colossal caryatides of stone cubes that were put on top of each other and treated with the greatest of economy of artistic means. The pre-Hispanic world owes to the Toltecs the invention of the column. In sculpture their most moving work is Chac-Mool, the deity of Rain, germination, and thunder. Its form is obviously intended as a function of architecture, and its various faces all wear an expression of intense tension. In Yucatán this art had a decisive influence on towns like Chichén-Itzá.

The Maya civilization reached its apogee between A.D. 300 and 900. In this period were created the sacred cities and the great architecture with its crenelated walls, its stucco facades and its arches with false vaults. Stelae and altars appeared in great numbers. Hieroglyphic writing was definitely established. Astronomical and mathematical knowledge reached a high point. The fronts of the temples and the interiors of the buildings were covered with paintings and reliefs. The figurines of Jaina (the "tanagras" of Mexico) testify to a similar mastership in the plastic art. After a period of cultural decline, during which several towns were deserted, the period inspired by the Toltecs began, from A.D. 900-1200. This was the great time of Chichén-Itzá and Uxmal. In architecture, palaces now assumed a greater importance than temples. A nationalist reaction put an end to the preponderance of Toltec elements. The last attempts to revive old values, however, could recreate neither the classic nor the Toltec splendor.

The cycle of pre-Hispanic art closes with the Aztec-Mexican culture. The Aztecs, being a people of conquerors, pushed the frontiers of their Empire all the way down to Guatemala. They were great strategists and warriors, and their battles with the Spanish conquerors and the fall of their Empire assumed true tragic proportions. Splendor was replaced by misery. Almost all monuments of their great architecture were destroyed. What we have left of their works in the various arts bear witness to a genius whose abundance of symbols is dominated by a synthetic conception of form. Still, not everything is dramatic religious symbolism. Aztec sculpture also offers realistic and aesthetically independent works.

This continuity of Mesoamerican cultures, unfolding through thirty-five centuries was based on certain common features and resources which were permanent: the cultivation of maize, tomatoes, cacao, chile, calabashes, a very precise knowledge of medicinal herbs, the use of the agave for production of *pulque* (a drink made of maguey juice) and paper; the use of cotton, leather and mosaics of feathers; the consumption, by certain tribes on certain ritual occasions, of hallucination-producing drugs like peyotl and sacred mushrooms. Their social organization shows, in almost all societies of this type, a great variety right from the start; on one hand the division into clans and families, on the other a corresponding division of the various workers and artisans. The classic period is, in this connection, characterized by the predominance of the great centers of theocracy. In the historical period proper, the warrior hierarchies appear, with their military orders and different ways of life. Religion does, however, remain the common source of power sacerdotal and military. On the technical level, although metallurgy was unknown, the gold and silversmith's art was highly developed. Wheels were not used, which can be explained by the lack of draft-horses. Armaments were not particularly developed. The artistic and pre-scientific developments offer strong contrasts by their amplitude and scope: urban architecture, sculpture in the hardest materials made with simple stone implements, ceramics, stone mosaics, arts of celebration and ceremony (dance, music etc.). No less remarkable is the scientific knowledge, which was connected with religion: a calendar, writing, numbering by the position of figures based on the number twenty and the use of zero, a very advanced astronomy, books (codices) of a religious character, historical annals, geographic maps and almanachs. In the field of natural sciences we should, of course, mention, botany and the use of medicinal herbs.

The civilization of old Mexico should not, however, be reduced to the material products of their arts and technical methods alone; the vision of the world they created is just as important. This vision was religious, religion being the original source, bathing everything in its atmosphere. But the image is also naturalistic in-so-far as it is a dramatic representation of the cosmic struggle, but one nourished by very exact astronomical knowledge. The architecture of the pyramids and the disposition of the ceremonial centers, the social organization and medecine, mathematics and wars, everything was subordinated to the religious presentation of the cosmos. Running the risk of oversimplification, we might say that it derives from a conception of the world as movement; of something that is doomed to perish. The movement is cyclic; time deteriorates and is reborn every day. The idea of time is inseparable from the idea of space. And each individual time-space complex appears, vanishes, returns as the product of a world of masked deities. It is a rhythmic universe whose law is analogy, the conflict of opposites, their fusion and dispersion. The world is like "a cosmic poem, every element of which is an image that fuses with other elements and separates from them again". In this world man is not the center, but without man the world would perish. Hence the idea of the sacrifice which re-established the equilibrium between life and death, between mobility and immobility.

*1521: the encounter between the Mesoamerican world and the West.* After the Conquest and during the following three centuries the historical construction of New Spain was on the ruins of the old civilization. In art three styles follow each other; soon after the Conquest the style of the 16th century, then the baroque, and finally neo-classicism. Very soon an interplay developed between the elements imported from Europe and the talents of the native inhabitants. This was to become the destiny and sign of the colonial world that thus found an original manner of expression which cannot be confused with the European models.

The churches and monasteries of the 16th century show a combination of elements imported from the romanesque and gothic styles a well as from the Renaissance. But less than a century later, and particularly throughout the 18th century, an original plastic vocabulary develops from the Spanish forms. The christianized native spirit manifests itself. A new sensibility, a new man is born: the Mexican. Thus we find, side by side with what can be called official buildings (churches, palaces etc.) the *folk-baroque* that is the spontaneous work of peasants and artisans. The neo-classic aesthetic reaction followed, reaching Mexico rather late in the day. It dominated from the end of the 18th and throughout the 19th century. On the margin of this official art, a popular art without aesthetic or political doctrines flourished in the provinces. It is the work of anonymous painters, whose pictures are full of charm and naivete. Only three artists' names have come down from this period that is so rich in art: José María Estrada, Hermenegildo Bustos and, above all José Guadalupe Posada.

Posada is one of the most important personalities of Mexican art. He expressed himself through the graphic media, working on wood or lead, with which he illustrated leaflets and papers that were sold in the markets. In the *dance macabre* of his "calaveras" Posada revealed all the corrosive force of his humor. He is supposed to have left thousands of engravings, in which melodrama was mixed with candor and the grotesque with the marvellous.

The Mexican Revolution of 1910 was a movement of profound renewal that touched on all aspects of life and society. One of the great conquests was the revision of the past and the rediscovery of the true essence and the real possibilities of the Mexican. As far as art is concerned, a survey, however brief, must comprise both the folk art and the works of the artists, for both categories are recognized as authentic expressions of the rediscovered country.

Painting, ever since the end of the revolution, has played a very dominant role, parallel to that of the novel and of poetry. At first the mural decorations were predominant. The painters, who had vast surfaces on public buildings at their disposal, made serious efforts to express the myths and history of both Mexico and the modern world. Artists of the first generation and those who succeeded them considered in a vast vision the universe of their heritage, without forgetting the conquests art on the other side of the Atlantic had made. Seeking the solution of their aesthetic problems, they too contributed to the art of the 20th century. At the same time folk art flourished in its old soil. Its variety seems unlimited, but it is still obvious that some piece of ceramic modelled yesterday in Oaxaca or some other province is faithful to the spirit of the oldest times. This art is outside history and the styles. In this respect Mexico is eternally present.

It is this presence, in all its variations and traditions, we have wanted to evoke for the American public with these Mexican treasures. It is with the greatest pleasure that the Mexican government has accepted the invitation of the Los Angeles County Museum of Art, after an extensive tour of great success through fifteen of the most prestigeous cities of Europe: among them, Paris, London, Moscow, Leningrad, Stockholm, Vienna, West Berlin, Rome and Copenhagen. We are sure that an exhibition of this kind will contribute to a better understanding between our two peoples. Our efforts have been rewarded with the most generous aid. In Mexico they have above all been supported by Adolfo López Mateos, President of the United States of Mexico, whose approval and high protection has made this exhibition possible; Manuel Tello, Secretary of Foreign Affairs; Dr.

Jaime Torres Bodet, Secretary of Education, who generously helped us to realize our enterprise; His Excellency Antonio Carrillo Flores, Mexican ambassador to the United States of America, whose participation in the undertaking was of decisive importance, and whose warm friendship has constantly facilitated our task.

In the USA we have obtained a most generous collaboration that testifies to a flattering interest in Mexico, for which we are infinitely grateful. First and foremost from President John F. Kennedy who has graciously conceded to sponsor the exhibition and for which honor we extend our warmest thanks. We do likewise to Warren M. Dorn, Chairman, and to the other distinguished members of the Los Angeles County Board of Supervisors, for the important backing they have given the exhibition, and to Lindon S. Hollinger, Chief Administrative Officer, and his staff who have given so much attention to the various phases of the realization of our project. Thanks also to His Excellency Thomas C. Mann, U.S. ambassador to Mexico; to Edward W. Carter, President, and to each and every member of the Board of Trustees of the Los Angeles County Museum of Art for the enthusiastic support they have given the exhibition. We also want to express our warmest gratitude to Richard F. Brown, to whose direct intervention and effort we owe the realization of this cultural manifestation of American-Mexican friendship. The dynamic action of this distinguished museum director has made Los Angeles one of the most important art centers of the U.S.A. We extend our most heartfelt thanks to him who has not only received us in his museum with a friendly consideration that we appreciate, but also offered his intelligent and untiring personal support and the very valuable help of his museum staff.

We would like to thank also, as warmly as possible, Mrs. Gloria Guinness for her courteous and valuable intervention, Mrs. Concha Romero James, cultural attaché at the Mexican Embassy in Washington D.C., for her cooperative efficiency, and the Hon. Edmundo González, Mexican consul general in Los Angeles, for his excellent help and support of our work.

We must finally thank with all our heart the institutes, and the persons in charge of them, both Mexican and American, that so generously have given us access to their collections and thus made possible the creation of this exhibition: Gustavo Baz, governor of the State of Mexico; Lic. Lernando López Arías, governor of the State of Veracruz; Prof. Juan Gil Preciado, governor of the State of Jalisco; Dr. Eusebio Davalos Hurtado, director of the Instituto Nacional de Antropología e Historia; Dr. Alfonso Caso, director of the Instituto Nacional Indigenista; Dr. Ignacio Bernal Y García Pimentel, director of the Museo Nacional de Antropología; Dr. Gonzalo Aguirre Beltrán, president of the University of Veracruz; Prof. Alfonso Medellín Zenil, director of the Institute of Anthropology of the University of Veracruz; Lic. Antonio Arriaga, director of the Museo Nacional de Historia; Dr. Daniel Rubín de la Borbolla, director of the Museo de Artes e

Industrias Populares; Monseñor Moisés Ugalde, Museo de Arte Religioso, the old convent at Tepotzotlán; Museo de Antropología and Museo Regional of Guadalajara, Jalisco; Museo Regional of San Luís Potosí; Museo Regional of Morelia, Michoacán; Museo Regional of Teotihuacán, Mexico; Museo Regional of Campeche, Campeche; Instituto Nacional de Bellas Artes; Museo Nacional de Arte Moderno; Taller de Gráfica Popular; Museo de Frida Khalo; the Library of the Mexican Ministry of Finance; J. O. Brew, director of the Peabody Museum, Harvard University; Alfred Barr, Jr., and Miss Dorothy Miller of the Museum of Modern Art in New York; the San Francisco Museum of Art; Henri Marceau, director and Henri Clifford, director of painting, of the Philadelphia Museum of Art; Sherman E. Lee, director of the Cleveland Museum of Art, Ohio; the Contemporaries Gallery of New York; and John Maxon, director of the Art Institute of Chicago.

Distinguished collectors in Mexico and the United States have generously lent us works of great value: Lic. Miguel Alemán Valdés; Raúl Anguiano; Gerónimo Bertrán Cusine; Emma Sohlther de Bracho; Dr. Alvar Carrillo Gil; Hermanos Castillo of Taxco; Lic. José María Dávila; Franz Feuchtwanger; Frederick V. Field; Marte R. Gómez; Salomón Hale; Dr. M. A. Leof; Ricardo Martínez; fam. Morillo Safa; Annette Nancarrow; Dolores Olmedo de Olvera; Lic. Gonzalo Pérez Salazar; Antonio Pineda, Taxco; Lic. Emilio Portes Gil; Juan Sordo Magdaleno and his wife; Dr. Kurt Stavenhagen; Rufino and Olga Tamayo; Margarita Valladares de Orozco and her daughter Lucrecia; Francisco Zúñiga, Mexico; Nicholas Murray, New York; Mr. and Mrs. Henry C. Rogers, Beverly Hills, Cal., and Mr. and Mrs. Selwyn S. Schwartz, Chicago, Ill.

We would finally like to express our gratitude to the Louisiana Museum, Humlebæk, Denmark, and particularly to its director Knud W. Jensen, and to Mrs. Kirsten Strømstad for the help this museum has given us in coordinating the catalog, which was edited and printed in Copenhagen. We likewise acknowledge our debt of gratitude to the East Asiatic Company, Ltd., Copenhagen and the Danish maritime shipping company, for the great care and attention shown in the loading and transport of the fragile and valuable art collections from Copenhagen to Los Angeles.

Will we succeed in showing the American public the changing picture of a country that is at the same time very young and very old, and whose art has always been one of the most authentic means of expression? If the visitor, when he leaves the exhibition at the Los Angeles County Museum of Art, thinks with friendship of Mexico of the past and present, the efforts made by our country and by the California museum will not have been in vain.

FERNANDO GAMBOA
*Director of the Mexican Art Exhibition*

# CONTENTS

| | EUROPE | U.S.A. | MEXICO | PACIFIC COAST North West and West regions |
|---|---|---|---|---|
| 1500 — | Minoan and Mycenean Cultures | | Early pre-classic period | |
| 1250 — | | | | |
| 1000 — | | Slow and prolongued migrations of people from eastern Asia, across Bering straits to Alaska and dispersal throughout north America, from the period about 20.000 B.C. | Middle pre-classic period | |
| 900 — | Etruscans Archaic Greece | | | |
| 800 — | | | | |
| 700 — | | | | |
| 600 — | | | | |
| 500 — | Classic Greece and Rome | | Late pre-classic period | |
| 400 — | | | | |
| 300 — | | | | |
| 200 — | | | | |
| 100 — | | | | |
| 0 — | Roman Empire | | | |
| 100 — | | | | |
| 200 — | | Basketweavers, Arizona | Beginning of classic period | Michoacán Guanajuato Guerrero Jalisco Colima Nayarit |
| 300 — | Theodosius I | | | |
| 400 — | | Corn growing brought from Mexico | | |
| 500 — | | | Classic or theocratic period | |
| 600 — | | | | |
| 700 — | | Hohokam culture, Arizona | | |
| 800 — | Rise of European Nations | | | |
| 900 — | | Leif Ericson to America, 1000 | Post-classic period and beginning of historical period | Toltec influence |
| 1000 — | | Mimbres culture, New Mexico | | |
| 1100 — | | Height of Pueblo culture, southwest | | |
| 1200 — | | Columbus discovers America 1492 | | Tarascans |
| 1300 — | | Beginnings of historical record | Historical period | |
| 1400 — | | Rodriguez Cabrillo in California 1542 | | |
| 1500 — | The Renaissance | Jamestown colony Virginia 1607 | | |
| 1600 — | | Massachusetts Bay colony 1620 | | |
| 1700 — | | U.S. independence 1776 | | |
| 1800 — | | | | |
| 1900 — | The Industrial Revolution | | | Independance: |

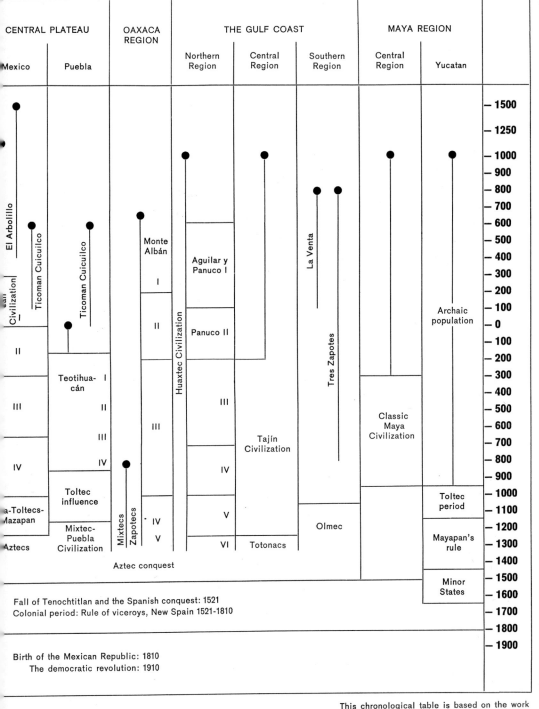

| CENTRAL PLATEAU | | OAXACA REGION | THE GULF COAST | | | MAYA REGION | | |
|---|---|---|---|---|---|---|---|---|
| Mexico | Puebla | | Northern Region | Central Region | Southern Region | Central Region | Yucatan | |

Archaic population

El Arbolillo
Ticoman Cuicuilco
Ticoman Cuicuilco

Monte Albán

I
II
III
IV

Civilization
I
II
III
IV

Teotihua- I
cán
II
III
IV

Toltec influence

a-Toltecs-Mazapan

Aztecs

Mixtec-Puebla Civilization

Mixtecs Zapotecs

IV
V

Huaxtec Civilization

Aguilar y Panuco I

Panuco II

III

IV

V

VI    Totonacs

Tajín Civilization

La Venta

Tres Zapotes

Olmec

Classic Maya Civilization

Toltec period

Mayapan's rule

Minor States

— 1500
— 1250
— 1000
— 900
— 800
— 700
— 600
— 500
— 400
— 300
— 200
— 100
— 0
— 100
— 200
— 300
— 400
— 500
— 600
— 700
— 800
— 900
— 1000
— 1100
— 1200
— 1300
— 1400
— 1500
— 1600
— 1700
— 1800
— 1900

Aztec conquest

Fall of Tenochtitlan and the Spanish conquest: 1521
Colonial period: Rule of viceroys, New Spain 1521-1810

Birth of the Mexican Republic: 1810
The democratic revolution: 1910

This chronological table is based on the work of Lothrop, G. Kutscher and Jimenez Moreno.

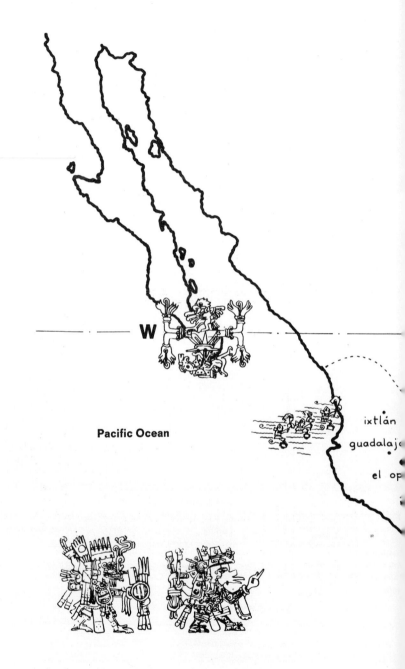

**W**

**Pacific Ocean**

ixtlán

guadalaj

el op

From: Marquina, I., "Arquitectura Prehispanica".

# THE PRINCIPAL CULTURES OF MESOAMERICA

**a** HIGH CENTRAL PLATEAU
(Mexico and Puebla)

**b** GULF COAST
(La Venta, Tajín, Huaxtec)

**c** PACIFIC COAST
(North-West and West zones)

**d** OAXACA REGION

**e** MAYA REGION

N

E

S

Gulf of Mexico

tampico
tamuín
teayo
**b**
tajín
chupícuaro
tula
teotihuacan
zintzuntzan
tenochtitlán
cempoala
atzio · calixtlahuaca · tenayuca
lima · xochicalco · cholula
**a** · tlaxcala
vera cruz
tres zapotes
la venta
**c**
tilantongo
**d**
oaxaca
palenque
monte alban
bonampak
mitla

uxmal
mayapán
chichen-itzá
cozumel
kabah
tulúm
jaina · sayil · labná
hochob
río bec
uaxactún
tikal
**e**
quirigua
copan
guatemala
· el baúl

**Key to abbreviations used in the text**

Works listed with and asterisk * are illustrated.

| Coll. | Collection | Jal. | Jalisco | S.L.P. | San Luís Potosí |
|---|---|---|---|---|---|
| Camp. | Campeche | Méx. | México | Tab. | Tabasco |
| Chis. | Chiapas | Mich. | Michoacán | Tamps. | Tamaulipas |
| D.F. | Distrito Federal | Mor. | Morelos | Tlax. | Tlaxcala |
| Gro. | Guerrero | Oax. | Oaxaca | Ver. | Veracruz |
| Gto. | Guanajuato | Pue. | Puebla | Yuc. | Yucatán |
| Hgo. | Hidalgo | | | | |

The place of origin of each work appears in parentheses, for example: (Veracruz, Ver.).
All dimensions are in inches, and height precedes width.
All works of ancient art which do not have the name of the collection indicated in the catalog listing belong to the National Anthropological Museum in Mexico City. In the section on graphics, where there is no indication of collection, the objects are the property of the National Museum of Modern Art or of the "Taller de Gráfica Popular" in Mexico City, and are so defined by the abbreviations: MNAM and TGP respectively.

# 1. Pre-Classic Cultures

*1500-100 B.C.*

*Sites*

*Pre-classic, early period* (1500-1100 B.C.) : El Arbolillo, Tlatilco and Zacatenco.

*Pre-classic, middle period* (1100-600 B.C.) : Tlatilco, Zacatenco, Atoto, Xalostoc, Copil-co, Tlapacoya and Coatepec.

*Pre-classic, late period* (600-100 B.C.) : Zacatenco, San Cristobal Ecatepec, Cerro del Tepalcate, Lomas de Becerra, Cuicuilco, Ticoman, Tetelpan, Tlapacoya, Contreras, Chi-malhuacan, Papalotla, Texcoco, Azcapotzalco, Xico, El Tepalcate, Cuanalan, Tepetla-oxtoc and Teotihuacan. All these places are situated in the area around Mexico City. Apart from the valley of Mexico there are other sites: Atlahuapan (the state of More-los) and Capula (the state of Michoacán) from the middle and late pre-classic period and Chupicuaro (the state of Guanajuato) and Santa Cruz (the state of Morelos) from early pre-classic to late pre-classic.

Knowledge of the pre-classic cultures (which are also called archaic, middle or forma-tive) is based on ceramics and small clay figures, classified according to the way in which they are made. These cultures are divided into various periods: early pre-classic, middle pre-classic and late pre-classic.

*Pre-classic, early period* (1500-1100 B.C.)

The oldest remains of cultures in Mesoamerica are found in the valley of Mexico (around Mexico City) and designated according to the places of discovery: El Arbillo, Tlatilco and Zacatenco. Life in these three places was dependent mainly on the culti-vation of corn; apart from that the population subsisted on hunting, fishing and har-vesting of fruit. Various crafts were already highly developed, but the tools found show that work, excluding the potter's work, was still only slightly specialized. The craft of weaving was only just beginning to be practiced. It was used for headgear and decora-tion for the costume of hides or plant materials that was the usual clothing.

Body and face were painted, earlobes and nose-wall were pierced so that hanging or-naments could be placed in them, and bracelets, necklaces and breast plates were used. A fertility cult, connected with agriculture, grave rituals and belief in a life after death (as manifested in the custom of placing small clay figures by the side of the dead, who were buried directly in the ground) constituted special features of life in these cultures. The potters made earthenware pots for household uses and these were mostly painted in monochrome. Decorations were carved in geometrical patterns covering the sides. The small figures were made by the so-called *pastillage* technique, i.e. by adding small lumps of clay in various shapes to the figures in order to produce details like facial fea-tures and various kinds of decorations.

*Pre-classic, middle period (1100-600 B.C.)*
This period is characterized by the transformation of several agricultural areas into more urbanized communities and the appearance of a new dominating influence from an important culture on the coast of the Gulf of Mexico, viz. the La Venta or the pre-classic Olmec culture. The settlements became more numerous, and the small communities already mentioned were increased by many more. To the products of the earlier period were added others in hitherto unknown materials, like jade, serpentine, hematite, turqoise, quartz and china-clay. Depictions of animals, like wild boars, ducks, frogs, turtles, water snakes, birds, fishes, rabbits and dogs became more frequent and testify to an increase in hunting and fishing. In this period hewing and shaping of the hard varieties of stone and production of objects of luxury was begun, while the ingenuity and skill of the ceramists increased. By barter with remoter regions, like Guerrero, Morelos and the Gulf coast, jade, sea shells, cotton, china-clay and turquoise were obtained. The art of decorating objects or adorning persons developed further at this time, and the painting of bodies and faces became more expressive and subtle. Patterns of a geometrical sort, or those inspired by nature, appeared — e.g. triangles, meanders, parallel lines, spirals. Prints of the human foot were made by special stamps, in black, red, yellow and white. The personal ornaments are particularly brilliant: breastplates, mosaics and masks. Teeth were filed and deformation of the skull was practiced. In Tlatilco where the cultural progress is obvious, the small clay figurines were put to distinguished use in the representation of individuals and scenes from daily life. There is a peculiar uniformity in these representations that have told us much of customs and social conditions in these societies. Religion was based on magic and comprised fertility rites. There were already rites in connection with astronomical phenomena and one deity symbolised water and agricultural work — a kind of heavenly dragon whose head was adorned with a comb. After the arrival of the Olmecs the attributes of the jaguar were added to this deity. Towards the end of the period we find a forerunner of the fire god. In Tlatilco a hunchbacked figure was made, the head of which served as a kind of vessel or brazier.

Ceramics show various local characteristics rather different from the black, cruder Olmec forms. The Olmec influence, however, resulted in vessels and containers with handles, in the shape of stirrups, vessels of a zoömorphic and anthropomorphic character, carved or engraved decorations and even the beginning of painting in the fresco manner. Certain types of decoration, which have been found on real clay sculptures combine both traditions.

*Pre-classic, late period* (600-100 B.C.)
This period is characterized by progress in the crafts and trades, specialization of work and development of the economic, political and religious organization of society. There

are numerous known localities from this period: Zacatenco, Cuicuilco, Ticoman and Teotihuacan. Some of these became early ceremonial centers of sorts with sacred and profane buildings. In times of changing climatic conditions, e.g. in periods of drought, agriculture on the terrace system was resorted to. In craftsmanlike techniques we witness the appearance of chisels of hard varieties of stone to cleave stone which is softer, (a process continued to Aztec times, which is to say throughout the whole period of Pre-Columbian people) boring tools and polishing tools of volcanic rock that could be used in the construction of buildings. From this period people dedicated to distinct vocations began to appear: magicians, priests, artists, masons, architects, astronomers, stonecutters and quarry men.

Religion was built up around the ceremonial and profane centers and the clergy. Although the wizard had not completely disappeared, he had lost all social importance and the priest had replaced him. The old god, or fire god (Huehueteotl), was always represented as an old hunchback with a brazier on his shoulder. An early representation of Tlaloc, the god of rain also appeared, represented on the neck of some vessels made of clay. The cult of the dead is manifest in the custom of placing distinguished persons in stone tombs with abundant sacrificial gifts. In ceramics the influence of the people of the West-coast of Mexico with the dominant polychrome painting is to be noted. The first temples were built and the small platforms serving as their bases acquired a certain monumentality and developed into the regular terrace-shaped bases that resemble truncated pyramids. Among these new constructions the pyramid at Tlapacoya in the state of Mexico stands out, its structure being a forerunner of the Sun Pyramid at Teotihuacan.

### 1-101. Female and male figurines*

Old and young, thick and thin, normal and hunchbacked, standing or sitting, nude or half-dressed. Many of them are adorned with fancy, highly varied headgear, have long plaits, earrings, necklaces, etc. and are dressed in skirts or costumes that resemble those of dancers. The last ones are called "pretty ladies". Since they are neither goddesses nor portraits they may have been produced with the magical purpose of augmenting the fertility of the soil and of man. Considering the Indian belief in the power of imitations of nature, one may imagine that they represent seeds or ears of corn. They are painted on face and body in yellows, reds, whites and purples, reminiscent of the colors of maize, which was the main staple food of the Mexican people. Some of the figures carry children, dance, cry, play with dogs, others represent acrobats, dancers, ball-players, wizards or chimeras. Others again have two heads, which seems to indicate the idea of twins, the symbol of the double fruit, or the principle of duality which is one of the roots of Mexican religious philosophy. All the figures are found among tomb offerings. They are made in terracotta, modelled in a technique known as pastillage. The largest of the figures measures $7^7/8 \times 3^7/8''$, the smallest $2^3/8 \times 7/8''$.

Pre-classic cultures: El Arbolillo 1500-600 B.C.; Zacatenco: 1100-600 B.C.; Tlatilco, which is divided into three periods, early period 1250-1000 B.C., middle period 1000-800 B.C., and late period 800-600 B.C. (The majority of the

Female and male figurines. Terracotta. Preclassic. Cat. 1-101.

Female and male figurines. Terracotta. Preclassic. Cat. 1-101.

Female and male figurines. Terracotta. Preclassic. Cat. 1-101.

Jar, shaped like an acrobat. Terracotta. Preclassic. Cat. 133.

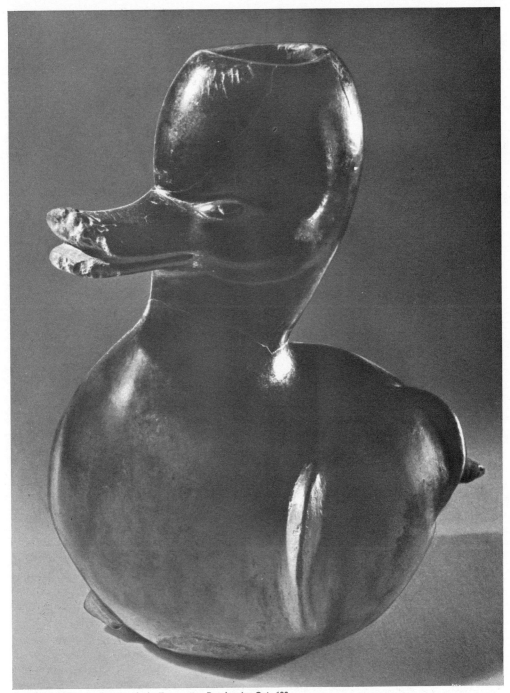

Jar, shaped like a swimming duck. Terracotta. Preclassic. Cat. 126.

figures shown belong to the middle period, when frontal representation was used and a movement, along with a certain spatial sense could be expressed, as for instance in the group of the four dancers). Collections: Museo Regional de Michoacán (the state of Michoacán), F. Feutchwanger and F. V. Field, Mexico.

**102. Sitting nude female figure**
With outstretched legs parted and very short arms; headgear in the shape of two frontlets. Hollow statuette. Terracotta with yellow and red painting. $7^1/4 \times 4^3/4''$. Tlatilco middle period: 1000-800 B.C. (Tlatilco, Mex.) Coll.: F. V. Field, Mexico.

**103. Sitting nude female figure**
Hunchbacked. Very short arms, outstretched legs parted and braided headgear. Ochre terracotta with red paint. $6^1/2 \times 4^3/4''$. Tlatilco middle period: 1000-800 B.C. (Tlatilco, Mex.).

**104. Sitting nude female figure**
High headgear; short arms and outstretched legs parted. Hollow statuette. Red polished terracotta. Tlatilco middle period: 1000-800 B.C. (Tlatilco, Mex.). Coll.: F. V. Field, Mexico.

**105. Sitting nude female figure**
The head halfway tonsured; short arms and outstretched legs apart. Hollow statuette. Red polished terracotta. $11^3/4 \times 7^1/2''$. Tlatilco middle period: 1000-800 B.C. (Tlatilco, Mex.). Coll.: F. V. Field.

**106. Standing nude female figure**
Smooth headgear with incisions. Hollow statuette. Red polished terracotta. $18^7/8 \times 7^7/8''$. Tlatilco middle period: 1000-800 B.C. (Tlatilco, Mex.). Coll.: F. V. Field, Mexico.

**107. Sitting nude female figure**
With a jar between the legs. Red polished terracotta. $10^5/8 \times 5^7/8''$. Tlatilco middle period:

1000-800 B.C. (Tlatilco, Mex.). Coll.: F. V. Field, Mexico.

**108. Nude female figurine**
With a child on her left arm. Ochre terracotta. $4^3/8 \times 2^3/4''$. Tlatilco middle period: 1000-800 B.C. (Tlatilco, Mex.). Coll.: F. Feuchtwanger, Mexico.

**109. Sitting nude female figurine**
With high headgear, short arms and outstretched legs apart. Ochre terracotta. $2 \times 1^1/8''$. Tlatilco middle period: 1000-800 B.C. (Tlatilco, Mex.). Coll.: F. Feuchtwanger, Mexico.

**110. Nude female figure**
Large headgear, carved with geometrical pattern. Hollow statuette. Ochre terracotta with decorations in red, yellow and white. $18^1/2 \times 8^5/8''$. Tlatilco middle period: 1000-800 B.C. (Tlatilco, Mex.). Coll.: F. V. Field, Mexico.

**111. Amphora**
In the shape of sitting woman, with outstretched legs apart and very short arms. Ochre terracotta, painted in yellow and red. $9 \times 4^3/4''$. Tlatilco middle period: 1000-800 B.C. (Tlatilco, Mex.). Coll.: F. V. Field, Mexico.

**112. Sitting bearded male figure**
With one hand on knee, the other under the chin, possibly a representation of Huehueteotl, the god of the first fire. Ochre terracotta. $12^5/8 \times 5^7/8''$. Tlatilco middle period: 1000-800 B.C. (Tlatilco, Mex.). F. Feuchtwanger, Mexico.

**113-117. Round masks**
Ochre terracotta with red and yellow paint. $5 \times 5^1/8''$ to $4 \times 5^1/8''$. Tlatilco middle period: 1000-800 B.C. (Tlatilco, Mex.). Coll.: F. V. Field, Mexico.

**118-120. Flutes**
Anthropo-zoömorphic. Representing dogs with human heads. Ochre terracotta. $4^1/2 \times 2^3/8''$.

Tlatilco middle period: 1000-800 B.C. (Tlatilco, Mex.). Coll.: F. V. Field and F. Feuchtwanger, Mexico.

### 121-124. Cylindrical stamps
With representations of plants and animals. Ochre terracotta. $3^1/8 \times 3^1/2''$ to $1^5/8 \times 2^1/2''$. Tlatilco middle period: 1000-800 B.C. (Tlatilco, Mex.).Coll.: F. V. Field, Mexico.

### 125. Cylindrical stamp
With motifs in the shape of tiger claws. Ochre terracotta with red paint. $3^1/4 \times 3''$. Tlatilco middle period: 1000-800 B.C. (Tlatilco, Mex.). Coll.: F. Feuchtwanger, Mexico.

### 126. Jar*
Shaped like a swimming duck. Representation of magical significance. This bird was part of the Indian food and lived in the large lakes (which at this period existed at the place where Mexico-City is now situated). The fact that it was an important means of nourishment indicate some magical purpose of these zoömorphic vessels. Black polished terracotta. $8^1/4 \times 4^3/4''$. Tlatilco middle period: 1000-800 B.C. (Tlatilco, Mex.). Coll.: F. V. Field, Mexico.

### 127. Jar
Shaped like a swimming duck. Black polished terracotta. $6^1/4 \times 6^1/2''$. Tlatilco middle period: 1000-800 B.C. (Tlatilco, Mex.). Coll.: F. Feuchtwanger, Mexico.

### 128. Small jar
Shaped like small swimming duck. Black polished terracotta. $1^3/4 \times 2^3/8''$. Tlatilco middle period: 1000-800 B.C. (Tlatilco, Mex.). Coll.: F. Feuchtwanger, Mexico.

### 129. Flute
Shaped like small swimming duck with its head turned. Black polished terracotta. $1^5/8 \times 3''$. Tlatilco middle period: 1000-800 B.C. (Tlatilco, Mex.). Coll.: F. V. Field, Mexico.

### 130. Jar
Anthropomorphic. Combination of man and duck for magical purpose. Black polished terracotta. The head of the man painted in red. $10 \times 5^1/4''$. Tlatilco middle period: 1000-800 B.C. (Tlatilco, Mex.). Coll.: F. Feuchtwanger, Mexico.

### 131. Jar
With high neck in the shape of armadillo. Pattern engraved on the shell. Black terracotta. $10 \times 5^7/8''$. Tlatilco middle period: 1000-800 B.C. (Tlatilco, Mex.). Coll.: F. V. Field, Mexico.

### 132. Small vessel
Shaped like a howling dog. Black polished terracotta. $4^1/2 \times 2^3/4''$. Tlatilco middle period: 1000-800 B.C. (Tlatilco, Mex.). Coll.: F. V. Field, Mexico.

### 133. Jar*
Shaped like an acrobat, short arms; one leg is bent, so that its foot rests on the head, the other serves as the spout of the vessel. Red polished terracotta. $11^1/4 \times 6^3/4''$. Tlatilco middle period: 1000-800 B.C. (Tlatilco, Mex.). Coll.: F. V. Field, Mexico.

### 134. Jar
Shaped like a human foot. Decorated with anklet in pastillage technique representing teeth. Rer terracotta. $3^1/4 \times 3''$. Tlatilco middle period: 1000-800 B.C. (Tlatilco, Mex.). Coll.: F. Feuchtwanger, Mexico.

### 135. Jar
Shaped like a human foot. Decorated with anklet of points in pastillage technique. Red terracotta. $5 \times 3^1/2''$. Tlatilco middle period: 1000-800 B.C. (Tlatilco, Mex.). Coll.: F. V. Field, Mexico.

### 136. Jar
Shaped like a stirrup. Red polished terracotta. Decorative motifs painted in red and yellow in

a geometrical pattern. $9^1/_4 \times 7^1/_2''$. Tlatilco middle period: 1000-800 B.C. (Tlatilco, Mex.). Coll.: F. V. Field, Mexico.

**137. Jar**

In a trapeze-like shape. Black polished terracotta. With engraved pattern, representing birds and snakes. $5^7/_8 \times 5^7/_8''$. Tlatilco middle period: 1000-800 B.C. (Tlatilco, Mex.). Coll.: F. V. Field, Mexico.

**138. Bottle**

Spherical, with a long neck. Brownish terracotta. Geometrical decoration in red and whites, presumably a representation of the Sun and Moon. One of the earliest examples of the pre-occupation of the preclassic cultures with cosmic phenomena. $11 \times 7^1/_2''$. Tlatilco middle period: 1000-800 B.C. (Tlatilco, Mex.). Coll.: F. V. Field, Mexico.

**139. Bottle**

With a long neck. Brownish polished terracotta. $14^1/_8 \times 6^1/_4''$. Tlatilco middle period: 1000-800 B.C. (Tlatilco, Mex.). Coll.: F. V. Field, Mexico.

**140. Small spherical bottle**

With a long neck. Pattern engraved, representing claws of jaguar. Black polished terracotta. $4^3/_4 \times 3^1/_8''$. Tlatilco middle period: 1000-800 B.C. (Tlatilco, Mex.). Coll.: F. Feuchtwanger, Mexico.

**141. Spherical bottle**

With a long neck. Pattern engraved, representing claws of jaguar. Black polished terracotta. $8 \times 6^1/_4''$. Tlatilco middle period: 1000-800 B.C. (Tlatilco, Mex.).

**142. Small bottle**

With long neck, shaped like a rabbit. Black polished terracotta. $4^3/_4 \times 3^1/_8''$. Tlatilco middle period: 1000-800 B.C. (Tlatilco, Mex.). Coll.: F. Feuchtwanger, Mexico.

**143. Large anthropomorphic mask**

Head of an ape-like man. Black polished terracotta, with traces of red paint. $6^1/_4 \times 5^1/_8''$. Tlatilco middle period: 1000-800 B.C. (Tlatilco, Mex.). Coll.: F. V. Field, Mexico.

**144. Bottle**

With a long neck and incised pattern. Red terracotta. $13^3/_4 \times 7^1/_8''$. Pre-classic, middle period: 800-600 B.C. (Santa Cruz, Mor.). Coll.: F. Feuchtwanger, Mexico.

**145. Sitting male figure***

With long deformed head. Infantile features, hands on knees and stretched legs. Terracotta, covered with white paint. $14^1/_4 \times 8''$. Pre-classic Olmec culture, Tlatilco middle period: 800-600 B.C. (Tlatilco, Mex.). Coll.: F. Feuchtwanger, Mexico.

**146. Standing female figurine**

Nude and with deformed head. Terracotta with traces of red paint. $7^1/_8 \times 3^1/_4''$. Pre-classic Olmec culture, Tlatilco middle period: 800-600 B.C. (Tlatilco, Mex.). Coll.: F. Feuchtwanger, Mexico.

**147-149. Small spherical votive jars**

Representing the powers of the sun. Inside, remains of a color like dark tile. White terracotta very delicate and clear. $2^3/_8 \times 2^3/_8$ and $1^5/_8 \times 1^5/_8''$. Pre-classic Olmec culture, Tlatilco middle period: 800-600 B.C. (Tlatilco, Mex.). Coll.: F. Feuchtwanger, Mexico.

**150. Small bird figure**

Representing a kingfisher. Jade. $2 \times 3/_4''$. Pre-classic Olmec culture, middle and late period: 800 B.C.-A.D.100 (Tlatilco, Mex.). Coll.: F. Feuchtwanger, Mexico.

**151. Sitting female figure**

Arms and legs short, outstretched and parted. Black terracotta with red paint. $15 \times 10^1/_4''$

Pre-classic late period: 600-100 B.C. (Santa Cruz, Mor.). Coll.: M. A. Leof, Mexico.

### 152. Sitting child figure with helmet

Short arms and outstretched legs parted. Ochre terracotta. $3^7/8 \times 2^3/4''$. Pre-classic late period: 600-100 B.C. (Santa Cruz, Mor.). Coll.: F. Feuchtwanger, Mexico.

### 153. Figure

Carrying a jar with a very large head and open mouth. Ochre terracotta. $7^1/8 \times 3^1/8''$. Pre-classic late period: 600-100 B.C. (Ozumba, Mex.). Coll.: F. Feuchtwanger, Mexico.

### 154-157. Small nude female figurines

With large headdresses and very finely finished necklaces. One of the figures has two heads and is in the last stage of pregnancy. The two heads are assumed to express the wish for fertility. Terracotta with traces of red and white paint. $6^1/4 \times 2^3/4''$. Pre-classic late period (Western region): 600-100 B.C. (Querendao, Mich.). Coll.: Museo Regional de Michoacán, Morelia, Mich.

### 158. Small standing nude female figure

Head looking upwards; the headdress is indicated by diagonal incisions, perforated ear-ornaments, the left arm is bent and holds a vessel in the shape of a calabash. Ochre terracotta. $3^3/4 \times 1^3/4''$. Pre-classic late period (Western region): 600-100 B.C. (Capula, Mich.). Coll.: Museo Regional de Michoacán, Morelia, Mich.

### 159. Small sitting female figure

With naked torso. The hair is divided into two parts, long earrings and eyes like "coffee-beans". The left arm rests on the knee and the legs are crossed. Ochre terracotta with traces of white paint. $6^7/8 \times 6^3/4''$. Pre-classic late period (Western region): 600-100 B.C. (Sahuayo, Mich.). Coll.: Museo Regional de Michoacán, Morelia, Mich.

### 160. Small male figure

With belt. Has a flat body, a flower in his hair, earrings and necklace. Ochre terracotta with red and white paint. $4^5/8 \times 2^1/4''$ Pre-classic late period (Western region): 300 B.C.-A.D. 300. (Chupicuaro, Gto.).

### 161. Small sitting female figure

With a part in her hair, eyes like "coffee-beans", earrings and necklace. Ochre terracotta with traces of red and white paint. $4^3/4 \times 3^3/8''$. Pre-classic late period (Western region): 300 B.C.-A.D. 300. (Chupicuaro, Gto.). Coll.: Museo Regional de Michoacán, Morelia, Mich.

### 162. Small nude female figure

With flat body, heavy breasts, part in her hair, eyes like "coffee-beans", necklace and earrings. Ochre terracotta with traces of red and white paint. $4^3/4 \times 2^5/8''$. Pre-classic late period (Western region): 300 B.C.-A.D. 300. (Chupicuaro, Gto.).

### 163-171. Small nude female figurines

With almost flat bodies, headdresses adorned with interlaced ribbons, the faces modelled in the pastillage technique; earrings, necklaces and bracelets. Ochre terracotta with traces of red and black paint. $2^5/8 \times 1''$. Pre-classic late period (Western region): 300 B.C.-A.D. 300. (Chupicuaro, Gto.).

### 172. Bottle

Square with round opening. The neck decorated with a braid. Black polished terracotta. $5^7/8 \times 6^1/4''$. Pre-classic, late period (Western region): 300 B.C.-A.D. 300. (Chupicuaro, Gto.).

### 173. Jar

Semi-spherical, with square opening. Black terracotta with carved ornaments. $6^1/4 \times 1^3/8''$. Pre-classic late period (Western region): 300 B.C.-A.D. 300. (Chupicuaro, Gto.).

# 2. The La Venta Civilization, Olmecs

*800 B.C.-A.D. 800.*
*Sites*
*Pre-classic, middle and late periods* (800-100 B.C.): Panuco, El Trapiche, Chacaltzingo, Atlihuayan, Tlatilco, Tlapacoya (the states of Tamaulipas, Veracruz and Mexico); La Venta (the State of Tabasco); Simojovel (the State of Chiapas), Tres Zapotes, Uxpanapa and San Lorenzo Tenochitlan Texistepec (the State of Veracruz).
*Classic* (100 B.C.-A.D. 800): Tres Zapotes and Cerro de las Mesas (State of Veracruz).

The large coastal plain, stretching along the Gulf of Mexico from the center of the state of Tamaulipas to the frontiers of the states of Veracruz and Tabasco, is a veritable mosaic of cultures and civilizations. In spite of an apparent similarity due to the geographic and climatic conditions (luxurious, tropical zone), we can distinguish here between three cultural areas, each with its own artistic style and religion. They are from north to south: the Huastec culture, the El Tajín culture and the La Venta culture, or the Olmec culture. The word *olmeca* means "people from the *hule* country", i.e. the rubber country, since rubber originates from this region. This civilization is also called the La Venta culture, after the place in the state of Tabasco where the most important archaeological remains have been found. It reached its climax in the pre-classic era.

The Olmecs had a strong influence on all of Mesoamerica. Their exceptional geographical dispersion was no doubt due to a migration that took place during the middle pre-classic period (1100-600 B.C.), and, starting in the region of Panuco, took them along the Gulf and towards the interior of the country to the state of Morelos and as far as the tableland. This group, which belongs to the middle pre-classic period, created very handsome earthenware, decorated with stylized feline motifs: claws, canines and jaguar's spots. The representations of human beings are no less typical: heads that expand upwards, slanting eyes, flat or very shapely noses, more or less fat lips that pout and doubtlessly correspond to actual physical types. The first Olmecs, who put their stamp on the Tlatilco culture were divided into totem clans. Their religion, based on magic, was dominated by a feline deity connected with rain and water.

In the late pre-classic period (600-100 B.C.) Olmec civilization developed in several centers. The most important ones were La Venta-Los Tuxtlas, Morelos-Puebla-Guerrero and Oaxaca-Chiapas. They had the treatment of hard stone (serpentine, basalt, jade) in common. But La Venta stands out from the others because of its monumental sculpture, its bas reliefs, its fine statuettes in greenish blue jade, its mosaic floors, its polished axes and its production of tile, a material that was invented in La Venta. The Morelos-Guerrero region is characterized by very remarkable masks and by colossal axes with schematic human representations, while the Oaxaca-Chiapas region created a synthesis of the two styles, particularly with regard to hewn stones and to the grayish-black ce-

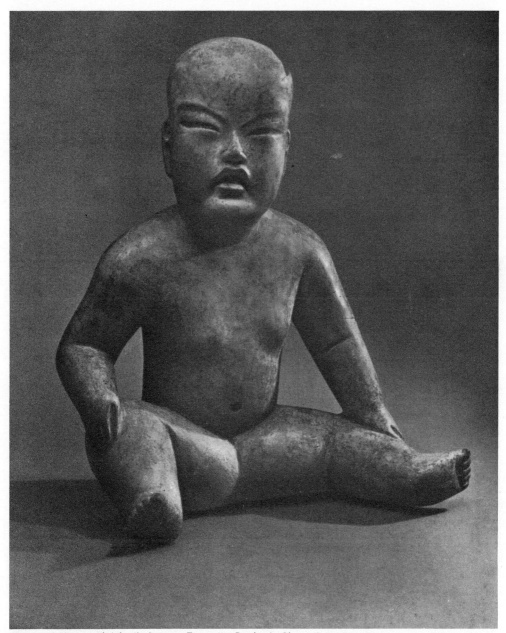

Sitting male figure with infantile features. Terracotta. Preclassic Olmec. Cat. 145.

Colossal male head. Basalt. Preclassic Olmec. Cat. 177.

Colossal male head. Basalt. Preclassic Olmec. Cat. 177.

Funeral mask. Green stone. Preclassic Olmec. Cat. 180.

Man's mask with feline features. Green stone. Preclassic Olmec. Cat. 182.

Dwarf-like child crying furiously. Greenish jade. Preclassic Olmec. Cat. 184.

Head with deformed skull and feline mouth. Jadeite. Preclassic Olmec. Cat. 210.

Offering of 16 male figures and 6 axes. Jade. Preclassic Olmec. Cat. 188-209.

Semi-ovoid breastplate with decoration of five heads. Serpentine. Preclassic Olmec. Cat. 186.

Seated smiling figurine. Jade. Preclassic Olmec. Cat. 214.

Ceremonial axe representing human figure. Jadeite. Preclassic Olmec. Cat. 226.

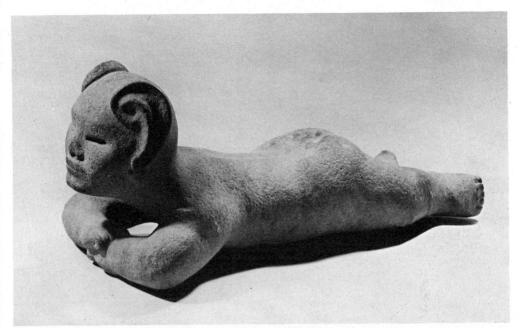

Young woman with feline features. Limestone. Preclassic Olmec. Cat. 234.

Young woman with feline features. Limestone. Preclassic Olmec. Cat. 234.

Monument shaped like a colossal mask. Basalt. Preclassic Olmec. Cat. 237.

Spherical head representing the sun. Basalt. Preclassic Olmec. Cat. 239.

ramics of the Monte Alban I period. It is assumed that it was through this region the Olmec civilization reached Guatemala and El Salvador towards the end of the late pre-classic period and the beginning of the classic period.

Although the Olmec civilization is still one of the most troubling enigmas of the Mexican past and nothing certain is known of its rise, it is now generally assumed that it is here where we find the origins of the great classic civilizations: Maya, Zapotec, El Tajín and Teotihuacán. The region in which the Olmec civilization reached its highest development is a vast alluvial plain, watered by the great rivers between Papaloapan and Grijalva. It is very warm almost all year round and the soil is extremely fertile. The richest centers of the "Olmec" world were La Venta, Tres Zapotes and San Lorenzo Tenochitlan. Almost no big buildings have been found here, a fact that can be explained by the lack of stone in the region. The sculptures, however, arouse our admiration. The Olmecs may be described as the true creators of sculpture in Mesoamerica. For the first time altars, sarcophagi, pillars, big stelæ, derivations of the stone axes, sacred tools, gigantic statues and monumental heads up to three yards high and weighing 18 tons are cut in stone with the stone axe, the sacred tool. The materials for these titanic works were obtained from sites remote from these centers. They were dragged over the beach, undoubtedly after having been shipped across the sea or by the rivers on large balsa-rafts.

The Olmec representations of human beings are almost always masculine, although generally without indication of the sex, in spite of the fact that they are nudes. They express a certain animality or ferocity, inspired by the Jaguar God. The faces are of two different kinds. The first and most common has a flat nose, thick lips, swollen eyes, strong chin and a disdainful mouth. It is a strange mixture of human and feline features. The other type has an elongated head, with an artificial, characteristic deformation, which seems to be inspired by the phallic image. It has an acquiline nose and shapely lips. The bodies are either straight and slender, or, contrariwise, squat and deformed. These two types are found, both in the monoliths and in the jade statuettes. Jade, that was to be such a valuable material among the pre-columbian peoples, came from the tropical zone.

The Olmecs seem to have ascribed great significance to deformed beings. They depicted fat children, crying frantically, or hunchbacks, or dwarfs without a lower jaw etc. Statuettes in an attentive attitude, holding their hands behind their ears and their legs slightly bent, are also found. They are all weird creatures, undoubtedly with some magical function and are the origin of the "Aztec imps", the *Tepeyolotl,* that lived in the mountains. Apart from those, we find supremely realistic figures, expressing true majesty and equipped with a smile that foreshadows the little impish heads that the later neighboring civilization of El Tajín was to produce in such numbers. The Olmecs treated jade in all its forms: as breastplates, masks, beads, little ships adorned with characters, caymans, rings etc. They liked smooth, well-polished surfaces, which they now and then provided with incisions to indicate tattoos, details of dress, ornaments or written characters.

Just as the Nahua-cultures were later to choose the eagle as their symbol, the Olmecs dedicated all their fervor of faith and all their terror to the Jaguar. It is found everywhere, as an animal and as a semi-human being. The idea of associating animals and people is, incidentally, of fundamental importance and significance in the Mesoamerican world of thought: it is a form of religious exchange which is necessary in its magical implications. Apart from the Jaguar cult, the Olmecs had a cult of fire and of the dead. Rich offerings of jade have been found in the excavations of the tombs. The colossal heads of warriors, distinguished persons or pelote-players were undoubtedly connected with cosmogenic ideas. The Olmecs were the first to represent the sun as a round human head with bristling hair symbolizing the rays and a cross in the eyes representing light. They were also the first to use the hieroglyph of the five-point cross to indicate the four corners of the world with heaven in the middle, an idea that later on was to inspire the construction of the truncated pyramids.

Olmec art is impressive by its monumentality. It combines a very strong sensuality with a will to form that is no less energetic. It is an art that is at the same time realistic and abstract.

The Olmecs worked out an alphabet of hieroglyphs, a calendar, a system of arithmetic, using points to indicate units and lines to indicate the individual numerals. We owe to them the oldest legible dates found in Mesoamerica. One of them, engraved into a small jade statuette called *estatuilla de Tuxtla,* gives the date year 162 B.C. According to carbon 14 analysis and comparison with the Maya calendar, this date should correspond to the year 97 B.C. Another date, that of the "C" stele of Tres Zapotes, should correspond to March 2, of the year 290 B.C.

After its decline the Olmec civilization lingered on for several centuries. Its artistic style which was so unique in its forcefulness and its loyalty to the material, was to have an enduring influence. A few evidences have survived from the last times of the Olmecs: their connection with the Toltecs, their migration to Central America, their expulsion from the Sanctuary of Cholula (the Puebla Valley) in the year A.D. 1168, the year that also marks the final dissolution and disappearance of their civilization.

**176. Reclining nude figure**

Probably representing an acrobat. The right arm and the lower extremities missing. Face with swollen eyes and mouth with feline lips. The jaguar (the animal called jaguar is actually an ocelot) is the most important deity of the Ol-mecs. It represents the earth. In Olmec art certain features of the jaguar, like the jaws and the fangs are very imaginatively combined with human features, thereby acquiring a symbolic character, like swollen eyelids that seem to refer to rain, just like the furrows in the cheeks. The large nose-ornaments suggest the fangs of the jaguar. These characteristics seem to be the beginning of what in later cultures was to develop into the god of rain: The Chac of the Mayas, the Tajin of the Totonacs, the Cocijo of the Zapotecs, the Tlaloc of Teotihuacan of the Mixtecs, of the Aztecs. Jadeite. $4^3/8 \times 2^1/8''$. Preclassic Olmec culture, middle and late period: 800 B.C.-A.D. 100. (Tzintzuntzan, Mich.). Coll.: Museo Regional de Michoacán, Morelia, Mich.

### 177. Colossal male head*

probably representing an earth deity, a warrior or a player of pelote, the ritual game that was connected with cosmic elements. Realistic features. Helmet of jaguar's hide with star signs. The stolid, impassive face changes its expression according to the light it receives: sometimes it is gently smiling, sometimes hard and energetic. The head is placed on a very low pedestal in the shape of a truncated pyramid. Stone was the best medium of expression in the great Mexican civilizations. The Olmecs were the first to use this material artistically. Until now 18 such heads have been found at La Venta, Tres Zapotes, Rio Chiquito (the state of Tabasco) and at San Lorenzo Tenochitlan (the state of Veracruz). To be sculptured, these enormous blocks of stone were shipped from very remote regions, around 100 km away. Basalt. $70^7/8 \times 53^1/8 \times 45^1/4''$. Pre-classic, Olmec culture, middle and late period: 800 B.C.-A.D. 100. (San Lorenzo Tenochitlan Texistepec, Ver.). Coll.: Museo de Antropología, University of Veracruz, Jalapa, Ver.

### 178. Mask

With realistic features, open mouth, sagging lower lip (the mask has been broken and was repaired in pre-Hispanic times). Green, veined Jade. $4^1/2 \times 3/8''$. Pre-classic, Olmec culture, middle and late period: 800 B.C.-A.D. 100. (unknown finding place).

### 179. Breastplate

In the shape of rectangular axe, representing a highly stylized jaguar's mask; deepset eyes, large nostrils, open mouth showing fangs. The headgear consists of bands with a smooth central piece and hanging ornaments at the sides. It is a representation of the jaguar, the old deity of the Olmecs. The material is jade, which was the highly valued emblem of the heart of the god of earth turning green under the rain, highly appreciated by the ancient peoples of Mexico. The Olmecs were the first to use it. The ancient Mexicans knew two sorts of precious stones, chalchihuitl, i.e. green serpentine, diorite and pale quartz, and "quetzaltli" that is green and luminous like the feathers of the quetzal bird, i.e. genuine jade, nephrite and rock-crystal, which is valued for its shining, translucid color. Green jade, $5^1/8 \times 4^1/4''$. Pre-classic Olmec culture, middle and late period: 800 B.C.-A.D. 100. (Veracruz, Ver.).

### 180. Funeral mask*

With very realistic expression. Oblong eyes and feline mouth. Green stone. $5^1/2 \times 6''$. Pre-classic Olmec culture, middle and late period: 800 B.C.-A.D. 100 (unknown finding place).

### 182. Man's mask*

With feline features. Green stone $7^1/2 \times 5^3/8''$. Pre-classic Olmec culture, middle and late period: 800 B.C.-A.D. 100 (Oaxaca, Oax.). Coll.: Peabody Museum, Cambridge, Mass., USA.

### 183. Mask

With incised pattern. Green stone. $4^1/2 \times 3^7/8''$. Pre-classic Olmec culture, middle and late period: 800 B.C.-A.D. 100. (Veracruz, Ver.). Coll.: Peabody Museum, Cambridge, Mass., USA.

### 184. Small figure*

Of dwarf-like child, nude and crying furiously; deformed head, wide nose and feline mouth. Greenish jade. $4^3/4 \times 3''$. Pre-classic Olmec culture, middle and late period: 800 B.C.-A.D. 100. (Cerro de las Mesas, Ver.).

### 185. Breast plate
In the shape of a barge. On the outside incised feline masks. Greenish jade. 8x2¹/₈″. Pre-classic Olmec culture, middle and late period: 800 B.C.-A.D. 100. (Cerro de Las Mesas, Ver.).

### 186. Breast plate*
Semi-ovoid, decorated with two heads in bas-relief, placed on top of each other, and three other incised heads. Wide noses, feline mouths. Five profiles in all. Dark green serpentine. 6x6¹/₂″. Pre-classic Olmec culture, middle and late period: 800 B.C.-A.D. 100. (the Gulf coast).

### 187. Breast plate
(Fragment), representing a crouching figure with flat nose and feline mouth. Gray jade, carefully carved and polished. 5¹/₄x3¹/₈″. Pre-classic Olmec culture, middle and late period: 800 B.C.-A.D. 100. (La Venta, Tab.).

### 188-209. Offering*
Consisting of 16 standing male figures and 6 axes representing stelæ (tall, flat monuments). The figures have deformed heads, oblong eyes and feline mouths and seem to be talking or commemorating some event. The stelæ have engraved patterns. The group was found at a depth of four feet. The significance of this offering, one of the four found that is not connected with a funeral, is unknown. Light green and white jade. 7¹/₈x10″. Pre-classic Olmec culture, middle and late period: 800 B.C.-A.D. 100. (La Venta, Tab.).

### 210. Head*
With deformed skull and feline mouth. Fragment of a statue. Jadeite. 8⁵/₈x3⁷/₈″. Pre-classic Olmec culture, middle and late period: 800 B.C.-A.D. 100. (Tenango del Valle, Mexico).

### 211. Small head
Fragment of figurine. Terracotta with traces of white paint. 1⁵/₈x1¹/₈″. Pre-classic Olmec culture, middle and late period: 800 B.C.-A.D. 100. (Gulf Coast, Ver.). Coll.: F. Feuchtwanger, Mexico.

### 212. Nude male figure
With long deformed head and flat body. Dark green jade with traces of vermilion. 4¹/₂x2¹/₄″. Pre-classic Olmec culture, middle and late period: 800 B.C.-A.D. 100. (La Venta, Tab.).

### 213. Sitting nude figure
With delicate facial features, hands on knees, crossed legs. Very dark green jadeite. 5¹/₂x3¹/₈″. Pre-classic Olmec culture, middle and late period: 800 B.C.-A.D. 100. (El Tejar, Ver.).

### 214. Sitting figure*
Smiling, probably one of the first representations of the god of joy and of the new maize. The hair is indicated by vertical lines, the delicate features suggest a smile. A disk of hematite on his breast. Hands and legs crossed. White jade, covered with vermilion. 3x1⁵/₈″. Pre-classic Olmec culture, middle and late period: 800 B.C.-A.D. 100. (La Venta, Tab.).

### 215. Small standing male figure
Deformed head, extremely stylized, deepset eyes and feline mouth, hands on the hips. White jade with vermilion. 2¹/₂x1¹/₈″. Pre-classic Olmec culture, middle and late period: 800 B.C.-A.D. 100. (La Venta, Tab.).

### 216. Kneeling male figure
Carrying a death mask. Left arm bent in front of the face. Jadeite, delicately carved and polished. 2³/₈x1⁵/₈″. Pre-classic Olmec culture, middle and late period: 800 B.C.-A.D. 100. (Cuanalan, Ver.). Coll.: F. Feuchtwanger, Mexico.

### 217-218. Fragments of nude female figurines
One sitting with open legs, the other holding

her hand to the back of her neck. Terracotta with traces of white paint. $3^7/8 \times 2^3/4''$, $3^1/8 \times 2''$. Pre-classic Olmec culture, middle and late period: 800 B.C.-A.D. 100 (Tlapacoya, Mex.). Coll.: F. Feuchtwanger, Mexico.

**219. Sitting child**
Fat, the head bent backwards, mouth open. Terracotta. $8^3/8 \times 5^1/4''$. Pre-classic Olmec culture, middle and late period: 800 B.C.-A.D. 100. (Veracruz). Coll.: Dr. M. A. Leof, Mexico.

**220. Figurine of child**
Standing with receding chin. The hair indicated by incisions. Representing a newly born, a frequent motif in Olmec culture. Dark brown stone. $2^1/8 \times 3/4''$. Pre-classic Olmec culture, middle and late period: 800 B.C.-A.D. 100. (Gulf Coast, Ver.). Coll.: F. V. Field, Mexico.

**221. Small ceremonial axe**
With representation of a very stylized human figure with receding forehead, the incised features emphasize the feline mouth. Green Jade with vermilion. $4^3/8 \times 2''$. Pre-classic Olmec culture, middle and late period: 800 B.C.-A.D. 100. (La Venta, Tab.).

**222. Torso of reclining child**
(Fragment). Terracotta, ochre. $9^1/2 \times 7^1/8''$. Pre-classic Olmec culture, middle and late period: 800 B.C.-A.D. 100. (Coatzacoalcos, Ver.). Coll.: F. V. Field, Mexico.

**223. Small figure of crouching, nude dwarf**
With crossed arms, head deformed and bent backwards. Eyes encrusted with stones. Green jade. $4^1/4 \times 2^1/8''$. Pre-classic Olmec culture, middle and late period: 800 B.C.-A.D. 100. (La Venta, Tab.).

**224 (A-B-C). Ritual axes**
Sacred tools and origin of the stele as memorial monument. Green stone, delicately polished and light gray jade. A. $10^1/4 \times 3^1/8''$, B. $7^1/2 \times 2^3/8''$.

Pre-classic Olmec culture, middle and late period: 800 B.C.-A.D. 100. (La Venta, Tab.).

**225. Ceremonial axe**
So-called "colossal axe", forerunner of the big memorial stelæ. Incised image of a person with flat nose, feline mouth, carefully elaborated headdress and hieroglyphs. Slate. $11^3/4 \times 3^1/2''$. Pre-classic Olmec culture, middle and late period: 800 B.C.-A.D. 100. (Simojovel, Chis.).

**226. Ceremonial axe***
So-called "colossal axe" with representation of a human figure with receding forehead. Eyes and eyelids incised, flat nose, feline mouth, hands on the chest. Jadeite. $8^5/8 \times 3^7/8''$. Pre-classic Olmec culture, middle and late period: 800 B.C.-A.D. 100. (Gulf Coast, Ver.).

**227. Necklace**
Consisting of 90 round beads in the shape of calabashes. Grass-green jade. Length $37^1/2''$. Pre-classic Olmec culture, middle and late period: 800 B.C.-A.D. 100. (La Venta, Tab.).

**228. Necklace**
Of 27 round and tubular beads. Light green jade, highly polished. Length $37^1/2''$. Pre-classic Olmec culture, middle and late period: 800 B.C.-A.D. 100. (La Venta, Tab.).

**229. Necklace**
Of 29 small and delicately carved beads, some of them smooth and of medium size. Limestone, gray and violet. Length $19^5/8''$. Pre-classic Olmec culture, middle and late period: 800 B.C.-A.D. 100. (La Venta, Tab.).

**230-233. Ritual disks and needles**
a) Dark green jade with cruciform perforations in the middle. $5^7/8 \times 2^3/4''$.
b) Dark green jade. $9^1/2 \times 1^1/4''$.
c) Needle, green jade, engraved. $10^3/4 \times 5/8''$.
d) Needle, grayish green jade. $7^7/8 \times 3/8''$. Pre-

classic Olmec culture, middle and late period: 800 B.C.-A.D. 100. (La Venta, Tab.).

#### 234. Young woman*
Nude, reclining and resting on her crossed arms, feline features, highly stylized jaguar's ears. Although the human representations of the Olmecs are always male, generally nude, but without indication of sex, this is one of the few figures of undoubted feminine character and endowed with great sensuality. Limestone. $4^{1}/_{2}\times16^{1}/_{2}''$. Pre-classic Olmec culture, late and early classic period: 300 B.C.-A.D. 300. (Veracruz, Ver.). Coll.: Cleveland Museum of Art, Ohio, USA.

#### 235. Vessel
Flat bottom. Cylindrical, slanting edge and four legs, shaped like human feet. Black stone, highly polished. $7^{1}/_{8}\times8^{3}/_{4}''$. Pre-classic Olmec culture; Cerro de las Mesas, late and early classic period: 300 B.C.-A.D. 300. (Jocotitla, Ver.).

#### 236. Vase
"Florero" with flat bottom, spherical and long conic neck with engraved decoration. The incisions filled with red paint. Gray terracotta. $7^{5}/_{8}\times4^{1}/_{4}''$. Pre-classic Olmec culture, late and early classic period: 300 B.C.-A.D. 300. (Cerro de las Mesas, Ver.).

#### 237. Monument*
Shaped like a colossal mask. Fleshless skull on which is placed a mask with the features of a living person. The forehead is adorned with a hieroglyph in relief, probably the sign of fertility. The swollen eyelids seem, as mentioned above, to represent rain, as do the furrows in the cheeks and the large nose-ornament suggests the fangs of the jaguar. On the back of the monument there is a bas-relief, representing a standing person who severely admonishes a sit-

ting woman in a very dejected attitude. Gray Basalt. $52^{3}/_{8}\times40^{1}/_{8}\times28^{3}/_{8}''$. Pre-classic Olmec culture, late and early classic period. 300 B.C.-A.D. 300. (Cerro de las Mesas Ver.). Coll.: Museo de Antropología, University of Veracruz, Jalapa, Ver.

#### 238. Mask
Representing the god of rain. Gray Basalt. $35^{3}/_{8}\times24^{3}/_{4}\times18^{1}/_{2}''$. Pre-classic Olmec culture, Cerro de las Mesas, late and early classic period: 300 B.C.-A.D. 300. (Medias Aguas, Sayula, Ver.). Coll.: Museo de Antropología, University of Veracruz, Jalapa, Ver.

#### 239. Head*
Spherical, representing the sun. Flat nose, feline mouth with long fangs, the attribute of the gods of rain. The front teeth are filed and form a V, the hieroglyph representing the breath of life. In the right ear appears the fivepoint cross, symbol of the light and of the four cardinal points, a forerunner of the truncated pyramid, the architectural monument that all later Mexican cultures had in common. The strange, wavy, bristling hair symbolizes the flames of the sun. Basalt. $29^{1}/_{2}\times27^{5}/_{8}\times27^{5}/_{8}''$. Pre-classic Olmec culture, Cerro de las Mesas, late and early classic period: 300 B.C.-A.D. 300. (Corral Nuevo, Acayucan, Ver.). Coll.: Museo de Antropología, University of Veracruz, Jalapa, Ver.

#### 240. Xipe-Totec
The god of spring and of renewal. Sitting with a monkey's mask and clad in the skin of a flayed person. Basalt. $53^{1}/_{8}\times34^{5}/_{8}\times34^{5}/_{8}''$. Pre-classic Olmec culture, Cerro de las Mesas: late and early classic period: 300 B.C.-A.D. 300. (Aparicio de la Vega de la Torre, Ver.). Coll.: Museo de Antropología, University of Veracruz, Jalapa, Ver.

# 3. The Cultures of the Pacific Coast

The region known as Western Mexico, or the Pacific Coast, comprises the states of Sinaloa, Nayarit, Colima, Jalisco, Michoacán and part of the states of Guanajuato and Guerrero. The scope of this region is determined by the relative uniformity of the cultures in pre-Hispanic times. The state of Guerrero is the outermost of the states involved.

The oldest place as yet discovered in Western Mexico is El Openo in the state of Michoacán, but the most important one is Chupicuaro in the state of Guanajuato. It dates back to the late pre-classic period. It seems to have been the most important settlement and one of the most important centers of ceramics of the epoch. Its highly developed crafts offer a large number of different forms, nuances and designs with their profusion of products: Monochrome and polychrome vases and jars with geometrical or naturalistic decorations such as butterflies, frogs, human hands and faces. Thanks to the wonderful hand made figurines it is known that inhabitants wore loin-cloths, which most often consisted of big sea-shells, held in place by a belt and covering the male sexual organs (possibly a fertility symbol), and that they painted their bodies, faces and hair in white, black and blue. We also know that men painted their hair white and women painted it red. Other features of life in these cultures are revealed by the statuettes of children sleeping in their cots, of women carrying their children, or of miniature jars used as toys etc. The influence from Chupicuaro has been felt way up into the central highland.

In the state of Guerrero in the Mezcala valley we find many figurines hewn in hard stone and polished afterwards, which in plastic power surpass the finest artistic manifestations of the larger centers. "The Mezcala" style is a synthesis of Olmec civilization and Teotihuacán. These sculptures are as a rule work tools — axes and hammers, representing deified persons — scrapers and handles of knives turned into temples and deities.

The inhabitants of the Colima and Tecomán valleys modelled admirable statues representing armadillos, roes, monkeys, wild turkeys and many other kinds of animals. Here one also finds scenes from daily life: women in childbirth or nursing their children or carrying water, grinding corn, or arranging their hair, groups of lovers, potters, hunters using slings, chieftains or important persons sitting on benches with backs, sick people and invalids, etc. The people of Colima were ruled by "caciques" who are depicted in covered stretchers, carried by naked bearers. The great number of representations of temples, dancers and musicians bear witness to a religion, stamped by magic, in which the spiritualized natural forces were undoubtedly dominant. So far the sculptures of deities found have been almost exclusively representations of Huehueteotl (fire god), presumably connected with terrestrial phenomena caused by the volcanoes, primarily by Jorullo in Colima.

The great significance of the cult of the dead is evident from the fact that the tomb offerings comprise statuettes in burned clay, representing fattened dogs, which are supposed to represent Xolotl accompanying the dead person on his way to the realm of the dead. But the myth of Xolotl belongs to later "Mexican" and Huastec cultures and it is possible that it is a matter of symbolic nourishment, since these dogs were actually bred and fattened for eating purposes.

In the period A.D. 1250 to 1521 stone buildings were erected in Colima, the style of which is reminiscent of the Mexican, though with local variations, like stairs and doors, decorated with animals and calendar figures.

The state of Jalisco and particularly the region around Autlán — Tuxcacuesco, offers several points of contact with the cultures of Colima, already at the beginning of the classic period, with the one difference that sculpture there was very smooth and came in nuances from white to cream.

The state of Nayarit is less known, apart from Ixtlán del Rio. It is distinguished by statuettes of humans in a very expressionistic style, particularly representations of sitting women with their children and of women in short capes with their breasts bare. They wore large earrings and nose-ornaments. One of the peculiarities of this style is the use of color in rendering skirts, capes, conical caps, clothing materials and hair, as well as the painted decorations on face and body.

In the state of Michoacán the population, that here too was agriculturist, created ceramics of great beauty, as well as remarkable woven materials. Their religion was complicated. For many years the archeological finds along the Pacific Coast were considered as belonging to the Tarasco-culture, but it is now conclusively demonstrated that the culture of the Tarascans is different and must be placed within the historical epoch. In the 13th century the Tarascans founded the kingdom of Michoacán, but nothing is known of their origins. Even their language is an enigma; it does not belong to the Me-

Warrior or a player of pelote. Terracotta. West Coast culture. Cat. 265.

Sitting female figure holding her breast. Terracotta.
West Coast culture. Cat. 273.

"The maiden of the West". Terracotta. West Coast culture. Cat. 291.

Pregnant female figure on the point of giving birth. Terracotta. West Coast culture. Cat. 296.

Amphora in the shape of a profoundly dejected man. Terracotta. West Coast culture. Cat. 284.

Important person. Terracotta. West Coast culture. Cat. 294.

Water-carrier. Terracotta. West Coast culture. Cat. 287.

Hunchbacked figure standing on a fish with two heads. Terracotta.
West Coast culture. Cat. 293.

Sitting howling dog with prominent ribs. Terracotta. West Coast culture. Cat. 322.

Fat hairless dog. Terracotta. West Coast culture. Cat. 314.

Sitting dog with human mask. Terracotta.
West Coast culture. Cat. 316.

soamerican family of languages, but shows pronounced phonetic similarities with the Peruvian languages. Their capital was Tzintzuntzan. Their works in ceramics, silver, copper and gold are characterized by great delicacy. As goldsmiths they excelled in producing fish with golden scales and silver bodies and cast metal bells in the shape of turtles adorned with metal threads or filigree. They also carved hard stones (mostly obsidian and rock crystal) and made feather mosaics. The precision and transparency of the large cylindrical and circular ear-ornaments made of obsidian are wonderful.

**241. Jar**

Boatshaped. On the keel a representation of a human face. Red terracotta, polished with decorations in ochre and carmine. $5^1/4$x$13^3/8''$. West Coast culture: 300 B.C.-A.D. 300. (Chupicaro, Gto.). Coll.: Museo Regional de Michoacán, Morelia, Mich.

**242. Jar**

Spherical, with a long neck, representing a duck. Ochre terracotta with black decoration, on red polished ground. 6x$5^7/8''$. West Coast culture: 300 B.C.-A.D. 300. (Chupicuaro, Gto.). Coll.: Museo Regional de Michoacán, Morelia, Mich.

**243. Jar**

With phallic forms. Narrow neck and wide rim. Ochre terracotta with decoration consisting of black and white bands on red polished ground. $6^1/4$x$11^3/8''$. West Coast culture: 300 B.C.-A.D. 300. (Chupicuaro, Gto.). Coll.: Museo Regional de Michoacán, Morelia, Mich.

**244. Jar**

Shaped like a human foot with hollow conical feet. Ochre terracotta with decoration consisting of black lines on red polished ground. $11^3/8$x$11''$. West Coast culture: 300 B.C.-A.D. 300. (Chupicuaro, Gto.).

**245. Bowl**

With kidney shaped container and pedestal in the shape of a truncated cone. Geometrical decoration in black and white on red polished ground. Red terracotta. $9^7/8$x$12^5/8''$. West Coast culture: 300 B.C.-A.D. 300. (Chupicuaro, Gto.). Coll.: Museo Regional de Michoacán, Morelia, Mich.

**246. Standing nude female figure**

Very fat. This little figure belongs to a group with a type of decoration that is not found in any other region of Mexico. Ochre terracotta polychrome with geometrical design in black and white on red polished ground. 9x$5^1/4''$. West coast culture: 300 B.C.-A.D. 300. (Chupicuaro, Gto.).

**247. Standing nude female figure**

Deformed head, divided into two parts. Ochre terracotta polychrome with geometrical design in black and white on red polished ground. $13^3/8$x$4''$. West Coast culture: 300 B.C.-A.D. 300. (Chupicuaro, Gto.). Coll.: Museo Regional de Michoacán, Morelia, Mich.

**248. Jar**

Shaped like a jug with spout. Ochre terracotta with geometrical design, white on red polished ground. $8^1/4$x$9^1/2''$. West Coast culture: 300 B.C.-A.D. 300. (Huandacareo, Mich.).

**249. Standing female figure**

Dressed in a skirt, with deformed head. Prominent pointed nose. Red polished terracotta with white paint. $13^3/8$x$6^3/4''$. West Coast culture: 300 B.C.-A.D. 300. (Guadalajara, Jal.). Coll.: M. A. Leof, Mexico.

**250. Small sitting female figure**

Nursing a child, dressed in a skirt. The head deformed, the nose prominent. Red terracotta with white paint. $9^1/2 \times 4^3/4''$. West Coast culture: 300 B.C.-A.D. 300. (Guadalajara, Jal.). Coll.: M. A. Leof, Mexico.

**251. Standing male figure**

Very stylized with crossed arms and ear-ornaments. Dark green serpentine, highly polished. $9^1/2 \times 3^1/8''$. West Coast culture: 300 B.C.-A.D. 300. (Mezcala Valley, Gro.). Coll.: M. A. Leof, Mexico.

**252. Standing male figure**

Ceremonial axe deifying the human shape with stylized features. Light green polished porphyry. $15^3/4 \times 5^1/2''$. West Coast culture: 300 B.C.-A.D. 300. (Mezcala Valley Gro.). Coll.: M. A. Leof, Mexico.

**253. Standing male figure**

Ceremonial axe deifying human shape. Green polished porphyry. $9 \times 3^1/4''$. West Coast culture: 300 B.C.-A.D. 300. (Mezcala Valley, Gro.). Coll.: M. A. Leof, Mexico.

**254. Standing male figure**

Ceremonial axe deifying human shape. Dark gray polished porphyry. $8^1/4 \times 2^3/4''$. West Coast culture: 300 B.C.-A.D. 300. (Mezcala Valley, Gro.). Coll.: M. A. Leof, Mexico.

**255. Sitting figure**

Ceremonial hammer deifying human shape, stylized features. Light green polished porphyry. $2^1/8 \times 3^7/8''$. West Coast culture: 300 B.C.-A.D. 300. (Mezcala Valley, Gro.). Coll.: M. A. Leof, Mexico.

**256. Sitting figure**

Ceremonial axe deifying human shape. Stylized features. Dark, highly polished diorite. $3^7/8 \times 5^1/8''$. West Coast culture: 300 B.C.-A.D. 300.

(Mezcala Valley, Gro.). Coll.: F. Feuchtwanger, Mexico.

**257. Standing male figure**

Ceremonial axe deifying human shape. Green, highly polished porphyry. $9^7/8 \times 2^3/4''$. West Coast culture: 300 B.C.-A.D. 300. (Mezcala Valley, Gro.). Coll.: Dolores Olmedo de Olvera, Mexico.

**258. Temple**

Scraper (tool), for sacred use. Green, highly polished porphyry. $6^1/4 \times 6^3/4''$. West Coast culture: 300 B.C.-A.D. 300. (Mezcala Valley, Gro.).

**259. Temple**

With a staircase and a deity in the middle of the temple. Light green porphyry, highly polished. $5 \times 3^1/2''$. West Coast culture: 300 B.C.-A.D. 300. (Mezcala Valley, Gro.).

**260. Handle of knife**

In the shape of a swimming man. Green, highly polished porphyry. $2^3/4'' \times 6^3/4''$. West Coast culture: 300 B.C.-A.D. 300. (Mezcala Valley, Gro.).

**261. Human head**

With eyes inlaid with mother of pearl. Very stylized representation. Green, highly polished porphyry. $4^1/2 \times 3^1/4''$. West Coast culture: 300 B.C.-A.D. 300 (Mezcala Valley, Gro.).

**262. Human head**

Very stylized. Green polished porphyry. $5 \times 4^1/2''$. West Coast culture: 300 B.C.-A.D. 300. (Mezcala Valley, Gro.).

**263. Brazier**

In the shape of a basket with representation of a contortionist, carrying a fire god, on whom a ray, shaped like a snake, is falling. Ochre terracotta. $21^1/4 \times 8^5/8''$. West Coast culture: A.D. 300-950. (Colima). Coll.: Museo de Antropología de Guadalajara, Jal.

**264. Brazier**

Shaped like a basket with representation of a contortionist, carrying a fire god, on whom a ray, shaped like a snake, is falling. Ochre terracotta. $13^3/8 \times 5^1/2''$. West Coast culture: A.D. 300-950. (Colima). Coll.: Museo de Antropología de Guadalajara, Jal.

**265. Figure***

Representing a warrior or a player of pelote, the sacred ball-game. Dressed in helmet and protective costume of padded cotton. Holds a club in his hand. Terracotta. $17^3/8 \times 10''$. West Coast culture: A.D. 300-950. (Tuxcacuesco, Jal.).

**266. Sitting hunchbacked figure**

With helmet and ornaments in the pastillage technique on his shoulders and legs. Magical powers were ascribed to dwarfs and hunchbacks, and they were often members of the court of the "caciques". Ochre terracotta with traces of brown and red paint. $21^5/8 \times 13^3/4''$. West Coast culture: A.D. 300-950 (Ocotlán, Jal.). Coll.: Dolores Olmedo de Olvera, Mexico.).

**267. Sitting female figure**

Very flat body, headdress, necklace with pendants and armrings. Ochre terracotta. $12^1/4 \times 6^1/4''$. West Coast culture: A.D. 300-950. (Colima). Coll.: M. A. Leof, Mexico.

**268. Two nude female figures**

Sitting in front of a work bench, making paper of woodpulp. White terracotta. $11 \times 9^1/2''$. West Coast culture: A.D. 300-950. (Tuxcacuesco, Jal.). Coll.: K. Stavenhagen, Mexico.

**269. Hunchbacked figure***

Leaning on the ground with very large hands, Ochre terracotta. $10^5/8 \times 11^3/8''$. West Coast culture: A.D. 300-950. (Tuxcacuesco, Jal.). Coll.: K. Stavenhagen, Mexico. ·

**270. Sitting hunchbacked figure**

With his hands on his knees and a purse on the left shoulder. Headdress with hair put up at the back of the neck and round ornaments on the shoulders. Ochre terracotta with traces of painting in white and red. $10^5/8 \times 9''$. West Coast culture: A.D. 300-950. (Tuxcacuesco, Jal.). Coll.: Museo de Antropología, de Guadalajara, Jal.

**271. Standing ball-player**

Large headdress, ear-ornaments and circular ornaments in pastillage technique on the shoulders. Terracotta with traces of white and red paint. $12 \times 7^1/8''$. West Coast culture: A.D. 300-950 (Ocotlán, Jal.).

**272. Man and woman**

Sitting down and embracing. White terracotta with traces of red paint. $9 \times 6^3/4''$. West Coast culture: A.D. 300-950 (Tuxcacuesco, Jal.). Coll.: K. Stavenhagen, Mexico.

**273. Sitting female figure***

Semi-nude, holding her left breast with one hand. The body decorated with paint. Light ochre terracotta. $15^3/8 \times 10^5/8''$. West Coast culture: A.D. 300-950. (Jalisco). Coll.: K. Stavenhagen, Mexico.

**274. Standing female figure**

Red terracotta with white decorations. $17^3/8 \times 7^1/8''$. West Coast culture: A.D. 300-950. (Jalisco). Coll.: Dolores Olmedo de Olvera, Mexico.

**275. Standing nude female figure**

Carrying a jar on her left shoulder. White terracotta. $19^5/8 \times 7^7/8''$. West Coast culture: A.D. 300-950. (Tuxcacuesco, Jal.) K. Stavenhagen, Mexico.

**276. Female figure with nude torso**

Holding her right breast. Ochre terracotta. $11^3/4 \times 10^5/8''$. West Coast culture: A.D. 300-950. (Tuxcacuesco, Jal.).

**277. Amphora**

Spherical, with a narrow neck. Decorated with mosaics in polychrome clay with delicately executed motifs of gods, priests and warriors. Ochre terracotta. $15^3/4 \times 15''$. West Coast culture: A.D. 300-950. (Jiquilpan, Mich.). Coll.: Museo de Jiquilpan, Mich. (Through the Museo Nacional de Antropología, Mexico).

**278. Warrior**

Holding a missile in his right hand. Dressed in helmet and protective costume, carrying a musical instrument in the shape of a sea shell on his shoulder. Red polished terracotta. $15^3/8 \times 9^7/8''$. West Coast culture: A.D. 300-950. (Los Ortices, Colima). Coll.: Dolores Olmedo de Olvera, Mexico.

**279. Warrior**

With sling and helmet. Red polished terracotta. $16^1/2 \times 12^1/4''$. West Coast culture: A.D. 300-950. (Los Ortices, Colima). Coll.: Dolores Olmedo de Olvera, Mexico.

**280. Figure representing a dancer**

In dancing position. Very tall and complicated headgear. Chin-strap and wide belt, engraved. Red polished terracotta. $16^7/8 \times 9^7/8''$. West Coast culture: A.D. 300-950. (Los Ortices, Colima). Coll.: Dolores Olmedo de Olvera, Mexico.

**281. Amphora**

In the shape of a dancer with a musical instrument. The headdress covers the head and part of the face. Eyes like coffeebeans. Red polished terracotta. $16^1/2 \times 10^1/4''$. West Coast culture: A.D. 300-1250. (Colima). Coll.: Dolores Olmedo de Olvera, Mexico.

**282. Bearded male figure**

Presumably representing an "aguamielero" (man who collects the juice of agaves, "maguey", which, when fermented, is called *pulque,* a religious drink and at the same time a very po-

pular secular drink). He has a cap on his head and holds an "acocote", (a kind of long-shaped calabash) in his hands to catch the juice. On his shoulder he carries a leather container, closed with the thorns of agaves. Ochre terracotta. $14^1/8 \times 9^1/2''$. West Coast culture: A.D. 300-1250. (Colima). Coll.: Dolores Olmedo de Olvera, Mexico.

**283. Small male figure**

Presumably representing an "aguamielero", bearded and with cap, holding in his hands an "acocote" for collecting juice. On his shoulder a leather container, closed with agave thorns. Necklace and anklets. Ochre terracotta. $5^1/2 \times 5^1/2''$. West Coast culture: A.D. 300-1250 (Colima). Museo de Antropología de Guadalajara, Jal.

**284. Amphora***

In the shape of a man, sitting with arms crossed on his knees, resting his head on his arm, looking profoundly dejected. Red polished terracotta. $11^3/4 \times 7^1/8''$. West Coast culture: A.D. 300-1250. (Colima). Coll.: Dolores Olmedo de Olvera, Mexico.

**285. Sitting figure***

Representing a prisoner with his hands bound at his back. Red polished terracotta. $9^1/2 \times 6^3/4''$. West Coast culture: A.D. 300-1250. (Colima). Coll.: Dolores Olmedo de Olvera, Mexico.

**286. Amphora**

In the shape of a sitting semi-nude man, leaning on his right hand and turning his head to one side. Red polished terracotta. $7^7/8 \times 9^3/4''$. West Coast culture: A.D. 300-1250. (Colima). Coll.: F. V. Field, Mexico.

**287. Naked figure representing a water-carrier***

With sack and jar on his back, holding a "mecapal" (headband to support burdens). Red polished terracotta. $16^1/2 \times 8^5/8''$. West Coast culture: A.D. 300-1250. (Colima). Coll.: Museo de Antropología de Guadalajara, Jal.

**288. Water-carrier**
Carrying a jar on his back by help of a "mecapal". Ochre terracotta. 26³/8x11″. West Coast culture: A.D. 300-1250. (Colima). Coll.: K. Stavenhagen, Mexico.

**289. Amphora**
In the shape of an acrobat with a jar on his stomach. Dark brown terracotta. 9⁷/8x12⁵/8″. West Coast culture: A.D. 300-1250. (Colima). Coll.: Dolores Olmedo de Olvera, Mexico.

**290. Jar**
In the shape of a bent acrobat. Red terracotta, partly polished on head, breast and pants. 9x 12⁵/8″. West Coast culture: A.D. 300-1250. (Colima). Coll.: Museo de Antropología de Guadalajara, Jal.

**291. "La doncella del occidente"\***
(The Maiden of the West). Nude woman, squatting. Ochre terracotta with red polished paint. 11³/4x7⁷/8″. West Coast culture: A.D. 300-1250. (Colima).

**292. Hunchbacked nude figure**
Sitting with his hands on his thighs. Red polished terracotta. 12⁵/8x9¹/2″. West coast culture: A.D. 300-1250. (Colima). Coll.: Museo de Antropología de Guadalajara, Jal.

**293. Hunchbacked figure\***
Regular features with incised tattoo. Necklaces with two canines, and "maxtlatl" (a kind of loin-cloth). He stands on a fish with two heads, leaning on a stick. Though it seems to have been characteristic of the West Coast cultures to represent human beings, rather than gods, this figure is apparently a mythical figure. Red polished ochre terracotta. 16¹/2x9¹/2″. West Coast culture: A.D. 300-1250. (Colima).

**294. Sitting figure, representing an important person\***
Very fat and semi-nude. Dressed in a slit tunic, circular ear-ornaments, nose-ornaments and bracelets. Nudity seems to have been a characteristic of the Nayarit peoples. It is not an expression of a lower culture, as appears from the refined artistry of jewellery and ornaments. Red polished terracotta. 20¹/2x14⁵/8″. West Coast culture: Colima. A.D. 300-1250. Coll.: K. Stavenhagen, Mexico.

**295. Sitting female figure**
With painted body and a jar in her right hand. Ochre terracotta. 23⁵/8x15³/8″. West Coast culture: A.D. 300-1250. (Colima). Coll.: K. Stavenhagen, Mexico.

**296. Nude pregnant female figure\***
On the point of giving birth. Symbol of fertility. Circular ear-ornaments, maize seeds on her shoulders. Red, polished terracotta with traces of black paint on her body. 19¹/4x8¹/4″. West Coast culture: A.D. 300-1250. (Colima). Coll.: Dolores Olmedo de Olvera, Mexico.

**297. Amphora**
In the shape of sitting woman, with her head bent, holding her left hand to her cheek. Semicircular headdress, dressed in a short skirt. Red polished terracotta. 13³/4x8⁵/8″. West Coast culture: A.D. 300-1250. (Colima). Coll.: Dolores Olmedo de Olvera, Mexico.

**298. Amphora**
In the shape of a nude, reclining, hydropic woman, lifting her right leg. Red polished terracotta. 5⁷/8x7⁷/8″. West Coast culture: A.D. 300-1250. (Colima). Coll.: M. A. Leof, Mexico.

**299. Amphora**
In the shape of a person lying on his side, resting his head on his left arm. Red polished terracotta. 4³/8x13³/4″. West Coast culture: A.D.

300-1250. (Colima). Coll.: Dolores Olmedo de Olvera, Mexico.

### 300. Jar
In the shape of reclining, sleeping woman, leaning on her left arm. Red terracotta. $7^1/8 \times 7^1/8''$. West Coast culture: A.D. 300-1250. (Colima). Coll.: K. Stavenhagen, Mexico.

### 301. Sitting female figure
Her left arm is against her right shoulder, the hair and bracelets engraved. Red polished terracotta. $13^3/8 \times 7^1/8''$. West Coast culture: A.D. 300-1250. (Colima). Coll.: K. Stavenhagen, Mexico.

### 302. Jar
Shaped like a stirrup, that is formed by the arms and the prominent breasts of a very fat woman. The opening is in the woman's head. She wears a necklace and has a decoration of round lumps on her shoulders. Red polished terracotta. $12^5/8 \times 11^3/4''$. West Coast culture: A.D. 300-1250. (Colima). Coll.: Museo de Antropología de Guadalajara, Jal.

### 303. Sitting figure, representing an old nude woman*
Red polished terracotta. $25^1/4 \times 7^7/8''$. West Coast culture: A.D. 300-1250. (Colima). Coll.: K. Stavenhagen, Mexico.

### 304. Flute
Shaped like a warrior, protecting himself with his shield, while throwing a stone. The helmet is decorated with an animal. Ochre terracotta. $2^3/4 \times 3^1/8''$. West Coast culture: A.D. 300-1250. (Colima). Coll.: Museo de Antropología de Guadalajara, Jal.

### 305. Small figure of a warrior
With his shield at his shoulder, in a position to throw an object with his right hand. Ochre terracotta. $5^1/8 \times 2^3/4''$. West Coast culture: A.D. 300-1250. (Colima). Coll.: Museo de Antropología de Guadalajara, Jal.

### 306. Flute
Shaped like a warrior, protecting himself with his shield and throwing a stone. The helmet is bi-partite and richly adorned. Ochre terracotta. $6^1/2 \times 3^1/8''$. West Coast culture: A.D. 300-1250. (Colima). Coll.: Museo de Antropología de Guadalajara, Jal.

### 307. Two women grasping each other's hair
Ochre terracotta. $4^3/4 \times 3^7/8''$. West Coast culture: A.D. 300-1250. (Colima). Coll.: K. Stavenhagen, Mexico.

### 308. Flute
Shaped like a sitting musician, beating a drum. Large headgear and necklace. Ochre terracotta. $4^3/8 \times 4^3/4''$. West Coast culture: A.D. 300-1250. (Colima). Coll.: Museo de Antropología de Guadalajara, Jal.

### 309. Small sitting figure
Presumably a potter. Holds a head in his left hand and a deep bowl in his right hand. Both headgears are decorated with incised patterns. Ochre terracotta partly polished. $5^1/2 \times 5^1/8''$. West Coast culture: A.D. 300-1250. (Colima). Coll.: Museo de Antropología de Guadalajara, Jal.

### 310. Sitting male figurine
Ear-ornaments, turban-like headgear and necklace. Holds a fan in his right hand and a deep bowl in his left hand. Ochre terracotta. $3^1/2 \times 3^1/8''$. West Coast culture: A.D. 300-1250. (Colima). Coll.: Museo de Antropología de Guadalajara, Jal.

### 311. Figurine representing a kneeling woman
Grinding maize. Ochre terracotta. $3^1/2 \times 2^1/8''$. West Coast culture: A.D. 300-1250. (Colima). Coll.: Museo de Antropología de Guadalajara, Jal.

### 312. Figurine representing an acrobat
With his head between his feet. Ochre terra-

cotta. $3^1/8 \times 2^3/8''$. West Coast culture: A.D. 300-1250. (Colima). Coll.: Museo de Antropología de Guadalajara, Jal.

### 313. Sitting female figurine
Has a child standing at her knees and holds her crossed arms around it. Ochre terracotta. $4^3/8 \times 3''$. West Coast culture: A.D. 300-1250. (Colima). Coll.: Museo de Antropología de Guadalajara, Jal.

### 314. Fat hairless dog*
These dogs of Mexican origin – now all but extinct – were called "izcuintli" and were connected with the tomb cult. They were placed in the tombs to accompany the dead person's soul on the journeys that were to take it along subterranean rivers, to the land of the dead. They were also put in the tombs as symbolic food and were actually eaten, as their meat was considered a delicacy. Because of the high temperature of their bodies they were used for medical purposes such as a cure for rheumatism. Ochre terracotta with red polished paint. $16^1/2 \times 9^7/8''$. West Coast culture: A.D. 300-1250. (Colima).

### 315. Sitting howling dog
Red polished terracotta. $13^3/8 \times 9''$. West Coast culture: A.D. 300-950. (Los Ortices, Colima). Coll.: Dolores Olmedo de Olvera, Mexico.

### 316. Sitting dog*
With human mask. Strange representation, the meaning of which is unknown. Red polished terracotta, the mask black. $13^3/8 \times 9''$. West Coast culture: A.D. 300-950. (Los Ortices, Colima). Coll.: Dolores Olmedo de Olvera, Mexico.

### 317. Two dogs entangled in play
Pattern in the skin indicated by incisions. Red polished terracotta. $11^3/8 \times 8^1/4''$. West Coast culture: A.D. 300-950. (Los Ortices, Colima). Coll.: Dolores Olmedo de Olvera, Mexico.

### 318. Small fat dog
Lying down. Red polished terracotta. $8^1/4 \times 11''$. West Coast culture: A.D. 300-950. (Los Ortices, Colima). Coll.: K. Stavenhagen, Mexico.

### 319. Small sitting dog
Ochre terracotta highly polished. $11 \times 10^1/4''$. West Coast culture: A.D. 300-950. (Los Ortices, Colima). Coll.: Dolores Olmedo de Olvera, Mexico.

### 320. Small sitting dog
Scratching his head with one paw. Red polished terracotta. $11 \times 17^3/8''$. West Coast culture: A.D. 300-950. (Los Ortices, Colima). Coll.: Dolores Olmedo de Olvera, Mexico.

### 321. Dog with scorpions
One scorpion on the nose, four on the body. Red polished terracotta. $11 \times 18^1/2''$. West Coast culture: A.D. 300-950. (Los Ortices, Colima). Coll.: Dolores Olmedo de Olvera, Mexico.

### 322. Sitting dog
Howling, prominent ribs. The pattern of the skin indicated by incisions. Red polished terracotta. $12 \times 16^7/8''$. West Coast culture: A.D. 300-950. (Los Ortices, Colima). Coll.: Dolores Olmedo de Olvera, Mexico.

### 323. Vessel in the shape of curled up dog
Ochre terracotta highly polished. $10^5/8 \times 5''$. West Coast culture: A.D. 300-950. (Los Ortices, Colimo). Coll.: Dolores Olmedo de Olvera, Mexico.

### 324. Vessel
Shaped like a dog lying on his back. Red terracotta. $5^1/8 \times 10^5/8''$. West Coast culture: A.D. 300-950. (Las Animas, Colima).

### 325. Vessel
With round spout, in the shape of a small curled up dog, lifting his head. Red polished terracotta. $5^7/8 \times 11^3/4''$. West Coast culture: A.D.

300-950. (Las Animas, Colima). Coll.: F. V. Field, Mexico.

### 326. Parrot

Eating. Red polished terracotta. $8^5/8 \times 14^1/8''$. West Coast culture: A.D. 300-950. (Los Ortices, Colima). Coll.: K. Stavenhagen, Mexico.

### 327. Vessel

Shaped like a fowl with flat head, whose tail serves as a spout. Red polished terracotta. The bill painted yellow. $7^7/8 \times 11^3/8''$. West Coast culture: A.D. 300-1250. (Colima). Coll.: M. A. Leof, Mexico.

### 328. Vessel*

Shaped like a fowl with flat head. Ochre polished terracotta. $7^7/8 \times 5^1/2''$. West Coast culture: A.D. 300-950. (Los Ortices, Colima). Coll.: K. Stavenhagen, Mexico.

### 329. Vessel

Shaped like two swimming ducks. Red polished terracotta. $5^7/8 \times 9^7/8''$. West Coast culture: A.D. 300-950. (Los Ortices, Colima). Coll.: K. Stavenhagen, Mexico.

### 330. Vessel

Shaped like coiled snake. Red polished terracotta with incisions. $7^1/2 \times 11''$. West Coast culture: A.D. 300-1250. (Colima). Coll.: Museo de Antropología de Guadalajara, Jal.

### 331. Chameleon

Red polished terracotta. $8^1/4 \times 11^3/4''$. West Coast culture: A.D. 300-950. (Los Ortices, Colima). Coll.: F. V. Field, Mexico.

### 332. Zoömorphic figure

In the shape of a bench with a parrot-profile. Representation of a piece of furniture made of roe-hide and used by the upper-class. Red polished terracotta. $9 \times 9^1/2''$. West Coast culture: A.D. 300-950. (Los Ortices, Colima).

### 333. Round vessel

Decorated with ten heads with headgear. Red polished terracotta. $8^1/4 \times 11^3/4''$. West Coast culture: A.D. 300-1250. (Colima). Coll.: Dolores Olmedo de Olvera, Mexico.

### 334. Round vessel

With flat bottom, decorated with calabashes. Red terracotta. $8^1/4 \times 13''$. West Coast culture: A.D. 300-1250. (Colima). Coll.: K. Stavenhagen, Mexico.

### 335. Round vessel

With narrow neck, decorated with an offering, consisting of five cactus leaves. Red terracotta. $7^1/2 \times 11^3/4''$. West Coast culture. A.D. 300-1250. (Colima). Coll.: Museo de Antropología de Guadalajara, Jal.

### 336. Calabash-shaped vessel

Supported by three small parrots eating the calabash. Red polished terracotta. $8^5/8 \times 14^1/8''$. West Coast culture: A.D. 300-1250. (Colima).

### 337. Standing warrior

Holding a lance in each hand, dressed in a protective armour-like costume. Adorned with ear and nose-ornaments and necklace and wearing a helmet. Ochre terracotta. $23^5/8 \times 11^3/8''$. West Coast culture: A.D. 300-1250. (Ixtlán, Nayarit). Coll.: Dolores Olmedo de Olvera, Mexico.

### 338. Warrior

With helmet, protective armour-like costume and lance. Red terracotta. $18^7/8 \times 8^1/4''$. West Coast culture: A.D. 300-1250. (Ixtlán, Nayarit). Coll.: Dolores Olmedo de Olvera, Mexico.

### 339. Sitting warrior

With a lance in his right hand and a shield in his left hand, wearing a helmet, nose- and ear-ornaments and bracelets. The body decorated with painted constellations. Terracotta with traces of white and red paint. $17^3/4 \times 12^1/4''$. West

Coast culture: A.D. 300-1250. (Ixtlán, Nayarit). Coll.: Dolores Olmedo de Olvera, Mexico.

### 340. Small "celestial" warrior

Apparently symbolizing the planet of Venus. Dressed in a protective armour-like costume and helmet and carrying a lance. Ochre terracotta with remnants of red and white paint symbolizing day and night. $6^1/4 \times 4^3/4''$. West Coast culture: A.D. 300-1250. (Ixtlán, Nayarit). Coll.: Museo de Antropología de Guadalajara, Jal.

### 341. Sitting nude male figure

Smoking. Very lean. Ribs and bones very prominent. Red polished terracotta. $16^7/8 \times 11''$. West Coast culture: A.D. 300-1250. (Ixtlán, Nayarit). Coll.: K. Stavenhagen, Mexico.

### 342. Sitting man and woman*

Embracing. A frequently occuring, very characteristic representation. Triangular headdresses, nose-ornaments, necklaces and richly painted bodies, red terracotta. $18^1/8 \times 14^1/8''$. West Coast culture: A.D. 300-1250. (Ixtlán, Nayarit). Coll.: K. Stavenhagen, Mexico.

### 343. Pregnant female figure

Holding her stomach with her hands, symbol of fertility. Standing, nude. Ear-ornaments, necklace and painted body. Red polished terracotta. $20^7/8 \times 8^5/8''$. West Coast culture: A.D. 300-1250. (Ixtlán, Nayarit). Coll.: Dolores Olmedo de Olvera, Mexico.

### 344. Nude male figure*

Apparently dead. Sitting on a three-legged bench. Headdress in the shape of the hair; nose-ornaments. Terracotta, partly polished. $22^1/2 \times 9^1/2''$. West Coast culture: A.D. 300-1250. (Ixtlán, Nayarit). Coll.: Museo de Antropología de Guadalajara, Jal.

### 345. Nude woman giving birth

Ear and nose-ornaments, bracelets. The shoulders decorated with maize seeds. Red polished

terracotta. $18^1/8 \times 11''$. West Coast culture: A.D. 300-1250. (Ixtlán, Nayarit). Coll.: Dolores Olmedo de Olvera, Mexico.

### 346. Old nude man

Sitting, holding a long-shaped gourd in his left hand and a small dish in his right hand. Red terracotta. $23^5/8 \times 11^3/4''$. West Coast culture: A.D. 300-1250. (Ixtlán, Nayarit). Coll.: K. Stavenhagen, Mexico.

### 347. Amphora*

Shaped like a sitting, very fat, important lady. The body sumptuously decorated as a polychrome robe; ear- and nose-ornaments and six necklaces. Very short legs. Brown, polished terracotta. $15^3/8 \times 11^3/8''$. West Coast culture: A.D. 300-1250. (Ixtlán, Nayarit). Coll.: K. Stavenhagen, Mexico.

### 348. Sitting figure

Representing old nude woman. Red terracotta. $15^3/4 \times 7^7/8''$. West Coast culture: A.D. 300-1250. (Ixtlán, Nayarit). Coll.: K. Stavenhagen, Mexico.

### 349. Sitting female figure*

With her chin resting on her knee. One of the most important evidences of thë expressionistic character of this art. Ochre terracotta. $9 \times 7^1/8''$. West Coast culture: A.D. 300-1250. (Ixtlán, Nayarit). Coll.: K. Stavenhagen, Mexico.

### 350. Small figure sitting

In the manner of important people, with limbs turned inwards, wearing headband and ear-ornaments. Terracotta, covered by white, yellow and red lines. $6^1/4 \times 5^1/8''$. West Coast culture: A.D. 300-1250. (Ixtlán, Nayarit).

### 351. Female figure

With nude torso. Strongly marked facial features and short limbs. Ornaments of maize seeds on her shoulders. Ochre terracotta. $16^7/8 \times 12^3/8''$.

West Coast culture: A.D. 300-1250. (Ixtlán, Nayarit).

### 352. House
With roof painted to look like thatch. Domestic scene with numerous persons inside and outside. An eloquent evidence of daily life in this culture. Terracotta with patterns painted in red and light brown. 11³/₄×7¹/₈″. West Coast culture: A.D. 300-1250. (Ixtlán, Nayarit).

### 353. A house
Constructed on four supporting pillars, with an outside staircase. Inside a family is assembled around a brazier. Ochre terracotta with remnants of light brown paint. 13³/₈×6³/₄″. West Coast culture: A.D. 300-1250. (Ixtlán, Nayarit). Coll.: Dolores Olmedo de Olvera, Mexico.

### 353. A. House
With seven persons inside. Ochre terracotta with remnants of light brown paint. 10³/₄×6¹/₄″. West Coast culture: A.D. 300-1250. (Ixtlán, Nayarit). Coll.: Dolores Olmedo de Olvera, Mexico.

### 354. Scene
With four houses and various persons, a large tree in the middle. Red terracotta. 7¹/₂×11³/₄″. West Coast culture: A.D. 300-1250. (Nayarit). Coll.: Dolores Olmedo de Olvera, Mexico.

### 355. Family
Consisting of parents and two children with a small dog. The woman is grinding maize. The figures are arranged on a base. Ochre terracotta. 2¹/₂×7¹/₄″. West Coast sulture: A.D. 300-1250. (Nayarit). Coll.: Dolores Olmedo de Olvera, Mexico.

### 356. Person carried on a litter
With a companion and four figures who carry them. Red terracotta. 6³/₄×6¹/₄″. West Coast culture: A.D. 300-1250. (Nayarit). Coll.: Dolores Olmedo de Olvera, Mexico.

### 357. Scene with a "palo volador" (flywheel)
Ritual dance of astronomical character. A tree-trunk is placed in the center of the scene, with a participant in flight, suspended by a rope. The rite consists in making 52 turns around the pole, which represents the Indian time cycle. The scene also comprises a house and spectators. Red terracotta. West Coast culture: A.D. 300-1250. (Nayarit). Coll.: Dolores Olmedo de Olvera, Mexico.

### 357 A. Round of dancers
With eight nude figurines and two musicians in the middle. Red terracotta. 8¹/₈×4″. West Coast culture: A.D. 300-1250. (Nayarit). Coll.: Dolores Olmedo de Olvera, Mexico..

### 358. Vessel
Circular, with 18 persons dancing in a double circle. Ochre terracotta. 7¹/₈×9¹/₂″. West Coast culture: A.D. 300-1250. (Ixtlán, Nayarit). Coll.: Museo de Antropología de Guadalajara, Jal.

### 359. Chac-mool*
God of rain. In Tarascan "Curicaueri" (the Great Priest), a representation of Quetzalcóatl. Reclining nude figure with a small table, functioning as an altar, between his hands. At the entrance of the sanctuaries of the pyramids offerings were placed on it. The figure is reclining, because it was believed that one day he would return from his journey or dream and reign again, as he actually has been a king and priest before he became a god. Basalt. 37¹/₂× 57¹/₈″. West Coast culture: Tarascan: A.D. 900-1300. (Tzintzuntzan, Mich.). Coll.: Museo Regional de Michoacán, Morelia, Mich.

### 360. Howling coyote*
God of the mountains, the shooting stars and the mysteries of the night. Judging from the flat back, the figure may have served as a throne or a sacrificial tabel. Gray basalt. 29¹/₂×47¹/₄″. West Coast culture, Tarascan: A.D. 900-1300.

Sitting man and woman, embracing. Terracotta. West Coast culture. Cat. 342.

Sitting female figure with her chin resting on her knee. Terracotta. West Coast culture. Cat. 349.

Chac-Mool, god of Rain. Basalt. West Coast culture. Cat. 359.

Chac-Mool, god of rain (detail). Basalt.
West Coast culture. Cat. 359.

Howling coyote. Basalt. West Coast culture. Cat. 360.

Old woman, sitting. Terracotta. West Coast culture. Cat. 303.

Sitting prisoner. Terracotta. West Coast culture. Cat. 285.

Amphora shaped like a very fat important lady. Terracotta. West Coast culture. Cat. 347.

Hunchbacked figure with very large hands. Terracotta. West Coast culture. Cat. 269.

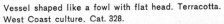

Vessel shaped like a fowl with flat head. Terracotta. West Coast culture. Cat. 328.

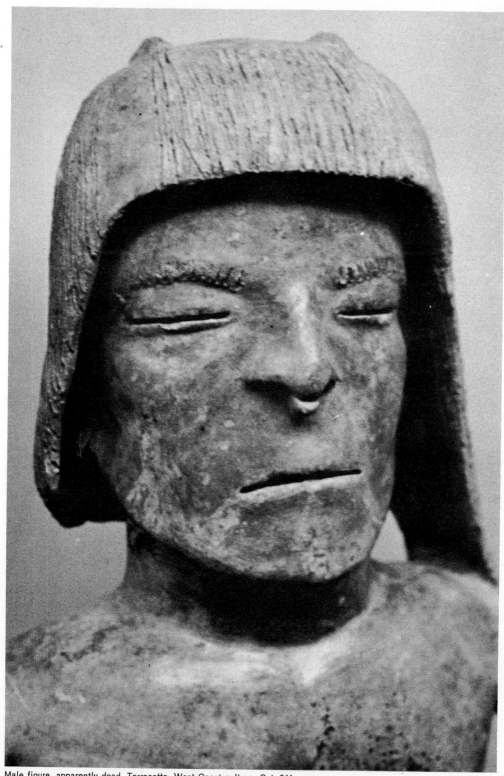

Male figure, apparently dead. Terracotta. West Coast culture. Cat. 344.

(Ihuatzio, Mich.). Coll.: Museo Regional de Michoacán, Morelia, Mich.

### 361. Small sitting figure

Representing "Curicaueri", the God of Rain. Wearing a mask with four plates, functioning as eyes and ear-ornaments, representing the four cardinal points. The canines characterize the deity of sacrifice. The headgear is decorated with the figure three: heaven, earth and the realm of the dead. Terracotta modelled in the pastillage technique. $4^5/8 \times 3^1/4''$. West Coast culture, Tarascan: A.D. 900-1300. (Michoacán). Coll.: Museo Regional de Michoacán, Morelia, Mich.

### 362. Spherical jar

With vertical flutings, long spout and basket-handles. White decoration on red polished ground. $8^1/4 \times 6^1/4''$. West Coast culture: Tarascan: A.D. 1300-1521. (Tzintzuntzan, Mich.).

### 363-372. Miniature jars

In various shapes: spherical, semi-globular and shaped like cushions and tripods. Spout with narow neck with basket-handles, three-legged shaped like baskets; three-legged shaped like human heads, hollow; four-legged, three-legged in the shape of spiders, with serrated rim; in the shape of duck, with handle. Terracotta with decorations in yellow and red, polished. The largest of these vessels measures $2^3/4 \times 3''$, the smallest $3/4 \times 7/8''$. West Coast culture, Tarascan: A.D. 1300-1521. (Tzintzuntzan, Mich.).

### 373. Mask representing the God of Rain

Eyebrows, nose and teeth shaped like snakes. Round eyes, representing clouds full of water. Volcanic tufa. $10 \times 9^3/4''$ West Coast culture, Tarascan, with Aztec influence: A.D. 1300-1521. (Arteaga, Mich.). Coll.: Museo Regional de Michoacán, Morelia, Mich.

### 374. Funeral mask

The back side of the mask has a glyph in the shape of an ara's head and the sign for the corresponding word. Polished obsidian. $7^1/4 \times 5^5/8''$. West Coast culture, Tarascan with Aztec influence: A.D. 1300-1521. (Sahuayo, Mich.). Coll.: Museo Regional de Michoacán, Morelia, Mich.

### 375. Necklace with 35 beads in one row

Shaped as truncated cones, highly polished and very close together. Rock crystal, weight 397 grammes. Length $17^5/8''$. West Coast culture, Tarascan: A.D. 1300-1521. (Michoacán), Coll.: Museo de Jiquilpan, Mich. (Through the Museo Nacional de Antropología, Mexico).

# 4. The Teotihuacán Civilization

*300 B.C.-A.D. 1000*
Divided into three periods:
Teotihuacán I:      300-0 B.C.
Teotihuacán II:     0-A.D. 300
Teotihuacán III:    A.D. 300-650
Teotihuacán IV:    A.D. 650-1000
*Sites*
San Juan Teotihuacán, Tenango, Otumba (the State of Mexico); Santiago Ahuizotla (Federal District); Calpulalpan (The State of Tlaxcala); Tehuacán (The State of Puebla); Huetamo (The State of Michoacán) and the State of Guerrero.

The Teotihuacán civilization in the center of Mexico is the most remarkable artistic manifestation of the plateau people. Its tradition starts with the pre-classic period, and before the Christian era the place had become the most important religious and cultural center in the Indian world of the time.

The Teotihuacán civilization, also called the "pyramid civilization", marks the beginning of the great cultural and urban centers, the creation of monumental sculpture and of an impressive architecture, in which the *tablero,* the rectangular wall and the *talud,* the diagonal wall, are combined, the creation of murals and of ceramics made in moulds and of a complex religious ceremonial.

The Teotihuacán valley slants gently towards the West from a height of 7500 feet, offering ideal conditions for social human life. At the beginning of the period known as Teotihuacán I (300 B.C. till the beginning of the Christian era), some groups belonging to the early pre-classic phase, undoubtedly coming from Tlatilco and Cuicuilco, settled in the middle of the valley, bringing their own cultural traditions. The figurines of this period are almost smooth and have very simple lines.

Side by side with this early culture (0-A.D. 300) it is possible, from the beginning of Teotihuacán II, to establish the presence of another tradition, characterized by a geometrical and symbolic art and by a spiritualized cult of the Water God (jaguar-serpent), whose origin is supposed to be the Gulf Coast. This group suppressed the agriculturists who had settled in the place at an earlier date, and its influence became from then on decisive. From this period date the sun and moon pyramids, built in the traditional architectural style. But at the same time a new type of building, of which the Quetzalcóatl-temple is an example, arises. Tlaloc-Quetzalcóatl or his attributes are found everywhere, as manifestations of the significance of the theocracy and of the religious interest of the people. Teotihuacán was not only a cultural center, but also the largest city so far known in Mesoamerica, and probably the capital of a theocratic empire. But primarily it was the Sacred City of old Mexico.

The center culminates in the period known as Teotihuacán III (A.D. 300-650). Towards the end of the 7th century, Teotihuacán was invaded by barbaric hordes and the temples were burned down. The following period, Teotihuacán IV (A.D. 650-1000) is characterized by a material and cultural revival and reconstruction, which does not, however, match the preceding period. In the 9th century the destruction of the culture is completed by a new wave of barbarians. But it is not implausible that the real cause of its demise was a crisis within the theocratic system. One of the aspects that are characteristic of the history of the great cultural centers of the classic period, both with the Mayans and with the peoples of the plateau, is the general crisis apparent from the fact that the towns were suddenly abandoned. Since these cultures were all theocratic, the cause can be either internal struggles (for power or for religious reasons) or a kind of petrification of the system and of the ruling class. All these signs of decline have been the prelude to the invasions of the barbarians.

The inhabitants of Teotihuacán used many different materials: andesite, granite, pyrite, serpentine, slate, basalt, "tecali", porphyry, mica, obsidian, jade, volcanic tufa, quartz, bone, horn, clay, sea shells, plant fibres, copal and wood. For ornaments they used lip and nose-plugs, ankle-rings, necklaces, breast-plates, bracelets, masks and mirrors. They wove their clothes of plant fibres, such as cotton, yucca and agave, dyeing the fibres in dyes made from vegetables and minerals. The dresses of the figurines mark certain social differences: the splendid costumes of the priests, headdresses with large feathers of the quetzal-bird, motley materials with appliqués of jade or sea shells, sandals, jewellery of expensive materials, as a contrast to the dress of the lower classes. The social stratification that had only been suggested in the early pre-classic period becomes apparent from the beginning of Teotihuacán II in a society whose members are divided into groups, according to their functions. It was presumably ruled by kings (priests), supposedly of divine origin.

The dead were either buried or burned. Together with human bones, either in the graves themselves or under the inner chambers and courtyards, numerous objects have been found which have been used as tomb gifts, among other things dogs that were to accompany the dead. In certain tombs the bones were not directly on the ground, but on splendid mother-of-pearl beds or on mica floors.

The natural phenomena: fire, thunder, rain, etc., were worshipped. There are renderings of the old god, or the Fire God (Huehueteotl), of Tlaloc, the rain god, Chalchiuhtlicue, the goddess of water and of Xipe, the god of fertility and renewal of nature. In connection with Tlaloc one finds Quetzalcóatl, the plumed serpent. The most important god was undoubtedly Tlaloc, who was considered the fecundator of the earth. He lived in the high mountains, where the clouds are formed and was represented with a mask, rings round the eyes, which symbolise the clouds heavy with rain, nose-ornaments, prominent canines and cleft tongue, i.e. with the attributes of the jaguar and the snake. The people of Teotihuacán did not reproduce material things, but created symbols and elaborated very complex religious ideas, as well as a theology that was to serve as the basis of that of their successors, until the Toltec and Aztec epoch.

The rain God had his dwelling in "Tlalocan", or Tlaloc's Paradise. There he was helped by "tlaloques" (clouds). The rain they spread was as precious as jade. Therefore water was expressed by the word "chalchihuitl" (a kind of emerald) and the colors most often used in the frescoes dedicated toTlaloc were green and turquois. The artists of Teotihuacán became masters of the fresco-art. The frescoes of Tepantitla are particularly admirable, a large composition representing the journey of the dead and his arrival at Paradise, the dwelling of Tlaloc, in a rapture of colors and flower motifs.

Teotihuacán was a gigantic town, constructed around a longitudinal axis, that was later named "the road of the dead", after the original nahuatl-word "Micaotli". Most of the religious buildings are in the shape of pyramids: truncated pyramids, with a staircase on one of the sides, pyramids put on top of each other, with landings (e.g. the Sun and Moon Pyramid), pyramids with rectangular walls, combining vertical and diagonal lines. Now and then they are adorned with paintings and sculptures, as for instance the pyramid called "the Citadel" and the Temple of the Plumed Serpent. The city has a surface of 55 square miles. The Sun Pyramid is 210 feet high. Its base is a square, the sides of which are 726 feet. The Moon Pyramid is 136 feet high and its base measures 486x389 feet. The large groups of buildings housed the multitudes of people participating in the religious celebrations, while the houses that were abundantly decorated with frescoes, were cult places for the priests.

Teotihuacán art was the simplest, the most severe and austere in ancient Mexico. It is far from any naturalism and expresses neither passion nor religious imagination, but contemplation and theological speculation. This culture created unprecedented symbols to express reality. The masks, these magical objects that both conceal and reveal the essence of the god or person, have a character that may be called abstract; they reduce the image to a sign, almost to an idea. The principles behind these sculptural and architectural works are concentration, interiorization, horizontal rhythm, a spatial construction reflecting the quincunx in its ideal form (the four cardinal points and the center, the immovable heaven, the axis of time and space). The whole is ruled by geometry, a vision of cosmic rest. If any Mesoamerican art deserves the name classic, it must be that of Teotihuacán.

**376. "Florero" (flower vase)**
Spherical. With neck and wide rim. Dark brown polished terracotta. $5^{1}/_{8} \times 3^{3}/_{4}''$. Teotihuacán I: 300 B.C.-o (Tenango, Mexico).

### 377. Head and nude torso
In realistic style, very expressive. Fragment of larger figure. Serpentine. 21$^1$/$_4$x9″. Teotihuacán I: 300 B.C.-o. (Teotihuacán, Mex.).

### 378. Male torso
Fragment of larger figure. Serpentine. 28x8$^5$/$_8$″. Teotihuacán I: 300 B.C.-o. (Teotihuacán, Mex.). Coll.: Museo Regional de Teotihuacán, Mex.).

### 379. Pendant of a necklace
In the shape of a small semi-circular mask with engraved headdress and eyes inlaid with copal. A strong Olmec influence is recognized in this style. Dark green jade. 2$^3$/$_8$x2$^3$/$_8$″. Teotihuacán I: 300 B.C.-o. (Teotihuacán, Mex.).

### 380. Small child's mask
Of Olmec type: Slanting eyes and mouth slit, upper lip drawn back. Green jade. 3x2″. Teotihuacán I: 300 B.C.-o. (Teotihuacán, Mex.). Coll.: Museo Regional de Teotihuacán, Mex.

### 381. Small figure
With rectangular headdress and loin-cloth. Headdress and hair incised. Green veined jade. 6$^3$/$_4$x2$^1$/$_2$″. Teotihuacán II: o-A.D. 300. (Yurecuaro, Mich.).

### 382-385. Small figures representing nude men
With arms and legs in dancing positions. Terracotta with traces of red and white paint. 4$^3$/$_8$x3$^1$/$_8$ and 4$^3$/$_8$x3$^3$/$_4$″. Teotihuacán II: o-A.D. 300. (unknown place of discovery).

### 386. Sitting female figure
Dressed in "huipil" (woman's triangular dress with an opening for the head). Terracotta with red paint. 3$^1$/$_8$x2″. Teotihuacán II: o-A.D. 300. (unknown finding place). Coll.: F. Feuchtwanger, Mexico.

### 387. Funeral mask
Representing a dead man. Delicate and well-proportioned features, the head deformed and tonsured. These masks were presumably put with the tomb equipment or used in religious ceremonies in connection with the death cult. Green granite. 9$^1$/$_2$x8$^5$/$_8$″. Teotihuacán II: o-A.D. 300. (Mexico Valley).

### 388. Small mask
Representing a fat man. Hair and eys incised. Light green jade. 2$^1$/$_8$x2″. Teotihuacán II: o-A.D. 300. (Teotihuacán, Mex.). Coll.: Museo Regional de Teotihuacán, Mex.

### 389. Brazier
Representing Huehueteotl (or the Old God), the god of the first fire. An old bent man with legs crossed and his hands on his knees. He was god of fire and light, "the father of gods and men", and he had numerous functions, specially in connection with the calendar. He is the oldest known god in the Mexican Pantheon. Volcanic rock. 14$^1$/$_2$x15$^3$/$_4$″. Teotihuacán II: o-A.D. 300. (Teotihuacán, Mex.). Coll.: Museo Regional de Teotihuacán, Mex.

### 390. Crenellated ornament*
From the front of a building, representing Tlaloc, the god of rain, sumptuously decorated with feathers of the quetzal bird, symbol of the creator of heaven and earth. One of the oldest Mexican deities. Red terracotta. 36$^5$/$_8$x29$^1$/$_8$″. Teotihuacán II: o-A.D. 300. (Teotihuacán, Mex.).

### 391-392. Two crenellated ornaments
Architectural elements, some of which adorn the sanctuary at the pyramid of Quetzalcóatl. Representing Quetzalcóatl, the god of rain in the Teotihuacán culture, with very stylized features. Basalt with traces of red paint. 59$^1$/$_2$x 57$^1$/$_8$″, 53$^1$/$_4$x65″. Teotihuacán II: o-A.D. 300. (Teotihuacán, Mex.). Coll.: Museo Regional de Teotihuacán, Mex.

### 393. Architectural element
Almost globular, with volutes representing "the

valuable water". Testifies to an Olmec influence still in existence. Sandstone. $15^3/_4$x$26''$. Teotihuacán II: o-A.D. 300. (Teotihuacán, Mex.). Coll.: Museo Regional de Teotihuacán, Mex.

### 394. Ceremonial knife
Shaped like a serpent. Obsidian. $2^1/_2$x$11''$. Teotihuacán II: o-A.D. 300. (Teotihuacán, Mex.).

### 395. Funeral mask
It is assumed that these masks were made to put on the mummy case after the mummy had been placed in a crouching position before burial or cremation. Realistic style, but all personal features have disappeared, which is characteristic of the periods II and III during which the Teotihuacán culture reached its full flowering. By reducing form to strictly geometrical proportions and by giving the mask a completely impassive expression, with the mouth forever half closed after the last sigh, the artist has tried to translate into stone the obsessive preoccupation with death and eternity. These basic features of the Teotihuacán style were taken over by the later Toltec and Aztec cultures. Stone. $9$x$11''$ Teotihuacán III: A.D. 300-650. (Teotihuacán Mex.).

### 396. Funeral mask
With realistic facial features. Ear-ornaments and perforated forehead. Stone. $11^3/_4$x$9''$. Teotihuacán III: A.D. 300-650. (Teotihuacán, Mex.).

### 397. Funeral mask
With realistic features. Green stone (damaged by fire) with remains of stucco. $11^3/_4$x$9^1/_2''$. Teotihuacán III: A.D. 300-650. (Teotihuacán, Mex.).

### 398. Funeral mask*
Covered with mosaic of small pieces of turquoise and red conches, stylised hieroglyph of Quetzalcóatl. Wears a necklace of beads, made of red conches, eyes inlaid with mother of pearl and obsidian. Green serpentine. $11^3/_4$x$9^1/_2''$. Teo-

tihuacán III: A.D. 300-650. (Teotihuacán, Mex.).

### 399. Funeral mask
With bands tattooed on eyes, nose and mouth, intended for a mosaic of semi-precious stones. Green veined stoned. $7^1/_2$x$7^1/_8''$. Teotihuacán III: A.D. 300-650. (Mexico Valley).

### 400. Funeral mask
Perforated forehead; nose and ears rectangular. Veined onyx. $7^1/_2$x$7^1/_2''$. Teotihuacán III: A.D. 300-650. (Otumba, Mex.).

### 401. Funeral mask
With realistic and very expressive features. Hair merely indicated. Red bands at the eyes, the mouth half open with teeth visible, large circular ear-ornaments. Terracotta with traces of paint in red and white $7^1/_4$x$9^7/_8''$. Teotihuacán III: A.D. 300-650. (Santiago Ahuizotla, D.F.).

### 402. Funeral mask
With realistic and very expressive features. Green veined, highly polished stone. $9^1/_2$x$8^5/_8''$. Teotihuacán III: A.D. 300-650. (Mexico Valley).

### 403. Funeral mask
Fragment. Granite-like, black, highly polished stone. $9^7/_8$x$9''$. Teotihuacán III: A.D. 300-650. (Teotihuacán, Mex.). Coll.: K. Stavenhagen, Mexico.

### 404. Small funeral mask
Eyes incrusted with mother-of-pearl and pyrites. Jade. $3^3/_8$x$3^7/_8''$. Teotihuacán III: A.D. 300-650. (Teotihuacán, Mex.).

### 405. Small funeral mask
Hollowed eyes, mouth incised and ears engraved. Jade. $2^5/_8$x$2^1/_2''$. Teotihuacán III: A.D. 300-650. (Teotihuacán, Mex.).

**406. Small funeral mask**
Eyes and mouth hollowed, ears engraved. Veined jade. $2^1/_8$x$2''$. Teotihuacán III: A.D. 300-650. (Teotihuacán, Mex.).

**407. Small funeral mask**
With small eyes and hollowed mouth. Green veined jade. $1^1/_2$x$1^5/_8''$. Teotihuacán III: A.D. 300-650. (Teotihuacán, Mex.). Coll.: Museo Regional de Teotihuacán, Mex.

**408. Pendant**
Of necklace, shaped like a small mask with distorted face and open mouth. Green veined jade. $2^3/_8$x$1^3/_4''$. Teotihuacán III: A.D. 300-650. (Teotihuacán, Mex.). Coll.: Museo Regional de Teotihuacán, Mex.

**409-410. Small masks**
Representing deities with paint on the faces. They were placed inside the ceremonial braziers in which copal or incense was burned. Polychrome terracotta. $3^1/_2$x$5^7/_8''$. Teotihuacán III: A.D. 300-650. (Teotihuacán, Mex.). Coll.: K. Stavenhagen, Mexico.

**411-412. Figurines with rectangular headdresses***
With ornaments at the back of the head, movable ear-ornaments and loin-cloth. Green jade. $2^1/_2$x$1^1/_4''$ and $2^3/_4$x$1^1/_2''$. Teotihuacán III: A.D. 300-650. (the Quetzalcóatl Temple, Mex.).

**413. Nude figurine**
With shaven head and loin-cloth. Green jade. $2^1/_2$x$1''$. Teotihuacán III: A.D. 300-650. (the Quetzalcóatl Temple, Mex.).

**414. Figurine**
With ornament at the back of the head. Green jade. $1^5/_8$x$1^1/_8''$. Teotihuacán III: A.D. 300-650. (the Quetzalcóatl Temple, Mexico).

**415-416. Figurines representing dwarfs**
With headdresses of feathers; ear-ornaments, loin-cloths and pants. Ochre terracotta with tra-

ces of white, yellow and brown paint. $7^1/_4$x$3^3/_4''$ and $6^3/_4$x$5^1/_8''$. Teotihuacán III: A.D. 300-650. (State of Mexico).

**417. Effigy jar representing Tlaloc***
The god of rain. On this jar, made out of one single piece of jade, Tlaloc is represented as sitting, wearing a headdress of double bands. The rings around his eyes symbolize clouds heavy with rain. The feline mouth is open, showing four long jaguar canines. Rectangular ear ornaments and a large breast-plate, covering the hands and legs. Green jade. $9^1/_2$x$6^3/_4''$. Teotihuacán III: A.D. 300-650. (Nanchititla, Mex.).

**418. Cylindrical vase**
With flat bottom. Cylindrical rounded legs and scratched decorations, representing two plumed serpents. Brown terracotta. $5$x$5^3/_4''$. Teotihuacán III: A.D. 300-650. (Unknown place of discovery).

**419. Cylindrical vase**
With flat bottom. Three cylindrical, rounded legs and incised decoration representing waves and glyphs. Brown terracotta. $4^3/_4$x$5^1/_8''$. Teotihuacán III: A.D. 300-650. (Unknown place of discovery).

**420. Cylindrical vase**
With flat bottom. Three cylindrical, rounded legs. Scratched decoration of two plumed serpents. Brown terracotta. $5^1/_8$x$5^3/_4''$. Teotihuacán III: A.D. 300-650. (Santiago Ahuizotla, Mex.).

**421. Cylindrical vase**
With flat bottom. The round bottom decorated with small heads. Three bell-shaped feet in the shape of calabashes. Brown terracotta. $6^3/_4$x$5^1/_4$x. Teotihuacán III: A.D. 300-650. (Teotihuacán, Mex.).

**422. Cylindrical vase**
With flat bottom and lid. Motifs representing

star symbols. Three flat, hollow, open-work legs, decorated with circular pattern. Brown terracotta, inlaid with white "tecal" and showing traces of vermilion paint. $9^7/8 \times 7^7/8''$. Teotihuacán III: A.D. 300-650. (Teotihuacán, Mex.).

### 423. Large tripod vase*
With lid. Three rectangular and open-work legs. Scratched decoration. Ochre terracotta with remnants of vermilion paint. $8 \times 11''$. Teotihuacán III: A.D. 300-650. (Teotihuacán, Mex.). Coll.: Museo Regional de Teotihuacán, Mex.

### 424. Cylindrical vase
With flat bottom and three flat legs. The bottom part decorated with small heads and a jaguar, modelled and mounted on the jar. Delicate orange terracotta. $5 \times 5^7/8''$. Teotihuacán III: A.D. 300-650. (Tehuacán, Pue.).

### 425. Cylindrical vase
With flat bottom. Three bell-shaped legs. Scratched decoration, representing the gods of agriculture. Brown terracotta. $9^7/8 \times 9^7/8''$. Teotihuacán III: A.D. 300-650. (Teotihuacán, Mex.).

### 426. Cylindrical vase
With flat bottom and three rounded legs. Fresco-decoration representing Tlaloc, the god of rain. Brown terracotta. $4^3/4 \times 4^3/4''$. Teotihuacán III: A.D. 300-650. (Teotihuacán, Mex.).

### 427. Large round vase
With flat bottom, decorated with glyphs in pastillage technique. Three hollow, spherical legs with open-work cross-pattern. Brown terracotta. $8^5/8 \times 12^5/8''$. Teotihuacán III: A.D. 300-650. (Teotihuacán, Mex.).

### 428. Vase
Polychrome painting in fresco technique. Motifs representing waves, butterflies and flowers. Delicate orange terracotta. $8^5/8 \times 7^7/8''$. Teotihuacán III: A.D. 300-650. (Teotihuacán, Mex.).

### 429-430. Fragments of vase
Painted in fresco technique. Representations of gods of agriculture and sun-signs. Brown terracotta. $3^7/8 \times 6^1/4''$ and $5^1/8 \times 4^3/8''$. Teotihuacán III: A.D. 300-650. (Teotihuacán, Mex.).

### 431. Bowl
Spherical. On the outside rich, engraved decoration, representing mythological scenes with gods, priests, warriors and animals. Ochre terracotta. $3 \times 5^1/4''$. Teotihuacán III: A.D. 300-650. (Calpylalpan, Tlax.).

### 432. Vessel
Almost spherical, with flat bottom, representing a fat hunchbacked dwarf. Dwarfs and hunchbacks played a great role as fools, wrestlers and acrobats. Delicate orange terracotta with a special absorbent preparation for fresco painting. $10^1/4 \times 9''$. Teotihuacán III: A.D. 300-650. (Tehuacán, Pue.). Coll.: K. Stavenhagen, Mexico.

### 433. Vessel*
Almost spherical, supported by a nude sitting figure, with his hair parted. Circular ear-ornaments and necklace. Hands on knees and crossed legs. Brown terracotta. $8^1/4 \times 9^1/2''$. Teotihuacán III: A.D. 300-650. (Teotihuacán, Mex.).

### 434. Small vessel
Shaped like a sitting figure with headdress and ornaments on the legs. Delicate orange terracotta. $5^1/2 \times 5^1/8''$. Teotihuacán III: A.D. 300-650. (Unknown place of discovery).

### 435. Small vessel
In the shape of a jaguar. Delicate orange terracotta. $3^7/8 \times 7^1/8''$. Teotihuacán III: A.D. 300-650. (Tehuacán, Pue.). Coll.: K. Stavenhagen, Mexico.

### 436-437. Small vessels
Shaped like small, curled up dogs. Delicate orange terracotta. $4^3/4 \times 9''$ and $1/2 \times 1^1/2''$. Teoti-

huacán III: A.D. 300-650. (Huejotzingo, Pue.).

### 438. Shell

Musical instrument with decoration in fresco technique, representing gods and calendar dates. Shell of a sea-snail. 13³/4×7⁷/8″. Teotihuacán III: A.D. 300-650. (Teotihuacán, Mex.).

### 439. Shell

Musical instrument with calendar dates engraved. Shell of a sea-snail. 7¹/8×16⁷/8″. Teotihuacán III: A.D. 300-650. (Teotihuacán, Mex.). Coll.: Museo Regional de Teotihuacán, Mex.

### 440. Small female figure

With large headdress, adorned with ribbons and feathers. Ear-ornaments, necklace and "quexquemitl" (Indian garment). Ochre terracotta with traces of white and brown paint. 4³/8× 2³/4″. Teotihuacán IV: A.D. 650-1000 (Teotihuacán, Mex.).

### 441. Small female figure

Headdress with jaguar's head; ear-ornaments, necklaces and feather-ornaments. Brown terracotta with traces of red and yellow paint. 2¹/2× 2¹/8″. Teotihuacán IV: A.D. 650-1000. (Teotihuacán, Mex.).

### 442-444. Miniature figurines

A dancer with polychrome headdress, a musician with a trumpet, a figure with removable headdress. Terracotta, modelled with pastillage technique. The largest of the figurines measures 5⁷/8″, the smallest 2³/8″. Teotihuacán IV: A.D. 650-1000. (Teotihuacán, Mex.). Coll.: K. Stavenhagen, Mexico.

### 445-449. Miniature figurines

A group of three figures, a person carried by two jaguars and three individual figures. Terracotta, pastillage technique. Average height 2″, width 1¹/8″. Teotihuacán IV: A.D. 650-1000. (Teotihuacán, Mex.). Coll.: K. Stavenhagen, Mexico.

### 450. Figurine

Representing a sitting dwarf, with his hands on his knees. Headdress, ear-ornaments, necklace. Terracotta with traces of paint. 2×³/4″. Teotihuacán IV: A.D. 650-1000. (Unknown place of discovery). Coll.: F. Feuchtwanger, Mexico.

### 451-452. Figurines

Sitting women with children. Terracotta with traces of paint. 2³/8×2³/8″. Teotihuacán IV: A.D. 650-1000. (Unknown place of discovery). Coll.: F. Feuchtwanger, Mexico.

### 453. Huehueteotl

The old God of the first fire. Standing, with a headdress, ear-ornaments, necklaces and a small skirt with ornaments. Brown terracotta. 4³/4× 2³/8″. Teotihuacán IV: A.D. 650-1000. (Unknown place of discovery).

### 454. Hunchbacked figurines

In wrestling position. Dressed only in loincloths. Terracotta with traces of white paint. 2³/4×3¹/2″. Teotihuacán IV: A.D. 650-1000. (Unknown place of discovery).

### 455. Sitting figurine

With deformed head, ear-ornaments and necklace. Ochre terracotta. 3¹/8×1⁵/8″. Teotihuacán IV: A.D. 650-1000. (Teotihuacán, Mex.).

### 457. Mask of old man

Representing Huehueteotl. Unique because of its technique, of which the composition still has not been analysed. Unburned gray clay. 11× 8⁵/8″. Teotihuacán IV: A.D. 650-1000. (Teotihuacán, Mex.). Coll.: K. Stavenhagen, Mexico.

### 458. Mask representing deity

Part of a large ceremonial brazier. Black terracotta with traces of paint in red, white and brown. 5⁷/8×8⁵/8″. Teotihuacán IV: A.D. 650-1000 (Teotihuacán, Mex.). Coll.: K. Stavenhagen, Mexico.

#### 459. Small mask representing eagle knight

Hollowed eyes, face placed in the open beak of an eagle. Terracotta with remnants of paint in red and yellow. $4^3/_4 \times 4^3/_8''$. Teotihuacán IV: A.D. 650-1000. (Unknown place of discovery).

#### 460. Xipe-Totec

"Our Lord the Flayed". Face and body dressed in a newly flayed human skin, symbol of spring and rebirth. Also called "the Great Expiator". Xipe-Totec was the god of sacrifice, repentance and of penance, i.e. purification. Also god of the sacrified warriors, and divine protector of the goldsmiths. Being corn god, the maize ears were dressed with yellow leaves like gold. Wears a headdress with the hair put up at the back of his neck and adorned with star symbols, a square shield on his left arm, and a bowl with eagle's claws in his right hand. The figure is composed of three distinct parts. Brown terracotta, with traces of paint in blue and brown. $43^1/_4 \times 19^5/_8''$. Late Teotihuacán (Mazapa-Toltec influence): A.D. 1000-1250. (Xolalpan, Mex.). Coll.: Museo Regional de Teotihuacán, Mexico.

Funeral mask covered with mosaic. Serpentine. Teotihuacán. Cat. 398.

Detail of the Temple of Quetzalcóatl. Teotihuacán, Mexico.

Pyramid of the Sun. Teotihuacán, Mexico.

Brazier representing Huehueteotl. Volcanic rock. Teotihuacán. Cat. 389.

Tripod vase with lid. Terracotta. Teotihuacán. Cat. 423.

Figurine with rectangular headdress. Jade. Teotihuacán. Cat. 411-412.

Jar representing Tlaloc. Jade. Teotihuacán. Cat. 417.

Crenellated ornament. Terracotta. Teotihuacán. Cat. 390.

Vessel representing sitting figure. Terracotta. Teotihuacán. Cat. 433.

# 5. The Zapotec Civilization

*650 B.C.-A.D. 1521*

Seven periods:

| | |
|---|---|
| Monte Albán I: | 650-200 B.C. |
| Monte Albán II: | 200 B.C.-A.D. 200. |
| Monte Albán II-III: | A.D. 200-350. |
| Monte Albán IIIA: | A.D. 350-700. |
| Monte Albán IIIB: | A.D. 700-1000. |
| Monte Albán IV: | A.D. 1000-1300. |
| Monte Albán V: | A.D. 1300-1521. |

*Sites*

Monte Albán, Mitla, Etla, Cuilapan, Teotitlán del Camino and Zachila (the State of Oaxaca).

"The Zapotecs constitute, with the Maya and the Toltecs, a third of the civilized pre-Hispanic peoples", the great Americanist Edouard Seler has said. The Zapotec group still exists within the geographical framework of the central valleys of Oaxaca, Etla, Tlacolula and Zimatlán. The center of this theocratic civilization is Monte Albán, a city constructed on terraces, situated as a veritable fortress on the highest point of a spectacular mountain range dominating the Oaxaca Valley.

Beginning about 200 B.C. the Zapotecs distinguished themselves by their handsome pottery urns representing deities, by their monochrome ceramics, their religious and funerary architecture and their tombs with angular vaults, many of which were covered with frescoes, by the strong, precise forms of their stelae and by the reliefs of their tombstones (e.g. the ones called "the Dancers"), as well as by their exact calendar, their hieroglyph writing and their contributions to the minor arts. The funeral urns represented sitting persons, with their hands on their knees and their heads adorned with plumed ornaments, gods of agriculture and of water, as well as other symbolic elements.

Through fossils of the giant mammals of the Pleistocene era have been found in the Oaxaca region, the existence of human life with this fauna has not been established with certainty. However, around Yanhuitlán, a pre-historical settlement of about 2000 B.C., exploration leads us to assume that groups of settlers have lived in Oaxaca since this remote period. The transition from the primitive phase to the Zapotec civilization proper still remains a profound mystery. But archeology has been able to demonstrate that the origins of this culture are to be found in other regions, perhaps deriving from the Olmecs or the Maya.

Around the tenth century the Zapotecs had to confront, and later come to terms with, a new people, the Mixtecs, who were slowly invading their valleys. For several centuries the peaceable Zapotecs thus co-existed with the belligerent Mixtecs. Later on the Zapotecs and the Mixtecs were to join forces against the invasion of the Aztecs, who eventually conquered them. Although the social organization of the Zapotecs in the beginning was essentially theocratic, the absolute autocrat, or "cacique" appeared shortly before the Spanish conquest.

The Zapotecs practiced deformation of the skull and filed their teeth, encrusting them with pyrites and turquoise. This can often be observed in their figurines and earthenware urns. The tutelary or malevolent spirits that lived in animals, trees, rocks, caves or the natural forces were the objects of their faith. Later on, with the rise of a sacerdotal organization a number of gods arose, making their religion a rather complicated affair.

Their astronomical knowledge was comprehensive; they possessed a very exact calendar and wrote on parchment and stone about history and geography. With the help of an ideographic and partly phonetic hieroglyphic writing they represented days, the deities of the year and conquests. All this was engraved in stone or painted within the tombs. The dead were buried, according to rank, in tombs or directly in the ground, and abundant offerings accompanied them. Slaves or dogs were frequently sacrified to accompany the dead on their journey to Lyobaa (the subterranean world). The religious celebrations and ceremonies were accompanied by dances, music, games and sacrifices.

The excavations at Monte Albán have made it possible to establish the development of ceramics and the approximative dates and variations within the civilization. In the Monte Albán I period (650-200 B.C.), we find for the first time a group with certain Olmec characters. The ceramics are gray, reddish brown, cream, black with white spots, pomegranate, white on red. It is the beginning of concave painting and fresco painting. The decorations are generally incised in the shape of geometrical motifs. But there are also representations of frogs, turkeys, ducks, snails, swimmers and of Cociji, the god of rain, as well as figurines. In the Monte Albán II period (200 B.C.-A.D. 200), after the settlement of some groups of people related to the Maya, jars and dishes with wide rims predominate, together with tripod vessels and terracotta jars with lids and handles decorated with frescoes. Later a marked period of transition, known in archeology as Loma Larga, seems to follow, and from this time we have twin bowls lids and jars with crenellated legs. This period can be determined as lasting from A.D. 200-350. Monte Albán III (A.D. 350-1000) shows an influence from Teotihuacán, particularly in ceramics. From this period we note vessels with effigy supports, large jars with stucco decorations, jars in the shape of bats claws and very elaborated urns. Monte Albán IV (A.D. 1000-1300) is the period of decline and the settlements are abandoned. Monte Albán V (A.D. 1300-1521) is stamped by the Mixtec influence.

In architecture the Zapotecs showed an extraordinary artistic sensitivity. Their skill as builders can be appreciated in the big ceremonial center Monte Albán, which is situated in a landscape of gigantic dimensions. But the beginnings of this center were modest. In period I we have the constructive system of large stone walls, placed in vertical rows and decorated with other stones, incised with figures of dancers and swimmers, as well as snake motifs in stucco. Then follows the use of mud bricks and real bricks with circular decorations in the friezes. During this second period the so-called Hill "J" was erected, presumably as an observatory. In period III buildings were placed on top of each other in two or more steplike formations and decorations in stucco and painting were executed. The intervals between the rectangular walls are decorated in the same way as the top part of the monolithic columns. The Monte Albán complex with its sober disposition of large masses and empty spaces possesses the unity of a living organism and the equilibrium of a geometrical construction. In his "Arte Antiguo de Mexico", Paul Westheim says: "While the ambition of Chinese architecture is to adapt the building to the surrounding landscape, Monte Albán is in framework and origin, non-nature. Not only have the architects not respected the configuration of the terrain, they have denied it, considering it as a chaos, on which man must impress order."

Mitla (in Zapotec: Lyobaa) was not a ceremonial center for the whole people like Monte Albán, but a city of the dead where the remains of kings and high-ranking priests were kept. Lyobaa means "the House of happiness or rest" and one might say that "never have the living dwelled so close to the dead". It was the most sacred of places and the seat of the high priest, or the "Great Seer". Mitla is a group of four buildings, closed towards the outside, with a patio in the middle. The Temple of Columns makes a calm and majestic impression with its rather limited proportions. But what particularly characterizes Mitla is the meandering patterns, made of bits of stone that are applied without mortar and combined so as to form mosaics, adorning the fronts of the buildings. These friezes of step-and-fret motifs were perhaps stylizations of snake skins and their repeated symmetrical forms in rhythmical arrangement may symbolize emphatic affirmation and exorcism with a magical propitiatory purpose. Westheim mentions that the walls of Mitla have little niches, halfway up. It is possible that one of these niches contained the relique that made Mitla famous, and was called "the heart of the world": a stone about 5 inches high, possibly a piece of transparent jade, in which were carved a bird and a snake. A Franciscan monk ordered this stone to be pulverized.

**461. Brazier**
Cylindrical. Represents a human face of Olmec type. Ochre terracotta. $6^1/4 \times 5''$. Monte Albán I: 650-200 B.C. (Nazareno, Oax.).

**462-463. Two cylindrical vases**
With flat bottoms. Each decorated with an engraved calendar glyph and a person with a bird's bill and a jaguar. Gray terracotta. $4^3/8 \times 3^1/2''$, $4^3/4 \times 3^5/8''$. Monte Albán I: 650-200 B.C. (Atzomba, Oax.).

**464. Round vessel**
With three rattle-supports in the shape of breasts

and carved decoration. Gray terracotta. 10x
12⁵/₈″. Monte Albán I: 650-200 B.C. (Monte
Albán, Oax.).

**465. Vessel\***

In the shape of a leg, adorned with glyphs in
bas-relief. Gray terracotta. 6³/₄x3⁷/₈″. Monte
Albán II: 200 B.C.-A.D. 200. (Monte Albán,
Oax.).

**466. Jar**

Representing *Cojico,* the god of rain, in haut-
relief. Gray terracotta. 7¹/₂x7¹/₈″. Monte Albán
II: 200 B.C.-A.D. 200. (Monte Albán, Oax.).

**467. Support of jar**

Spool-shaped. The tubular part with pierced
decoration. Gray terracotta. 11³/₈x6¹/₄″. Monte
Albán II: 200 B.C.-A.D. 200. (Monte Albán,
Oax.).

**468. Circular brazier**

With tall, cylindrical base. Representing a jaguar
with a bow at its neck. The rim of the vessel
decorated with a band of jaguar's claws, the
base has three bands with sun-hieroglyphs. Gray
terracotta. 14⁵/₈x9⁷/₈″. Monte Albán II: 200
B.C.-A.D. 200. (Oaxaca, Oax.).

**469. Jar**

Almost spherical, with long neck and spout.
Shaped like an old sitting man. Gray terracotta.
7¹/₂x6¹/₄″. Monte Albán II: 200 B.C.-A.D. 200.
(Monte Albán, Oax.).

**470. Jar**

Almost spherical with flat bottom, long neck
and carved pattern. Representing a sitting man,
who presses his hands against his chest. Gray
terracotta. 9x10¹/₄″. Monte Albán II: 200 B.C.-
A.D. 200. (Paso de Ovejas, Ver.).

**471. Jar**

Almost spherical, with flat bottom, long neck
and spout, representing a man with a jaguar's

mask. Gray terracotta. 9¹/₄x7¹/₂″. Monte Albán
II: 200 B.C.-A.D. 200. (Paso de Ovejas, Ver.).

**472. Jar**

With flat bottom and double spout, representing
a dancer with shaved head and a headdress in
the shape of a comb. Gray terracotta, adorned
with pastillage technique and with traces of
vermilion. 6x6″. Monte Albán II: 200 B.C.-
A.D. 200. (Monte Albán, Oax.).

**473. Bat's head**

The bat being the delegate of the god of darkness and death. With stylized and strongly
pronounced features, open mouth and protruding tongue. Ochre terracotta. 15³/₈x13³/₄″.
Monte Albán II: 200 B.C.-A.D. 200. (Ocotlán,
Oax.).

**474. Jaguar\***

Deity of Earth and Death. The head turned in
a defiant attitude. Necklace with breast-plate.
Gray terracotta. 15x19⁵/₈″. Monte Albán II:
200 B.C.-A.D. 200. (Oaxaca, Oax.).

**475. Sitting jaguar-bat**

With a necklace with pendant of three bells.
Gray terracotta. 12¹/₄x12″. Monte Albán II:
200 B.C.-A.D. 200. (Oaxaca, Oax.). Coll.: F. V.
Field, Mexico.

**476. Large breast-ornament**

In the shape of a mask, representing the Bat
God, a mixture of human elements and features
of the delegate of the god of Darkness and
Death, an animal that may have had direct
connection with the gods of agriculture, since
it fought against the plagues and pests of the
cultivated land. It was carried by a priest who
played the role of the god and invoked the fruits
of the earth, particularly the maize. The mouth
is thick-lipped in the shaped of flowers, eyes and
teeth are incrusted with mother-of-pearl, three
pendants of slate in the shape of a beard. It
is made in mosaic technique and consists of 25

Palace of Mitla, Oaxaca. Zapotec culture.

Standing priest. Terracotta. Zapotec. Cat. 478.

Jaguar, deity of Earth and Death. Terracotta. Zapotec. Cat. 474.

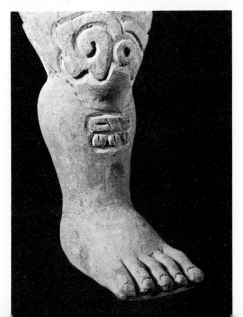

Vessel in the shape of a leg. Terracotta. Zapotec. Cat. 465.

The Priest of Cuilapan, also called the Scribe. Terracotta. Zapotec. Cat. 479.

arge funeral urn representing Cocijo. Terracotta. Zapotec. Cat. 485.

Funeral urn: half human, half jaguar-bat. Terracotta. Zapotec. Cat. 503.

Xochipilli. Terracotta. Zapotec. Cat. 495.

Funeral urn representing a goddess of the earth. Terracotta. Zapotec. Cat. 488.

Small funeral urn representing a sitting figure. Terracotta. Zapotec. Cat. 482.

Large funeral urn representing a sitting person. Terracotta. Zapotec. Cat. 500.

plates of jade, delicately worked and carved and fitted to each other. Apart from the Zapotecs, only the Olmecs and the Maya knew this unusual technique of jade-mosaic. Bluish green jade. $9^1/2 \times 6^1/4''$. Monte Albán II-III: 200 B.C.-A.D. 350. Monte Albán, Oax.).

#### 477. Support for a jar
In the shape of a vertebral column. Terracotta with fresco-painting. $16^1/8 \times 7^7/8''$. Monte Albán II-III: 200 B.C.-A.D. 350. (Monte Albán, Oax.).

#### 478. Standing priest*
With outstretched arms. Richly decorated with a high headdress, ornaments at the back of the head, pendants in the ears and a necklace of teeth. Dressed in loin-cloth, bracelets, ankle-rings and sandals. Terracotta with remnants of fresco-paint. $24^3/8 \times 12^5/8''$. Monte Albán II-III: 200 B.C.-A.D. 350. (Monte Albán, Oax.).

#### 479. The priest of Cuilapan*
Also called *the Scribe*. Naked figure, sitting with crossed legs and his hands on his knees. The features are realistic, the head deformed. On his forehead is engraved the calendar glyph "13 water", on his breast the date "13 eyes of the monster" (to each day corresponded a number, followed by a symbol). Ochre terracotta with traces of red paint. $13 \times 7''$. Monte Albán II-III: 200 B.C.-A.D. 350. (Cuilapan, Oax.). Coll.: Museo Regional de Oaxaca, Oax.).

#### 480. Small funeral urn
Representing a nude person, sitting with his arms crossed. Round headdress and ear-ornaments. The Zapotecs had a cult of the dead and buried them, according to social status, either in tombs or directly in the ground. According to circumstances, abundant offerings were placed in the tombs to accompany the dead. Sometimes the tombs were constructed of stone, in the interior of small burial mounds, in the shape of rooms with flat ceilings and walls de-

corated with frescoes. Sometimes the rooms had an antechambre, whose entrance was closed with a stone on which was placed an urn representing the patron god of the dead person and containing the ashes of his forefathers. In the tomb the body was placed pointing east-west, accompanied by offerings and small funeral urns with the ashes of forbears. Gray terracotta, with traces of vermilion. $8^1/4 \times 5''$. Monte Albán II-III: 200 B.C.-A.D. 350. (Monte Albán, Oax.).

#### 481. Small funeral urn
Representing an old man, the god of Fire, sitting, with a high headdress. Ear-ornaments, necklace with a large breast-plate, bracelets and facial decoration. Red painted terracotta. $12^5/8 \times 5^7/8''$. Monte Albán II-III: 200 B.D.-A.D. 350. (Monte Albán, Oax.).

#### 482. Small funeral urn*
Representing a sitting figure. The eyes incrusted with mother-of-pearl. The headdress symbolizes Cocijo, the god of Rain. Terracotta with red paint. $7^7/8 \times 5''$. Monte Albán II-III: 200 B.C.-A.D. 350. (Tomb 109, Monte Albán, Oax.).

#### 483. Small funeral urn
Representing a sitting deity with the high headdress of Cocijo. Terracotta with traces of vermilion. $7^1/2 \times 4^3/8''$. Monte Albán II-III: 200 B.C.-A.D. 350. (Oaxaca, Oax.).

#### 484. Small funeral urn
Representing a sitting figure, with a jaguar's mask, from which a small jaguar bat stands out, surrounded by rays of the sun. Gray terracotta with traces of white paint. $11^3/8 \times 8^5/8''$. Monte Albán II-III: 200 B.C.-A.D. 350. (Oaxaca, Oax.). Coll.: K. Stavenhagen, Mexico.

#### 485. Large funeral urn*
Painted with frescoes. Representing Cocijo. With graded headdress, round ear-ornaments, rings around the eyes, prominent canines and a necklace. Dark brown terracotta. $22^1/2 \times 24^3/4''$.

Monte Albán III A: A.D. 350-700. (Tomb 137, Monte Albán, Oax.).

### 486. Large funeral urn

Life size head of a person, representing an owl's head, with round ear ornaments, a large headdress with wings extended at the sides, and with ornaments at the back of the head. Ochre terracotta with traces of fresco-painting. 32$^{1}$/$_{4}$x 26″. Monte Albán III A: A.D. 350-700. (Tomb 77, Monte Albán, Oax.).

### 487. Funeral urn

Representing a sitting person with the face painted in red, richly adorned. High headdress, consisting of a large jaguar's head, a head of Ehecatl (a bird), the god of the wind, another jaguar's head, fragmentary and splendidly adorned with plumes. Ear-ornaments, necklace with pendant in the shape of a duck's head, and belt consisting of ears of maize. Ochre terracotta with traces of paint. 18$^{7}$/$_{8}$x15$^{5}$/$_{8}$″. Monte Albán III A: A.D. 350-700. (Monte Albán, Oax.).

### 488. Funeral urn*

Representing "13 Serpent", a goddess of the earth. Headdress consisting of entwined snakes. Face with delicate features, filed teeth, ear-ornaments and necklace, round-bordered shirt. Sitting position, Indian style. Dark brown terracotta. 13$^{3}$/$_{4}$x9$^{7}$/$_{8}$″. Monte Albán III A: A.D. 350-700. (Monte Albán, Oax.).

### 489. Funeral urn

Representing a sitting person, with crossed legs and his hands on his knees. Large headdress of feathers, necklace, ear-ornaments, dressed in a "maxlatl", a kind of loin-cloth. Terracotta. 13$^{3}$/$_{4}$x8$^{5}$/$_{8}$″. Monte Albán III A: A.D. 350-700. (Oaxaca, Oax.). Coll.: Dolores Olmedo de Olvera, Mexico.

### 490. Small funeral urn

Representing Cocijo with a mouth-mask shaped like serpents. Ochre terracotta with vermilion paint. 12$^{1}$/$_{4}$x7$^{1}$/$_{8}$″. Monte Albán III A: A.D. 350-700. (Tomb 77, Monte Albán, Oax.).

### 491. Vessel

In the shape of a fish. The tail is the spout. Red, polished terracotta. 3$^{1}$/$_{8}$x11″. Monte Albán III A: A.D. 350-700. (Zachila, Oax.).

### 492-493. Figurines representing dancers

With removable headdresses, consisting of birds' heads with large feathers. Equipped with prominent nose-plugs, round ear-ornaments, necklaces and small skirts, each holding a bag of copal, the emblem of the priests. Terracotta with traces of paint. 10$^{1}$/$_{4}$x5$^{1}$/$_{8}$″. Monte Albán III A: A.D. 350-700. (Monte Albán, Oax.).

### 494. Head

Fragment of funeral urn. Realistic features, large headdress with glyph. Gray terracotta. 10$^{5}$/$_{8}$x 5$^{7}$/$_{8}$″. Monte Albán III A: A.D. 350-700. (Monte Albán, Oax.).

### 495. Xochipilli*

The Flower Prince, god of Joy, Music and Dance. High headdress and necklace. The body decorated with geometrical plant and wave motifs. Dark brown terracotta. 18$^{1}$/$_{2}$x12$^{1}$/$_{4}$″. Monte Albán III A: A.D. 350-700. (San Lorenzo Albarradas, Oax.).

### 496. Musician blowing a shell

Standing, richly adorned with necklaces, bracelets, belt with bells and ankle-rings. Gray terracotta with traces of white paint. 24$^{3}$/$_{4}$x13″. Monte Albán III A: A.D. 350-700. (Oaxaca, Oax.). Coll.: K. Stavenhagen, Mexico.

### 497. Model of a temple

On a base, with a central staircase. Over the entrance is placed a deity in haut-relief with headdress adorned with bats and plumes, and in the skylight is seen a bird, flying towards the sun. The old Mexicans prepared plans both for the construction of their cities and of individual buildings. They also made very exact models in clay and stone. Andesite. $12^5/8 \times 13^3/4''$. Monte Albán III A: A.D. 350-700. (Oaxaca, Oax.).

**500. Large funeral urn***

Representing a person, sitting on a pedestal, with his hands on his knees. Very elaborate headdress, with a mask of Cocijo, the god of Rain and a sumptuous display of plumes. Also a large necklace, ear-ornaments and a belt of small bells. Terracotta. $24^3/4 \times 19^5/8''$. Monte Albán III B: A.D. 700-1000. (Oaxaca, Oax.). Coll.: Dolores Olmedo de Olvera, Mexico.

**501. Funeral urn**

Representing an important person, sitting with a jar in his hands. Large headdress, representing Cocijo and sumptuous display of plumes. Dark brown terracotta. $20^7/8 \times 15''$. Monte Albán III B: A.D. 700-1000. (Oaxaca, Oax.). Coll.: K. Stavenhagen, Mexico.

**502. Funeral urn**

In the shape of a sitting bat with stretched out claws. The body is of human shape. Large necklace with pendant representing a jaguar's head. Gray terracotta. $18^1/8 \times 10^1/4''$. Monte Albán IV: A.D. 1000-1300. (Oaxaca, Oax.). Coll.: K. Stavenhagen, Mexico.

**503. Funeral urn***

Half human, half jaguar-bat, in sitting position. The left hand is at the neck. Representing a supernatural being. Adorned with necklace and belt. Gray terracotta. $18^1/2 \times 10^5/8''$. Monte Albán IV: A.D. 1000-1300. (Oaxaca, Oax.). Coll.: K. Stavenhagen, Mexico.

# 6. The Mixteca-Puebla Civilization

*A.D. 800-1521*

*Sites*

Coixtlahuaca, Tilantongo, Yanhuitlán, Nazareno, Noehixtlán, Tuxtepec, Teotitlán del Camimo, Monte Albán and Mitla (the State of Oaxaca); Cholula (the State of Puebla); Tlaxcala (the State of Tlaxcala) and Texmelincan (the State of Guerrero).

The high mountains of Oaxaca were occupied by the Mixtecs, "the inhabitants of the cloud country", whose influence on the Zapotec culture is felt from around A.D. 1000. The Mixtecs, who have survived to this day, created certain particularly brilliant art forms: highly refined polychrome ceramics, precious geometrical decoration in town architecture, e.g. at Yagul and Mitla, refined gold jewellery, a perfect mastery of bone, wood and alabaster, codices that were folded like screens, and mosaics of precious stones.

The Mixtecs maintained that they descended from some trees in the region of Apoala, the branches of which were supposed to have produced their first "caciques" (chiefs) – men and women – who multiplied and succeeded in populating a very extensive realm. They must have been Nahuas. They practiced agriculture, hunting, fishing, collected fruits and provided themselves with raw materials and manufactured products, of which they were short, by means of commerce. They manufactured paper for the codices, baskets and cloth, garments, earthenware for domestic and funeral uses, ornaments, nets and boats and drums.

The Mixtec women wore blouses, skirts of dyed materials, and "huipiles", capes and "quexquemitl's". The men wore cotton materials, tied over the shoulder, loin-cloths, "xicolli's" (a sort of long shirt). Both men and women wore sandals and jewellery of shell, gold, silver, jade, turquoise and coral.

The Mixtec society was divided into two main classes. The upper class consisted of the chiefs or "caciques", the nobility, the merchants and the rich people; the lower class of artisans and peasants. The country was divided into principalities, ruled by chiefs with hereditary titles. The chief was the leader in war-time, and he was surrounded by counsellers and governors who belonged to the nobility.

The Mixtecs were primarily a warrior people. Their traditions and manuscripts retain the memories of a series of conquests, e.g. the Apoala ruler's conquest of Tilantongo, on which occasion the first Mixtec fought with the Sun about dominion over the territory. The warriors were recruited from the districts of the chiefs, and their captains were chosen from the upper class. Before they went to war, they consulted oracles and had propitiatory ceremonies. The Mixtecs used ornaments for noses and ears, plugs for under the lower lip and wore bracelets and ankle-rings. They painted their bodies and faces in various colors and wore red tattoos. The high priest wore a dyed mantle, a sleeveless shirt, or "xicolli", and a kind of mitre. The other priests painted their faces black. The priesthood occupied high civil and military positions.

The numeral system, based on the number twenty, astronomy and the calendar corresponded to the same systems of the other peoples from Mexican antiquity. In their admirable folded manuscript on roe-hides, the Mixtecs registered their genealogy, their conquests, their gods and their every day occupations. They had a large number of deities and some of their names have been preserved: Huituayuta (the god of life), Yozotoyua (the god of merchants), Cohuy (the god of maize), Qhuay (the god of hunters). These deities also had names of the calendar: Quecosagua: 7 deer, Nuchi: 6 wind, Ganacuu: 5 lizard. All the deities descended from a divine couple. The Mixtecs worshipped the Sun (Taandoco), to whom they sacrificed prisoners of war. Quetzalcoátl was one of their most important gods.

There seems to have been no Mixtec architecture proper, but we can speak of a transitional stage in architecture, in which Zapotec constructions on Mixtec soil resulted in a style, reminiscent of Zapotec architecture, but with the precious Mixtec decorations added to it, as is apparent in Yagul and Mitla. Many architectural elements that had originated in the III B epoch of Monte Albán show up at Yagul, where there are altars decorated with stone-mosaics, mainly frets, tombs with fronts decorated in the same style and rooms covered with paintings of the Mixtec type. These mosaics, with their step-and-fret motifs, with their cruciform, wavy, serrated and rhomboid motifs on red ground, so that the white colors of the geometrical motifs stand out clearly, are characteristic of Mitla. So is the Hypostyle Hall of the Temple of the Columns, where the pilasters made out of one block lend the place a truly majestic aspect.

The Mixtec ceramics from Tilantongo and Yucunco are related to those of Monte Albán I; and those of Yucunudahui with those of Monte Albán II. The Mixtec ceramics proper begin around A.D. 1000, at the time when the monochrome, often black or gray, lead-like vessels appear. In the last period appear the polychrome and bichrome ceramics. The bichrome earthenware is rich in bowls with fret motifs, reminiscent of the decorative art of Mitla, e.g. the small dishes decorated with skulls and crossed bones. The colors used are vermilion, black and dark red on white ground. The polychrome ceramics comprise jars and tripod dishes with supports ending in animals' heads, particularly snakes' heads, handsome zoömorphic vessels, eagles and jaguars, biconic braziers with a skull on the front. The Mixtec codices follow the same style. Among the most remarkable objects in Mixtec gold jewellery must be mentioned the ones from tomb 7 in Monte Albán: Plugs of gold for under the lower lip, necklaces with globular, oval or carapace-shaped beads, always ending in bells, filigree-rings, ending in jaguars' or eagles' heads, nose-ornaments shaped like butterflies, handles for sticks or scepters, pendants decorated with filigree. The patience and skill of the Mixtec artisans is also manifest in their works in stone, bone and wood.

The delicately worked jaguar's bones may be compared to Oriental ivory miniatures.

We find here a whole register of information: signs for days, figures of rabbits, crocodiles, reeds, flintstone, eagles, flowers, proper names, dates, star motifs. Other examples of Mixtec art offer the "atlatls" (propellers of arrows) and the "teponaxtles" (drums) carved in wood, handles of sacrificial knives, pectorals and plates of jade, "penates" or small idols of jade and serpentine, and vases and cups of rock-crystal. Dürer's astonishment, when he saw, at Charles V's court, some pieces of gold jewellery from Mexico, is well-known. These pieces were probably Mixtec. And Mixtec, certainly, was the silver fish, encrusted with gold, which the emperor gave to the pope, and which filled Benvenuto Cellini with admiration and surprise at its execution.

**504. Macuilxochitl**

An incarnation of Xochipilli, the patron god of Music, Singing, Dance and the emerging Sun, of the court-nobles, of Poetry, Games and Joy, represented as a nude man with his body painted in red and disguised as Quetzalcocochtli, a bird that sings at dawn. Wears a dancer's headdress. Red terracotta with traces of fresco painting. 15³/₄×11³/₄″. Mixteca-Puebla: A.D. 1300-1450. (Teotitlán del Camino, Oax.).

**505. Macuilxochitl**

Disguised as Quetzalcocochtli, a bird that sings at dawn. With dancer's headdress. Ochre terracotta with fresco painting. 15³/₄×8⁵/₈″. Mixteca-Puebla: A.D. 1300-1450. (Unknown finding place). Coll.: K. Stavenhagen, Mexico.

**506. Censer**

With hemispherical receptacle and pierced decoration; handle shaped like a snake. Two round supports. Ochre terracotta with traces of red and brown paint. 3⁷/₈×8¹/₄″. Mixteca-Puebla: A.D. 1300-1450. (Oaxaca Valley, Oax.).

**507. Bowl**

Hemispherical with flat bottom and simple rim. Decorated with carvings on polished red ground. Ochre terracotta. 3⁷/₈×6¹/₄″. Mixteca-Puebla: A.D. 1300-1450. (Nazareno, Oax.).

**508. Polychrome vessel***

With flat bottom and three legs in the shape of snakes' heads. Decorated with stellar motifs and a symbol of "the precious water". Ochre terracotta. 3⁷/₈×5⁷/₈″. Mixteca-Puebla: A.D. 1300-1450. (Nochixtlán, Oax.).

**509-510. Two polychrome vessels**

With flat bottoms and each three legs shaped like snakes' heads and stylized plumes. Decoration with eagles' profiles, step motifs, and richly adorned deities in conversation. Ochre terracotta. 4¹/₈×6″, and 4¹/₈×7″. Mixteca-Puebla: A.D. 1300-1450. (Tejuanilco, Oax. and Acatlan, Pue.).

**512. Circular polychrome lid of jar**

Decorated with motifs like points, circles, arrows and rectangles of solar significance. Ochre terracotta, with fresco painting. ³/₈×5″. Mixteca-Puebla: A.D. 1300-1450. (Oaxaca, Oax.).

**513. Small jar**

With flat spout and handle, decorated with stellar signs. Ochre terracotta with painting. 3¹/₈×2³/₄″. Mixteca-Puebla: A.D. 1300-1450. (Oaxaca, Oax.).

**514. Small jar**

With concave spout and handle in the shape of a snake. Decorated with three signs: eagle, human face and death. Polychrome terracotta. $4^{3}/_{4} \times 4^{3}/_{4}''$. Mixteca-Puebla: A.D. 1300-1400. (Etla, Oax.).

### 515. Small bowl
Polychrome, of the "florero" type, wide rim, handle-spout. Decorated with stylizations of a bird and an insect. Ochre terracotta. $5^{1}/_{4} \times 5^{5}/_{8}''$. Mixteca-Puebla: A.D. 1300-1450. (Oaxaca, Oax.).

### 518. Small polychrome jar
Polished and with flat spout and handle. Because of the rich decorations similar to those of the Mixtec codices with various deities. This jar might have belonged to the household of some Mexican ruler. Ochre terracotta. $6 \times 5^{5}/_{8}''$. Mixteca-Puebla: A.D. 1300-1450. (Nochixtlán, Oax.).

### 519. Bowl
With three rounded rattle-supports. Decorated with three snakes and various signs, similar to those of the codices. Ochre polychrome terracotta. $9 \times 8^{1}/_{4}''$. Mixteca-Puebla: A.D. 1300-1450. (Etla, Oax.).

### 520. Breast-plate
Representing *Xiuhtecuhtli* (Xiuh: turquoise, Tecutli: prince), the god of Fire, with ear-ornaments in round, square and triangular shapes. Gold (lost wax technique). $3^{1}/_{8} \times 2''$. Mixteca-Puebla: A.D. 1300-1450. (Coixtlahuaca, Oax.). Coll.: Museo Regional de Oaxaca, Oax.

### 521. Breast-plate*
Representing Xipe-Totec, "Our Lord the Flayed", god of Spring and Vegetation. The skin of a flayed person covers the head of the deity, the mask is fastened with cords, and at the top we see the hair and the tuft that the warriors wore on one side. Gold (lost wax technique). $4^{3}/_{4} \times 7^{1}/_{8}''$. Mixteca-Puebla: A.D. 1300-1450. (Coixtlahuaca, Oax.).

### 522. Necklace
Of five calabash-shaped beads, six round gold beads and 73 cylindrical beads of mother-of-pearl. Gold and mother-of-pearl. Weight $6^{5}/_{8}$ oz., length $15^{3}/_{4}''$. Mixteca-Puebla: A.D. 1300-1450. (Coixtlahuaca, Oax.).

### 523. Large breast-plate*
For distinguished person, representing *Mictlantecutli*, god of Darkness and Death, luxuriously adorned on a plate divided into two squares, the left of which contains the head of the god of Wind, while the right one has a Mixtec sign of the year and two dates, Gold (lost wax technique). Weight 4 oz., length $4^{3}/_{4} \times 3^{1}/_{2}''$. Mixteca-Puebla: A.D. 1300-1450. (Tomb 7, Monte Albán, Oax.). Coll.: Museo Regional de Oaxaca, Oax.

### 524. Mask representing Xipe-Totec
"Our Lord the Flayed". With round ear-ornaments and a nose-ornament in the shape of a butterfly. Gold (lost wax technique) – Weight $3^{1}/_{2}$ oz., length $2^{3}/_{8} \times 3^{1}/_{2}''$. Mixteca-Puebla: A.D. 1300-1450. (Tomb 7, Monte Albán, Oax.). Coll.: Museo Regional de Oaxaca, Oax.

### 525. Ring with eagle's head
Representing the rising sun, with nine rattle-supports. Gold (lost wax technique). Weight $^{5}/_{8}$ oz., length $1^{3}/_{8} \times 3/_{4}''$. Mixteca-Puebla: A.D. 1300-1450. (Tomb 7, Monte Albán, Oax.). Coll.: Museo Regional de Oaxaca, Oax.

### 526. Ring
Representing an eagle descending, the symbol of the setting sun. As a pendant the sign for "precious water" and seven bells. Gold (lost wax technique). Weight $^{7}/_{8}$ oz., length $1^{3}/_{8} \times 3/_{4}''$. Mixteca-Puebla: A.D. 1300-1450. (Tomb 7, Monte Albán, Oax.). Coll.: Museo Regional de Oaxaca, Oax.

### 527. Breast-plate
With representation of Xochipilli, the Flower

Large breast-plate representing Mictlantecutli, god of Darkness and Death. Gold. Mixtec. Cat. 523.

Large decorated vase. Terracotta. Mixtec. Cat. 546.

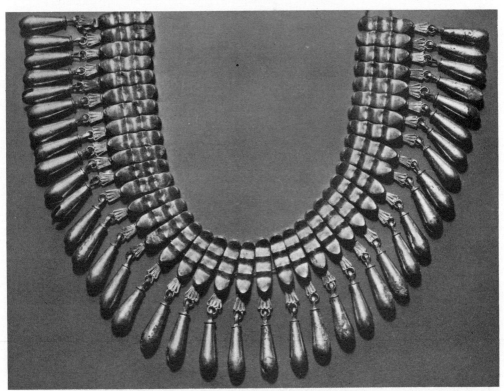

Necklace. Gold. Mixtec. Cat. 529.

Polychrome vessel with legs in the shape of snakes' heads. Terracotta. Mixtec. Cat. 508.

Breast-plate representing Xipe-Totec. "Our Lord the Flayed". Gold. Mixtec. Cat. 521.

Teponaztli. Wooden drum. Mixtec. Cat. 550.

Tlaloc, god of Rain. Terracotta. Mixtec. Cat. 551.

Large vase in the shape of a human skull. Terracotta. Mixtec. Cat. 555.

Prince, deity of Vegetation and the new Maize, and god of Games, Plays, Music and Dance. He is also called "Centeotl" in aztec songs and poems. Gold (lost wax technique). Weight $^5/_8$ oz., length $3^1/_8 \times 2^3/_8''$. Mixteca-Puebla: A.D. 1300-1450. (Tomb 7, Monte Albán, Oax.). Coll.: Museo Regional de Oaxaca, Oax.

### 528. Large breast-plate
For important person, shaped out of bits of turquoise, mother-of-pearl, gold and gold-bells. Weight 13 oz., length $7^7/_8 \times 15^3/_4''$. Mixteca-Puebla: A.D. 1300-1450. (Tomb 7, Monte Albán, Oax.). Coll.: Museo Regional de Oaxaca, Oax.

### 529. Necklace*
Of 39 beads, shaped like jaguar's teeth and bells. Gold (lost wax technique). Length $15^3/_4''$. Mixteca-Puebla: A.D. 1300-1450. (Tomb 7, Monte Albán, Oax.). Coll.: Museo Regional de Oaxaca, Oax.

### 530-532. Three round breast-plates
On two of them representations of a monster's face, concentric circles and sun rays; on the third sun signs. White jade. $3^1/_2 \times 3^1/_2''$ to $3 \times 2^3/_4''$. Mixteca-Puebla, late period: A.D. 1375-1521. (Mexico Valley).

### 532-535. Three "penates"
With representations of death seated, with the hands on the chest. Green stone. $6^3/_4 \times 2^1/_2''$, $5^1/_4 \times 2''$ and $4^3/_8 \times 1^3/_4''$. Mixteca-Puebla, late period: A.D. 1375-1521. (Oaxaca, Oax.).

### 536-538. Three masks
Pendants of necklace, representing Tlaloc, the god of Rain. Light green stone. One $3^1/_2 \times 3^1/_4''$ the other two $3^1/_4 \times 2^3/_4''$. Mixteca-Puebla, late period: A.D. 1375-1521. (Oaxaca, Oax.). Coll.: S. Hale, Mexico.

### 539. Necklace
With seventy round beads. Light gray jade with some beads of dark green jade. Length $15^3/_4''$. Mixteca-Puebla, late period: A.D. 1375-1521. (Oaxaca, Oax.).

### 540. Necklace
Of 64 round and tubular beads. Light green jade, very finely polished. Length $16^1/_2''$. Mixteca-Puebla; late period: A.D. 1375-1521. (Oaxaca, Oax.).

### 541. Necklace
Of 106 round beads. Rock-crystal. Length $15^3/_4''$. Mixteca-Puebla, late period: A.D. 1375-1521. (Oaxaca, Oax.).

### 542. Small sculpture
In the shape of a hand, with holes for hanging it as a pendant. Rock-crystal. $2^1/_8 \times 1^1/_8''$. Mixteca-Puebla, late period: A.D. 1375-1521. (Oaxaca, Oax.).

### 543-544. Small sculptures
With holes for hanging them as pendants. A skull, B frog. Rock-crystal. $1^3/_4 \times 1^3/_8''$, $2^1/_8 \times 1^5/_8''$. Mixteca-Puebla, late period: A.D. 1375-1521. (Unknown finding place).

### 545. Vase for tomb gifts
In the shape of two cones, the top rim is wide. Decoration with skulls, hands and flint stone. Polychrome terracotta. $9 \times 4^1/_2''$. Mixteca-Puebla, late period: A.D. 1375-1521. (Oaxaca, Oax.).

### 546. Large vase*
Decorated with skulls and crossed bones. Terracotta with cream and dark brown paint. $12^1/_4 \times 5^1/_2''$. Mixteca-Puebla, late period: A.D. 1375-1521. (Tlaxcala).

### 547-548. Censers
In the shape of hemispherical receptacles, representing masks of gods of Rain. With long handles, decorated at the end with eagle's head and claws of a bird. Polychrome, polished terra-

cotta. 24×9⁷/₈″, 25¹/₄×10³/₈″. Mixteca-Puebla, late period: A.D. 1375-1521. (Mexico City).

### 549. Censer
Of complicated form, with two flat handles. The round top part adorned with two snakes' heads. Decorated with eagles' heads and other signs. Polychrome ochre terracotta. 5¹/₈×8⁵/₈″. Mixteca-Puebla, late period: A.D. 1375-1521. (Cholula, Pue.).

### 550. Teponatzli*
Wooden drum with two tongs, representing a person lying on his stomach, adorned with an elegant headdress and a necklace of plumes. The eyes inlaid with mother-of-pearl and pyrites. Carved out of a trunk. 23⁵/₈×5⁷/₈″. Mixteca-Puebla, late period: A.D. 1375-1521. (Tlaxcala, Tlax.).

### 551. Tlaloc*
God of Rain and Germination. Seated, with crossed arms over his knees. Rings around his eyes, symbolizing clouds. Nose and mouth of the jaguar-serpent, which is connected with the myth of the earth and agriculture. Large headdress, necklace and decorated sandals. Ochre terracotta, originally richly painted. 18⁷/₈×9″. Mixteca-Puebla, late period: A.D. 1375-1521. (Tlaxcala, Tlax.).

### 552-553. Two vases
With flat bottoms, wide rims, narrow legs. One shows a symbolical decoration: water and sun rays. The other a monkey talking. Polychrome terracotta. 3¹/₈×9¹/₄″ and 3¹/₂×7³/₄″. Mixteca-Puebla, late period: A.D. 1375-1521. (Tepeaca, Pue. and Veracruz).

### 554. Tripod polychrome vase
Decorated with motifs of plumes, scrollwork patterns and stripes. Terracotta. 8⁵/₈×5¹/₈″. Mixteca-Puebla, late period: A.D. 1375-1521. (Cholula, Pue.).

### 555. Large vase*
In the shape of a human skull. Protruding eyes, the nose mutilated, the mouth fleshless, support in the shape of a truncated cone. Terracotta with fresco painting. 7⁷/₈×12″. Mixteca-Puebla, late period: A.D. 1450-1521. (Mexico City).

### 556. Brazier with four hemispherical protuberances
With two flat handles. Decoration of incised lines, representing monkeys, on red polished ground. Ochre terracotta. 3³/₄×8¹/₄″. Mixteca-Puebla, late period: A.D. 1450-1521. (Mexico Valley).

# 7. The Huaxtec Civilization

*Northern part of the Gulf of Mexico*
*1100 B.C.-A.D. 1521*
Comprises seven periods:
Pavon and Ponce: 1100-600 B.C.
Aguilar and Pánuco I: 600-100 B.C.
Panuco II: 100-B.C.-A.D. 200
Panuco III: A.D. 200-700
Panuco IV: A.D. 700-1000
Panuco V: A.D. 1000-1250
Panuco VI: A.D. 1250-1521

*Sites*
Pavon and Las Flores (The State of Tamaulipas); El Ebano, Tamuin, Tantoc, Tancan-
huitz, Tampozoque, Cuatlamayan and Xilitla (the State of San Luís Potosí), and Hue-
jutla (the State of Hidalgo).

The Huaxtec civilization developed in a zone that comprises the southern part of the
present State of Tamaulipas, the large coastal plain on the Gulf of Mexico, the eastern
part of the State of San Luís Potosí, and the northern part of the State of Veracruz, as
well as part of the neighboring states of Hidalgo and Queretaro. From an ethnological
and linguistic point of view, the Huaxtecs belong to the Maya family.

The pre-classic Huaxtec culture originated in the region of Tampico, in the so-called
"Sitio Pavón". The ceramics of this period are in certain features reminiscent of that of
the pre-classic peoples from the plateau. Later on the Huaxtecs had an independent development.

The architecture of the Huaxtecs is inferior to that of the other pre-Hispanic civilizations, but it is possible that the discoveries of future archeologists will prove surprising in
that respect. It should be mentioned that the dimensions of certain buildings are quite
exceptional. The Tantoc-pyramids (in the State of San Luís Potosí) which have not yet
been explored surpass the Sun Pyramid of Teotihuacán, both in height and volume.
The altars are of great interest, because they sometimes are constructed on circular, semi-
circular or rectangular bases, with rounded corners, in a "streamlined" style, that seems
to connect them with the cult of Quetzalcóatl, in his role of "God of the Wind". One
of the hieroglyphic representations of this deity is the spiral of a conch in longitudinal
section.

In sculpture the Huaxtecs show preference for the stone stela, which they carved in
bas-reliefs of extremely complicated mythological scenes, like the one of the god Xolotl,
the devine monster who was the twin of Quetzalcóatl. Their detached sculptures are al-

Large stela of Xolotl, the evening star. Limestone. Huaxtec. Cat. 564.

Xilonen, goddess of Maize. Limestone. Huaxtec. Cat. 565.

Centeocihuatl, goddess of Maize. Limestone. Huaxtec. Cat. 561.

most two-dimensional. Certain volumes of a great tenderness are surrounded by a simple and sober geometrical frame.

Among the Huaxtec sculptures one piece is often mentioned as outstanding and with much justification: that of an adolescent to whose back a child is clinging. In spite of the realism of this figure, it is a representation of Quetzalcóatl, the evening star, on his way to the lower world with his son, the setting sun. The ceramics are divided into six periods (Panuco I to VI). The cream colored jars tinged with green, are the most common. They are smooth and decorated with black paint, with incised decoration or even with frescoes. The anthropomorphic tendency is dominant (breasts of women). The handmodelled figurines of clay, are of great elegance.

The Huaxtecs put much store on the adornment of the body. They practised tattooing and several artificial deformations of the skull and the teeth. Apart from that they dyed their teeth with chapopote, a kind of black unrefined oil. They liked ornaments of feathers, gold, jade and turquoise, and, even more, of mother-of-pearl which they treated with a skill that has not been surpassed anywhere.

They constantly had to fight hordes coming from the North, and towards the middle of the XVth century they were partly conquered by the Aztecs, on whose religion they had considerable influence. The Huaxtec government was centralized, but from all territories there were representatives. The Huaxtecs lived in a very fertile region. Their material wealth is reflected in their attitude towards life, which is more cheerful and sensual than that of the other groups who lived on the plateau. This explains their reputation in old Mexico. Sahagún relates that "they did not consider voluptuousness a sin". They loved splendor and luxury, and men and women were attracted by rich materials and ornaments of precious stone, and their neighbors on the plateau were scandalized by their way of dressing and the looseness of their morals. The cult of the Phallus had a central place in their religion.

Several of the deities and the religious ideas of the plateau derive from the coastal regions of the Gulf. Tlazolteotl, the queen of the harvest and the ripe maize, is a Huaxtec goddess. Her cult, which is connected with sexual and fertility rites, is strangely reminiscent of that of the archaic Artemis. Here too we find the sacrifice by arrow. The moon goddess Tlazolteotl is also the one who hears confessions and pardons carnal sins. Quetzalcóatl too comes from the coast of the Gulf, though the peoples of the plateau have transformed and recreated him. The Huaxtecs worshipped him, both as the god of the wind and as the morning and evening star (Venus). As already mentioned the Huaxtecs distinguished themselves by their works in mother-of-pearl. Some archeologists have maintained that all gods who have attributes of mother-of-pearl are of Huaxtec origin. It is known that one of the attributes of Quetzalcóatl-Ehecatl (the wind) is a sea shell, or conch, whose spiral is reminiscent of whirlwinds.

The many religious celebrations of the Huaxtecs were accompanied by ritual dances with music, songs, sacrificial ceremonies and games of pelote. To this very day one of them survives, viz. the dance of *El Volador,* which is celebrated annually in the mountainous regions of Puebla and Papantla (in the State of Veracruz). A thirty meter high tree trunk is erected, crowned by a round platform of about one meter in diameter. The six persons who participate in the dance are placed on this platform. One of them plays the flute and the drums. The other five participants disguised as birds all throw themselves from the platform at the same time. They are tied by one foot with a long, heavy rope that unrolls gradually as they rotate around the pole till they touch the ground, having done 52 turns, which represents the years of their century. *El Volador* also represents the descent to earth of the dead warriors who have been transformed into stars.

### 557. Jar
In the shape of a calabash, with handle and spout. Creamcolored terracotta. $7^5/8$x$8^5/8''$. Huaxtec, Panuco V: A.D. 1000-1250. (San Luís Potosí, S.L.P.). Coll.: F. V. Field, Mexico.

### 558. Jar
Shaped with five female breasts. With spout and handle shaped like a stirrup. Creamcolored terracotta. $8^3/8$x$8^1/4''$. Huaxtec, Panuco V: A.D. 1000-1250. (San Luís Potosí, S.L.P.). Coll.: F. V. Field, Mexico.

### 559. Large jar
Shaped with ten female breasts, Braided handle and spout. Creamcolored terracotta. $9^7/8$x$13''$. Huaxtec, Panuco V: A.D. 1000-1250. (San Luís Potosí, S.L.P.). Coll.: Museo Regional de San Luís Potosí, S.L.P.

### 560. Centeocihuatl
Deity of maize (fragment). Conical cap, ear-ornaments, and mouth in the shape of a snake. Limestone. $19^5/8$x$19^1/4''$. Huaxtec, Panuco V: A.D. 1000-1250 (from the mouth of the Panuco River, S.L.P.). Coll.: Museo Regional de San Luís Potosí, S.L.P.

### 561. Centeocihuatl*
With large headdress, shaped like sun rays, and joined hands. Limestone. $55^5/8$x$21^5/8''$. Huaxtec, Panuco V: A.D. 1000-1250. (Cd. de las Flores, Tampico, Tamps.). Coll.: Museo Regional de San Luís Potosí, S.L.P.

### 562. Breast plate
With engraving, representing a priest and a person piercing his tongue, as a sacrificial gesture to secure the fertility of the earth. Section of a conch. $6$x$3^3/8''$. Huaxtec, Panuco V: A.D. 1000-1250. (Tamaulipas, Tamps.).

### 563. Centeotl
God of maize. Nude, standing, with a high headdress. Limestone. $59$x$19^5/8''$. Huaxtec, Panuco V: A.D. 1000-1250. (San Luís Potosí, S.L.P.).

### 564. Large stela of Xolotl*
The evening star. The deity is represented in his quality of the heavenly body that accompanies the sun on its nocturnal journey through the cold, subterranean world, till the meeting with Quetzalcóatl, the morning star and the twin brother of Xolotl, who, in the shape of the god of Wind, helps the sun to rise again. In the bas-relief Xolotl seems to fall menacingly from

the firmament and plunge his claws into the horizon. The figure is half skeletal and richly dressed. The face with the heavily emphasized eyes, is adorned with sumptuous ear and nose ornaments with chronological and mathematical signs. A necklace repeats the same motifs. The open mouth bares the canines and a tongue that hangs down like that of a dying animal, viz. of a dog, an animal that was closely connected with the tomb cult. The head is crowned with a triangular cap, representing a ray of light emerging from a diadem of precious stones, with a large circle of stylized rays as a background at the neck. The arms and ankles are adorned with elegant rings, and the skeletal chest is covered by a broad belt, adorned with plumes and precious stones. The dress is rounded off with a kind of skirt with circular border motifs that become smaller and smaller towards the ends to symbolize the last vibrations of the light. Xolotl was also the god of monsters and twins. At the center of the stele on both sides of the belt, can be seen Xolotl's twin brother, Quetzalcóatl, represented in profile as the god of Wind, with the mouth mask he used to produce wind. Limestone. $65^3/4 \times 43^1/4 \times 7^7/8''$. Huaxtec, Panuco V: A.D. 1000-1250. (Tepetzintla, Ver.).

### 565. Xilonen*

Goddess of the germination of maize, or "the young Mother of Maize", seated in the traditional sitting posture of native women. Headdress of multiple ribbons and ears of maize, and ornaments at the back of the head, representing rays of the sun, with two bands at the sides, a large necklace of jade, symbolizing the earth turning green after rain. Dressed in "huipil" (triangular garment) and short skirt. Limestone. $25^1/4 \times 15''$. Huaxtec, Panuco V: A.D. 1000-1250. (Tuxpan, Ver.).

# 8. The Tajín Civilization

*The middle part of the coast of the Gulf of Mexico
1000 B.C.-A.D. 1521.
Pre-classic, middle and classic period* (1000 B.C.-A.D. 300): Trapiche, Early Remojadas and Late Remojadas I (the State of Veracruz).
*Classic and post-classic* (A.D. 200-1250): Tajín I, Tajín II, Tajín III, Remojadas II, Isla de Sacrificios (the State of Veracruz).
*Historical period* (A.D. 1250-1521): Zempoala, Quiahuitzlán and Cerro Montoso (the State of Veracruz).

The most important remains of this civilization are found in the middle of the State of Veracruz, where the cities of Misantla, Zempoala, Castillo de Teayo, Quiahuitzlán, and El Tajín were built. The last mentioned became the center and home of this culture that is supposed to have sprung from the La Venta civilization (Olmec), from Teotihuacán and from the Mayas.

Its artistic manifestations are often designated as *Totonac* because they are found in a territory that until our time has been inhabited by the Totonac ethnic group, which has preserved its own language and traditions in a relatively unmixed form. The flourishing of the El Tajín civilization took place between the 7th and 14th century of our era. After that the Totonac came under political and military dominion of the Aztecs, entertaining fruitful cultural contacts with them as evidenced by the religion, sculpture, architecture and crafts of both peoples. As far as daily life and customs are concerned, this people resembled its neighbors to the north, the Huaxtecs. Nevertheless its artistic forms of expression were different and show a clearly delineated personality. We don't know much about the religious beliefs and customs, but it is almost certain that the most important god was Tajín, the local version of Tlaloc, the god of Rain. Tajín gave his name to the culture and the city, whose impressive architecture bears comparison with that of the greatest Maya centers.

The art of ceramics was highly developed, as is obvious from the wonderful polychrome jars from Remojadas and Isla de Sacrificios (the State of Veracruz). On these jars are shown deities, hunting scenes and stylized animals of extremely refined design. Remarkable sculptures in terracotta represent the mother deity, Cihuateteo, or goddesses for women dead in childbirth, sumptuously dressed warriors, musicians, an entire community of figurines, full of life and highly expressive, most of them decorated with chapopote, i.e. bitumen.

The architecture also reached a highly advanced stage, to which the numerous big buildings and ball-game grounds, bear witness, as does the truncated pyramid at El Tajín, that contains so many harmoniously arranged elements (e.g., the rectangular and diagonal walls with ledges). It measures 246 ft. on each side and 190 ft. in height, and

**117**

contains 365 niches, one for each day of the year. It is not known if these niches ever contained statues or other objects. The purpose of their hollowness was to convey a sense of "chiaroscuro", and thus symbolize the cosmic movement of light and dark, death and life. The symbolic character is also apparent from the 52 planes that constitute the horizontal spaces (52 years of the Indian Century), and from the ramp of the impressive central staircase with its plumed serpents, formed by 13 fret motifs reminiscent of the days of the week. The obsession with light and darkness is also at the root of the refined patterns of frets and bas-reliefs, which incidentally reveal a subtle knowledge of the technique of lighting.

The Totonacs particularly emphasized the magical significance of the pelote game, at the cost of its athletic aspect. The enclosure, representing the cosmos, was constructed along a longitudinal axis pointing north-south, and the stone rings along an axis pointing east-west. The ball passed along this axis, that symbolized the rise and the setting of the sun, the ball itself, clearly representing the sun. When the players on the light side won, it was considered a good omen, because they had supplemented the power of the sun with their own. When the players on the dark side won there was reason to fear the future. There were ceremonies centered on the court, in which the players wore richly adorned dresses, on which could be seen the attributes of the gods, they were assumed to represent. The chief of the winning side was sometimes sacrificed, as on the great occasions of the turn of a century or exceptional dates, but his death meant return to the cosmic life. On the walls around the enclosure at Tajín, there are four large stone reliefs, describing the sacrifice of a player. It is a masterpiece in which the shape and the economic use of line indicate the sacred austerity of the place.

The most characteristic sculptures of the Tajín culture are the "yokes", "palmas", and "axes", so-called because of their shapes. The "yokes" are symbolical representations in stone of an ornamental belt, worn by the pelote player during the ceremony and during the game, and made, for that use, of light materials. The stone yokes are of porphyry, greenish granite, jadeite or diorite, and admirably carved and polished with a perfection corresponding to the taste of the Olmec ancestors. They frequently represent a frog, a death symbol of the earth, or a jaguar whose body is carved in the two "arms" of the yoke, while the head is carved on the front. Apart from the main motif there are often complementary figures and volutes. The latter formal ornaments are of Olmec origin, and may also be stylizations of a tiger's skin or snake's movements. The volute permeates everything and signifies, like the frets, an element of propitiatory magic repetition. "Palmas" which were also among the attributes of the pelote players, were also made of very hard stone and represent human beings, deities, symbolic animals, and even abstract ideas. The "axes" generally represent heads of persons, who were presumably deified by their death, or of deities. Their very special form, the most notable example of

Pyramid of the Niches. El Tajín, Mexico.

Head of Huehueteotl, the old god of the fire. Terracotta. El Tajín. Cat. 614-616.

Cihuateotl, goddess of women dead in childbirth. Terracotta. El Tajín. Cat. 568.

Cihuateotl. Terracotta. El Tajín. Cat. 569.

Cihuateotl. Terracotta. El Tajín. Cat. 570.

Yoke, so-called of the owl. Stone. El Tajín. Cat. 625.

Ceremonial axe, representing a skull. Basalt. El Tajín. Cat. 642.

Palma representing a woman's head. Basalt. El Tajín. Cat. 631.

Palma representing a prisoner of war. Basalt. El Tajín. Cat. 632.

Ceremonial axe, profile of a person. Basalt. El Tajín. Cat. 640.

Jar, sitting monkey. Terracotta. Totonac. Cat. 661.

Jar, sitting monkey. Terracotta. Totonac. Cat. 661.

Jar, monkey. Terracotta. Totonac. Cat. 664.

Seated smiling old man. Terracotta. Totonac. Cat. 659.

Xochipilli, features of a child. Terracotta. Totonac. Cat. 645.

Chalchiuhcihuatl, goddess of fecundity. Terracotta. Totonac. Cat. 587.

Chalchiuhcihuatl. Terracotta. Totonac. Cat. 588.

two-dimensional art, arises from the fact that both sides of the head were rendered in profile. The "axes" were presumably also used as architectural elements, fastened to the walls, always with the purpose of symbolizing light and dark.

Unique of their kind are the polished, incised onyx-jars, on which are found representations of fruits and animals. Special attention should also be drawn to the "small smiling heads". They are clay figurines, made in moulds and hollow, but finished by hand, and represent old and young people, women and children. They are very handsome sculptures, and their laughing or teasing expression testifies to the spirit of festivity and leisure that has inspired them. They represent the forces of fertility and joy, and anticipate Xochipilli in his capacity of the god of the new maize.

Midway between the opulence of the Mayas and the severity of the Teotihuacáns, the Tajín art combines vitality and imagination in a certain equilibrium. Its dominating element is the rhythm. Geometry stylizes the lines of the volutes with frets and spirals without ever making them immobile. The smiling figurines are at one extreme of this art, which did not disown gracefulness. At the other extreme we find the "yoke", the "axes", and the "palmas", the Xipe-sculptures, and the stone reliefs from the pelote court. It is a sensual art which does not, however, cease to be religious; the stone breathes.

**566. Chalchiuhcihuatl**
Goddess of fecundity and nourishment, seated in an attitude of inner concentration. Ear-ornaments, necklace and skirt. Right hand on knees and crossed legs. Ochre terracotta. $17^3/8 \times 11^3/8''$. Tajín I (Olmec influence): A.D. 200-650. (Veracruz, Ver.). Coll.: F. V. Field, Mexico.

**567. Head and shoulder**
(Fragment of a larger figure). High headdress, divided into two parts, eyes narrowed, mouth half-open. Greenish, veined serpentine. $12^5/8 \times 5^1/8''$. Tajín I (Olmec and Teotihuacán influence): A.D. 200-650. (Veracruz, Ver.). Coll.: F. V. Field, Mexico.

**568. Cihuateotl***
Goddess of women dead in childbirth. These women were honored like warriors who died in battle. At their death they ascended to heaven where they sang the praise of the sun. Ochre terracotta. $24^3/4 \times 18^7/8''$. Totonac, Remojadas II:

A.D. 300-800. (Remojadas, Ver.). Coll.: K. Stavenhagen, Mexico.

**569. Cihuateotl***
Carrying on her head a brazier, decorated with three beaks. Outstretched arms, face and mouth decorated with black paint. Ochre terracotta. $17^3/8 \times 9^1/2''$. Totonac, Remojadas II: A.D. 300-800. (Berren region of Veracruz). Coll.: Museo de Antropología, University of Veracruz, Jalapa, Ver.

**570. Cihuateotl***
Wearing helmet with bells and belt of sea shells. The emphasis on the breasts symbolizes frustrated motherhood. Terracotta. $30^3/4 \times 13''$. Totonac, Remojadas II: A.D. 300-800. (Dicha Tuerta, Tierra Blanca, Ver.). Coll.: Museo de Antropología, University of Veracruz, Jalapa, Ver.

**571. Cihuateotl**

Standing, with arms stretched out. Hair done up in tufts, and diadem with beaks. Terracotta. 16$^{1}$/$_{2}$x11$^{3}$/$_{4}$″. Totonac, Remojadas II: A.D. 300-800. (El Faisán, Paso de Ovejas, Ver.). Coll.: Museo de Antropología, University of Veracruz, Jalapa, Ver.

**572. Seated male figure**

Richly adorned, fanning himself. Headdress, necklace, bracelets and ankle rings. Black paint on mouth and arms. Ochre terracotta with traces of red paint. 15$^{3}$/$_{4}$x8$^{1}$/$_{4}$″. Totonac, Remojadas II: A.D. 300-800. (Veracruz, Ver.). Coll.: Dolores Olmedo de Olvera, Mexico.

**573. Xipe-Totec**

Sitting on a throne, with a large headdress of feathers, ear-ornaments, mask and necklace. Ochre terracotta. 9$^{7}$/$_{8}$x5$^{7}$/$_{8}$″. Totonac, Remojadas II: A.D. 300-800. (Nopiloa, Ver.). Coll.: Museo Regional de Michoacán, Morelia, Mich.

**574. Xipe-Totec**

Standing figurine with outstretched arms, leaning on a bench. Terracotta. 5$^{7}$/$_{8}$x5$^{7}$/$_{8}$″. Totonac, Remojadas II: A.D. 300-800. (Nopiloa, Ver.). Coll.: Museo de Antropología, University of Veracruz, Jalapa, Ver.

**575. Seated female figure**

Ear-ornaments, eyes and mouth painted black, necklace, arm-ornaments, and a little knitted skirt. Terracotta. 11$^{3}$/$_{8}$x7$^{1}$/$_{2}$″. Totonac, Remojadas II: A.D. 300-800. (Semi-arid zone of Veracruz, Ver.). Coll.: Museo de Antropología, University of Veracruz, Jalapa, Ver.

**576. Jar**

In the shape of a female figure with black paint on her headdress, eyes, mouth, breasts and skirt. Terracotta. 15x10$^{5}$/$_{8}$″. Totonac, Remojadas II: A.D. 300-800. (Remojadas, Ver.). Coll.: Museo de Antropología, University of Veracruz, Jalapa, Ver.

**577. Small sculpture**

Representing a seated person, dressed in "maxtlatl" (a kind of loin-cloth) and a large cotton helmet, with ankle-rings, necklace and tubular ear-ornaments. Terracotta. 4$^{3}$/$_{4}$x2$^{3}$/$_{4}$″. Totonac, Remojadas II: A.D. 300-800. (Los Cerros, Tierra Blanca, Ver.). Coll.: Museo de Antropología, University of Veracruz, Ver.

**578-579. Two whistles**

In shape of women; one standing and the other seated. Terracotta with red polished paint on cream-colored ground and black paint on headdress, cheeks and teeth. 12$^{5}$/$_{8}$x9$^{7}$/$_{8}$″, 7$^{7}$/$_{8}$x4$^{3}$/$_{8}$″. Totonac, Remojadas II: A.D. 300-800. (El Faisán, Paso de Ovejas, Ver.). Coll.: Museo de Antropología, University of Veracruz, Jalapa, Ver.

**580. Rattle**

Representing the goddess Cihuateotl. With large headdress and upraised arms. Terracotta. 9$^{7}$/$_{8}$x 5$^{7}$/$_{8}$″. Totonac, Remojadas II: A.D. 300-800. (Nopiloa, Tierra Blanca, Ver.). Coll.: Museo de Antropología, University of Veracruz, Jalapa, Ver.

**581-583. Family group**

(Small figures representing woman, child and man). Terracotta, painted black. 17$^{3}$/$_{4}$x10$^{1}$/$_{4}$″, 10$^{3}$/$_{4}$x3$^{7}$/$_{8}$″, 14$^{5}$/$_{8}$x9$^{7}$/$_{8}$″. Totonac, Remojadas II: A.D. 300-800. (Remojadas, Ver.). Coll.: Museo de Antropología, University of Veracruz, Jalapa, Ver.

**584. Seated female figure**

Headdress with fringes, necklace, bracelets and short skirt. Decorated with black paint on eyes and mouth. Terracotta. 16$^{1}$/$_{8}$x10$^{1}$/$_{4}$″.• Totonac, Remojadas II: A.D. 300-800. (El Faisán, Paso de Ovejas, Ver.). Coll.: Museo de Antropología, University of Veracruz, Jalapa, Ver.

**585. Sitting female figure**

Half-nude, deformed head without hair. Terracotta. $15^3/4 \times 9^7/8''$. Totonac, Remojadas II: A.D. 300-800. (El Faisán, Paso de Ovejas, Ver.). Coll.: Museo de Antropología, University of Veracruz, Jalapa, Ver.

**586. Small fantastic sculpture**
In the shape of a head on a foot. Ochre terracotta. $4^3/8 \times 3^7/8''$. Totonac, Remojadas II: A.D. 300-800. (Veracruz, Ver.). Coll.: K. Stavenhagen, Mexico.

**587. Chalchiuhcihuatl***
Goddess of fecundity and nourishment. Seated with half-open mouth in a contemplative attitude. Adorned with large ear-ornaments and a large strict headdress of geometrical shape. Breasts and torso nude, crossed legs, and the delicate hands placed on the knees. Ochre terracotta. $33^7/8 \times 26''$. Totonac, Remojadas II: A.D. 300-800. (El Faisán, Ver.). Coll.: K. Stavenhagen, Mexico.

**588. Chalchiuhcihuatl***
Goddess of nourishment and fecundity. Represented as a young woman, with budding breasts, sitting with her legs crossed and her delicate hands resting on her knees. Necklace with three bells and bracelets. With holes in the head and ears for the precious plumes sacrificed to her. Polished ochre terracotta. $19^1/4 \times 14^1/8''$. Totonac, Remojadas II: A.D. 300-800. (Remojadas, Ver.). Coll.: K. Stavenhagen, Mexico.

**589. Priest**
Nude man with conical headdress that reaches his shoulders, and rounded ear-plugs. Ochre terracotta, with black painted decoration. $27^1/8 \times 12^1/4''$. Totonac, Remojadas II: A.D. 300-800. (Remojadas, Ver.). Coll.: K. Stavenhagen, Mexico.

**590. Sitting nude female figure**
With large headdress, painted black; crossed legs and hands on knees. Terracotta. $18^1/2 \times 10^1/4''$. Totonac, Remojadas II: A.D. 300-800.

(Remojadas, Ver.). Coll.: K. Stavenhagen, Mexico.

**591. Standing priest**
With the attributes of the god Tezcatlipoca, the evening star. Painted black all over and holding a stick in his right hand. Deformed head, and ears with large holes in the lobes, for the purpose of adorning them with large, round ornaments of jade. Ochre terracotta, with black paint. $18^1/8 \times 9^1/2''$. Totonac, Remojadas II: A.D. 300-800. (Remojadas, Ver.). Coll.: M. A. Leof, Mexico.

**592. Small figure with large headdress**
Representing a musician who wears a mask and seems to beat his drum with energy and joy. Ochre terracotta. $7^1/8 \times 4^3/4''$. Totonac, Remojadas II: A.D. 300-800. (Centro de Veracruz). Coll.: M. A. Leof, Mexico.

**593. Seated male figure**
With filed teeth and necklace with pendant in the shape of a bell. Terracotta with black, red, and yellow paint. $11^3/4 \times 12^1/4''$. Totonac, Remojadas II: A.D. 300-800. (Veracruz, Ver.). Coll.: M. A. Leof, Mexico

**594. Warrior**
With helmet in the shape of a bird and shield in his right hand. Eyes and fringe of hair painted black. Ochre terracotta. $18^1/8 \times 7^1/8''$. Totonac, Remojadas II: A.D. 300-800. (Nopiloa, Tierra Blanca, Ver.). Coll.: Museo de Antropología, University of Veracruz, Jalapa, Ver.

**595. Standing warrior**
With two bells in the shape of human skulls. Large headdress and necklace. Ochre terracotta with black paint. $21^5/8 \times 10^1/4''$. Totonac, Remojadas II: A.D. 300-800. (Remojadas, Ver.). Coll.: K. Stavenhagen, Mexico.

**596. Warrior**
With two missiles in his hands. Large headdress,

ear-plugs, necklace and belt. Black decoration. Ochre terracotta. 20$^{1}$/$_{2}$x16$^{1}$/$_{2}$". Totonac, Remojadas II: A.D. 300-800. (Remojadas, Ver.). Coll.: K. Stavenhagen, Mexico.

**597-608. Twelve small whistles in zoömorphic and antropomorphic shapes**
Terracotta. From 2" to $^{3}$/$_{4}$". Totonac, Remojadas II: A.D. 300-800. (Nopiloa and Los Cerros, Tierra Blanca, Ver.). Coll.: Museo de Antropología, University of Veracruz, Jalapa, Ver.

**609. Small running jaguar**
With movable limbs which were placed on wheels with axels. These amusing toys represent the only application of the principle of the wheel in the New World. Ochre terracotta. 3$^{7}$/$_{8}$x4$^{3}$/$_{4}$". Totonac, Remojadas II: A.D. 300-800. (Tres Zapotes, Ver.).

**610. Censer**
With human head, and grains of maize in pastillage-technique. Terracotta. 4$^{3}$/$_{4}$x4$^{3}$/$_{4}$". Totonac, Remojadas II: A.D. 300-800. (Cozomoalapan, Ver.). Coll.: Museo de Antropología, University of Veracruz, Jalapa, Ver.

**611. Woman's head**
(Fragment of a larger figure). Round headdress, ear-ornaments and filed teeth. Polished ochre terracotta. 7$^{1}$/$_{2}$x6$^{3}$/$_{4}$". Totonac, Remojadas II: A.D. 300-800. (Mesillas, Ver.).

**612. Warrior's head**
(Fragment of a larger figure), with headdress, chin-strap and nose-plug. Eye-brows, eyes and mouth painted black. Ochre terracotta. 9$^{7}$/$_{8}$x 6$^{1}$/$_{4}$". Totonac, Remojadas II: A.D. 300-800. (Mesillas, Ver.).

**613. Head**
(Fragment of a large figure). Ochre terracotta. 9x8$^{1}$/$_{4}$". Totonac, Remojadas II: A.D. 300-800. (Los Cerros, Tierra Blanca, Ver.). Coll.: Museo

de Antropología, University of Veracruz, Jalapa, Ver.

**614-616. Three heads of old men\***
Representing Huehuetotl, the god of the First Fire. (Fragments of figures). Terracotta. 7$^{7}$/$_{8}$x9", 5$^{1}$/$_{2}$x6$^{1}$/$_{4}$" 6$^{3}$/$_{4}$x4$^{3}$/$_{4}$". Totonac, Remojadas II: A.D. 300-800. (Remojadas, Ver.). Coll.: K. Stavenhagen, Mexico.

**617. Cylindrical seal**
Representing a person with a fan and headdress of feathers. Ochre terracotta. 6$^{3}$/$_{4}$x2$^{3}$/$_{8}$". Totonac, Remojadas II: A.D. 300-800. (Huachínx, Ver.). Coll.: F. V. Field, Mexico.

**618-623. Six cylindrical seals and twelve flat ones**
With representations of water, plant and animal motifs; deer, snakes, fishes, eagles, monkeys and frogs. Terracotta. Some of the seals have traces of paint. The size varies between. 3$^{1}$/$_{2}$" and 3$^{1}$/$_{8}$" and $^{3}$/$_{4}$" and 1$^{1}$/$_{8}$". Totonac, Remojadas II: A.D. 300-800. (Remojadas, Ver. and 4 from Zempoala, Ver.). Coll.: F. V. Field, Mexico.

**624. Large seal**
Spiral-shaped, representing the "precious water", or the blood. Ochre terracotta, with traces of red paint. 5$^{1}$/$_{2}$x9$^{1}$/$_{2}$". Totonac, Remojadas II: A.D. 300-800. (Remojadas, Ver.). Coll.: F. V. Field, Mexico.

**625. Yoke\***
So-called of the "owl", the bird of night, a forerunner of death. It is assumed that these yokes were imitation in stone of a leather-belt upholstered with cotton, and worn by the pelote players. The designation "yoke" refers to the shape and dimension that is reminiscent of the yoke of oxen. These richly elaborated, strange sculptures in stone were probably used in the ceremonial "Tlachtli" or pelote game, in honor of the players, who often risked their lives in the game. This religious game was at the same time a representation of the fight between the

cosmic elements and a ritual of a magic, divinatory character. The players were dressed as gods and symbolized the elements, their fights and their various periods. The priests in their capacity of intermediaries between celestial and temporal powers, interpreted the future according to the fortunes of the game, which was very difficult and dangerous, and took place in a rectangular enclosure of 131×10 ft., with either vertical or slanting walls along one side. In the middle of this wall, about 16 ft. from the ground, was a vertical ring or a marker of stone, in the shape of a snake or a bird's head, through which the hard rubber ball, which symbolized the sun, had to pass. The ball could not be touched with hands or feet, but had to be controlled exclusively with the hip, the arms and the right leg. None of these "yokes" have yet been found on the site, but their significance seems obvious from the sculptures in which the players are equipped with this yoke, and from descriptions by the chroniclers of the Spanish conquest, who were present at this ritual game, which was also played as an ordinary game for sports or betting purposes. The old Mexicans were passionately interested in this game. In the north-eastern part of Mexico, in the States of Sonora and Sinaloa, a similar game, called "hulama", still exists. Sandstone. 19$^1$/$_4$x16$^1$/$_8$″. Tajín II: A.D. 650-1000. (Veracruz, Ver.).

### 626. Yoke

Representing of swimming figure. Headdress in the shape of a bird, that carries in its beak a coiled serpent with two heads. Water symbolized by volutes. The exterior of the yoke has two human profiles engraved in relief. Green granite. 16$^1$/$_8$x15$^3$/$_8$″. Tajín II: A.D. 650-1000. (Veracruz, Ver.).

### 627. Yoke

In the shape of a jaguar lying in wait, with cleft snake's tongue. An animal incarnation of Tezcatlipoca, the god of night. The hide is represented by volutes. Animal and human figures

in bas-relief on the extremities and the inside. Green granite. 16$^1$/$_8$x14$^3$/$_4$″. Tajín II: A.D. 650-1000. (Costa del Golfo).

### 628. Palma

In the shape of a bird's wing. Representation in stone of an ornament (ritual) which the players wore on their chest during the ceremony. The name "palma" derives from the form, which is reminiscent of a palm leaf. Stylized bird's wing with four large feathers and at the sides entwined ribbons, decorated with volutes symbolizing water. Basalt. 26$^3$/$_8$x7$^1$/$_8$″. Tajín II: A.D. 650-1000. (Coatepec, Ver.).

### 629. Palma

In the shape of a reptile, with its body vertical and its tail coiled in a circle. Head and forelegs very stylized. Basalt. 20$^5$/$_8$x8$^7$/$_8$″. Tajín II: A.D. 650-1000. (Coatepec, Ver.).

### 630. Palma

Representing a richly adorned prisoner of war. He is tied and here the volutes that surround him seem to indicate his captivity. Basalt. 22x 8$^1$/$_2$″. Tajín II: A.D. 650-1000. (Veracruz, Ver.).

### 631. Palma*

Representing a woman's head with hair combed back and comb-shaped ornaments. Perfectly proportioned features. Round ear-ornaments, necklace and ribbon at the back of her head. Basalt. 7$^1$/$_8$x4$^3$/$_8$″. Tajín II: A.D. 650-1000. (Costa del Golfo).

### 632. Palma*

Representing an important prisoner of war, seated on a pedestal and dressed in a "maxtlatl" (kind of loincloth). His arms are bent backwards. His headdress is typical of the prisoner. He is wounded in the breast. Basalt. 22x8$^1$/$_2$″. Tajín II: A.D. 650-1000. (Costa del Golfo).

**633. Palma**

In the shape of a stylized pelican. Andesite. $15^1/2$x$6^1/4$". Tajín II: A.D. 650-1000. (Coatepec, Ver.).

**634. Ceremonial axe**

Representation in stone of an ornament (a kind of clasp) worn at the belt by priests in connection with the pelote games. Head of predatory bird with rings around the eyes and feather decoration on the front. Diorite. 13x$8^5/8$". Tajín II: A.D. 650-1000. (Teotihuacán, Mex.).

**635. Ceremonial axe**

In the shape of the head of an iguana with engraved features. Green granite like stone. $7^7/8$x$9^1/2$". Tajín II: A.D. 650-1000. (Veracruz, Ver.).

**636. Ceremonial axe**

With open-work representation of a sitting figure, wearing a deer's mask with a hieroglyph and volutes symbolizing vegetation. Andesite. $18^1/2$x$9^7/8$". Tajín II: A.D. 650-1000. (Costa del Golfo, Ver.).

**637. Ceremonial axe**

With representation of an important person, sumptuously adorned, who is talking to a naked man, whose heart he seems to be on the point of tearing out. Both are covered with volutes. Onyx with remains of red paint. $17^3/4$x$10^3/8$". Tajín II: A.D. 650-1000. (Veracruz, Ver.). Coll.: Dolores Olmedo de Olvera, Mexico.

**638. Ceremonial axe**

Representing the profile of an important person with a moustache and a headdress in the shape of a bird's head whose beak reaches down over the forehead. Diorite. $10^3/8$x$7^5/8$". Tajín II: A.D. 650-1000. (Costa del Golfo, Ver.).

**639. Ceremonial axe**

Representing the head of a predatory bird with large round eyes and perforated beak. Greenish stone. $7^7/8$x$6^1/4$". Tajín II: A.D. 650-1000. (Veracruz, Ver.). Coll.: S. Hale, Mexico.

**640. Ceremonial axe***

Representing the profile of an important person with a large rectangular headdress. Basalt with traces of red paint. $18^1/2$x$7^1/8$". Tajín II: A.D. 650-1000. (Veracruz, Ver.). Coll.: K. Stavenhagen, Mexico.

**641. Ceremonial axe**

(Fragment) representing Xolotl, the evening star Venus, in its nightly phase, as a dying dog or jaguar with hanging tongue. Headdress of plumes showing palms of human hands. Stone. $9^7/8$x9". Tajín II: A.D. 650-1000. (El Viejón, Ver.). Coll.: Museo de Antropología, University of Veracruz, Jalapa, Ver.

**642. Ceremonial axe***

Representing a fleshless skull with highly stylized features. Basalt. $8^5/8$x$11^3/8$". Tajín II: A.D. 650-1000. (Costa del Golfo), Ver.). Coll.: K. Stavenhagen, Mexico.

**643. Padlock**

Reproduction in stone of a belt-clasp for a pelote player. Round shaped, pierced decoration, engraved and carved in bas-relief. On each of the sides a representation of the sun in the shape of frontal human faces. Sandstone. $12^5/8$x$12^5/8$". Tajín II: A.D. 650-1000. (Veracruz, Ver.).

**644. Smiling male figure**

Representing Xochipilli, God of joy, music, dance, procreation and the new maize. Ochre terracotta. $16^7/8$x$8^5/8$". Totonac, Remojadas II, late period: A.D. 300-800. (Nopiloa, Tierra Blanca, Ver.). Coll.: Museo de Antropología, University of Veracruz, Jalapa, Ver.

**645. Xochipilli***

With the features of a child, seated, naked and smiling. Ochre terracotta. $12^5/8$x$10^1/4$". Totonac,

Remojadas II: A.D. 300-8000. (Tierra Blanca, Ver.). Coll.: F. V. Field, Mexico.

### 646. Smiling female figure

Goddess of joy and procreation. Dressed in a "huipil" (triangular garment) that is richly adorned. Ochre terracotta. $13^3/8 \times 8^1/4''$. Totonac, Remojadas II: A.D. 300-800. (Tierra Blanca, Ver.). Coll.: K. Stavenhagen, Mexico.

### 647-656. Ten different small smiling faces

(Fragments of figures) representing Xochipilli. The different expressions vary from the most delicate smile to the mocking grimace. Various headdresses, adorned with wavy lines, volutes, birds and fish, as part of their eighteen different types of ornaments. Ochre terracotta. $3^7/8 \times 5^7/8''$. Totonac, Remojadas II: A.D. 300-800. (Los Cerros, Dicha Tuerta, Tierra Blanca, Ver.). Coll.: Museo Nacional de Antropología, Mexico and Museo de Antropología, University of Veracruz, Jalapa, Ver.

### 659. Seated old man*

With smiling mask. Terracotta. $13^3/4 \times 10^5/8''$. Totonac, Remojadas II: A.D. 300-800. (Remojadas, Ver.). Coll.: K. Stavenhagen, Mexico.

### 660. Small sculpture

Representing a deity seated on a throne. Headdress of plumes, cotton ribbons and two large disks. Face, breast-plate and headdress painted black. Ochre terracotta. $4^3/4 \times 4^3/4''$. Totonac, Remojadas II: A.D. 300-800. (Tierra Blanca, Ver.).

### 661. Jar*

In the shape of a sitting monkey, whose tail is the spout of the jar. Ochre terracotta. $7^1/4 \times 9^7/8''$. Totonac, Remojadas II: A.D. 300-800. (Veracruz, Ver.). Coll.: F. V. Field, Mexico.

### 662. Jar

In the shape of a sitting hare, with its front paws joined. Stylized anatomy. Translucent alabaster. $8^1/2 \times 7^1/8''$. Totonac, Isla de Sacrificios: A.D. 800-1250. (Veracruz, Ver.).

### 663. Jar

Pearshaped. With a ring engraved on the neck; three legs and vertical decorations. Translucent alabaster. $13^5/8 \times 6^1/2''$. Totonac, Isla de Sacrificios: A.D. 800-1250. (Isla de Sacrificios, Ver.).

### 664 Jar*

With effigy of a monkey, carrying a receptacle in its tail. Eyes inlaid with pieces of pyrites and perforated ears. Translucent alabaster. $10 \times 8^5/8''$. Totonac, Isla de Sacrificios: A.D. 800-1250. (Veracruz, Ver.).

### 665. Head of Xipe-Totec

Fragment. Terracotta with traces of paint. $5^7/8 \times 5^7/8''$. Totonac, Isla de Sacrificios: A.D. 800-1250. (Mesillas, Ver.).

### 666. Jar

Hemispherical, decorated with two sea animals. Ochre terracotta with vermilion paint on orange ground. $6^1/8 \times 6^3/4''$. Totonac, Isla de Sacrificios: A.D. 800-1250. (Otates, Ver.).

### 667. Jar

Pearshaped. Decorated with symbols of water and glyphs with reference to the calender. Support in the shape of an extended ring. White paint emphasized with vermilion on orange ground. Delicate orange terracotta. $7^7/8 \times 4^7/8''$. Totonac, Isla de Sacrificios: A.D. 800-1250. (Isla de Sacrificios, Ver.). Coll.: F. V. Field, Mexico.

### 668. Jar

In the shape of a truncated cone. Wide rim and base. Polychrome decoration: skulls and bones, white, black and red lines. Orange terracotta. $11^3/4 \times 5^1/8''$. Totonac, Isla de Sacrificios: A.D. 800-1250. (Isla de Sacrificios, Ver.). Coll.: F. V. Field, Mexico.

**669. Jar**

Hemispherical, with deep bottom; decorated with painted jaguars and people in white and red on ochre ground. Delicate orange terracotta. 5⁷/₈×7⁷/₈″. Totonac, Isla de Sacrificios: A.D. 800-1250. (Isla de Sacrificios, Ver.). Coll.: F. V. Field, Mexico.

**670. Jar**

Hemispherical, with head of armadillo. The tail of the animal is the spout. Painted decoration: signs symbolizing the cosmic movements and time. White, red and brown on ochre ground. Delicate orange terracotta. 5³/₈× 9¹/₂″. Totonac, Isla de Sacrificios: A.D. 800-1250. (Isla de Sacrificios, Ver.). Coll.: F. V. Field, Mexico.

**671. Large jar**

With high, cylindrical receptacle, handle and spout; decorated with human head and body in white, brown and ochre. Delicate orange terracotta. 11×9″. Totonac, Isla de Sacrificios: A.D. 800-1250. (Isla de Sacrificios, Ver.). Coll.: F. V. Field, Mexico.

**672. Jar**

With convergent bottom and three cylindrical rattle-supports. Adorned with motifs symbolizing the earth; and plumes in red, white and ochre. Delicate orange terracotta. 4¹/₈×10¹/₈″. Totonac, Isla de Sacrificios: A.D. 800-1250. (Isla de Sacrificios, Ver.). Coll.: F. V. Field, Mexico.

**673. Cup**

With high receptacle, divergent rim and base in the shape of a truncated cone. Polychrome decoration: white and red lines, representing a snake. Ochre terracotta. 9⁷/₈×4⁷/₈″. Totonac, Isla de Sacrificios: A.D. 800-1250. (Isla de Sacrificios, Ver.). Coll.: F. V. Field, Mexico.

**674. Cup**

With cylindrical receptacle, divergent rim and truncated cone as base. Decorated with red,

brown and white lines, representing plumed serpents, and glyphs in connection with the time calculation. Delicate orange terracotta. 5¹/₂×8⁵/₈″. Totonac, Isla de Sacrificios: A.D. 800-1250. (Isla de Sacrificios, Ver.). Coll.: F. V. Field, Mexico.

**675. Dish**

Decorated in the bottom with stylized human head, adorned with a serpent. Delicate orange terracotta with polychrome paint. 2×11⁵/₈″. Totonac, Isla de Sacrificios, Ver.: A.D. 800-1250. (Isla de Sacrificios, Ver.). Coll.: F. V. Field, Mexico.

**676. Dish**

Decorated in the bottom with stylized representation of a rabbit being devoured by a snake. Delicate orange terracotta with red, brown and white paint. 2³/₄×11¹/₄″. Totonac, Isla de Sacrificios: A.D. 800-1250. (Isla de Sacrificios, Ver.). Coll.: F. V. Field, Mexico.

**677. Dish**

With decoration in red, brown and white on creamcolored ground. In the bottom a stylized flower. Delicate orange terracotta. 2×7⁷/₈″. Totonac, Isla de Sacrificios: A.D. 800-1250. (Isla de Sacrificios, Ver.). Coll.: F. V. Field, Mexico.

**678. Dish**

Decorated in the bottom with motifs of concentric bands and a skull. Polychrome decoration in red, white and orange on creamcolored ground. Delicate orange terracotta. 1⁵/₈×7¹/₂″. Totonac, Isla de Sacrificios: A.D. 800-1250. (Isla de Sacrificios, Ver.). Coll.: F. V. Field, Mexico.

**679. Small dish**

In the bottom representation of a person in profile. Delicate orange terracotta. 1⁵/₈×5¹/₈″. Totonac, Isla de Sacrificios: A.D. 800-1250. (Isla de Sacrificios, Ver.). Coll.: Museo de

Antropología, University of Veracruz, Jalapa, Ver.

### 680-682. Small polychrome dishes

Terracotta. a) diam. $3^7/_8''$, b) diam. $3^7/_8''$, c) diam. $5^7/_8''$. Totonac, Isla de Sacrificios: A.D. 800-1250. (Isla de Sacrificios, Ver.). Coll.: Museo de Antropología, University of Veracruz, Jalapa, Ver.

### 683. Rattle

In the shape of a woman, painted in red, white and black. Braided headdress, dressed in "quezquemitl" (a kind of native shirt). Delicate orange terracotta. $6^1/_4 \times 3^1/_8''$. Totonac, Isla de Sacrificios: A.D. 800-1250. (Isla de Sacrificios, Ver.). Coll.: Museo de Antropología, University of Veracruz, Jalapa, Ver.

### 684-685. Two cups

a) polychrome decoration with a snake and glyphs symbolizing the cosmic movements, b) with orange, red and brown paint. Terracotta. $6^1/_4 \times 3^7/_8''$, $7^1/_8 \times 3^1/_8''$. Totonac, Mixtec style, Puebla: A.D. 1250-1521. (Zempoala, Ver.). Coll.: Museo de Antropología, University of Veracruz, Jalapa, Ver.

### 686. Cup

With legs and large opening. Polychrome terracotta. Decorated on the top part with sun glyphs and snakes. $5^7/_8 \times 5^7/_8''$. Totonac, Mixtec style, Puebla: A.D. 1250-1521. (Zempoala, Ver.). Coll.: Museo de Antropología, University of Veracruz, Jalapa, Ver.

### 687. Tripod jar

With supports in the shape of eagle heads. The top part decorated with sun glyphs and snakes. Polychrome terracotta. $7^7/_8 \times 9^1/_2''$. Totonac, Mixtec style, Puebla: A.D. 1250-1521. (Zempoala, Ver.). Coll.: Museo de Antropología, University of Veracruz, Jalapa, Ver.

### 688. Quetzalcóatl

The name derives from the roots "quetzal", a bird symbolizing heaven, and "cóatl", the snake of earth. The deity is represented, sitting with his arms on his knees. The headdress is of quetzal feathers with the symbol "Ehécatl" (the god of wind), a spiral-shaped shell representing the wind as forerunner of the rain. Ochre terracotta. $26 \times 11^3/_4''$. Totonac, Quiahuiztlán: A.D. 1250-1521. (Veracruz, Ver.). Coll.: Museo de Antropología, University of Veracruz, Ver.

# 9. The Toltec Civilization

*A.D. 856-1250*
*Comprises three periods:*
Transitional period (from classic to Toltec): A.D. 856-950.
Local period: A.D. 950-1168.
Expansive period: A.D. 1150-1250.
*Sites*
Tula (the State of Hidalgo); Xochicalco (the State of Morelos) and Chichén Itzá and
Uxmal (the State of Yucatán).

The problem of the Toltecs has always been, and still is, one of the most fascinating in
the old history of Mexico. For many years they were considered the creators of the Teotihuacán civilization. But certain scholars maintained that Teotihuacán represented an
older culture. The discovery and exploration of the ruins of Tula, the Toltec capital, ini-
tiated about twenty years ago, ended the quarrel, for it established that the Toltec culture of Tula was different from, and several centuries younger than, that of Teotihuacán. On the other side it should be emphasized that the nahuatl word *tolteca* does not
designate a nation. It means artist, civilized man, as opposed to *chichimeca,* barbarian
or nomad. This is why this group is also called *tolteca-chichimeca,* for they were nomads from the north who invaded the plateau, settled in the old centers of civilization
and assimilated the civilization of their predecessors. Although the Tula culture is, in a
certain way, a development of the heritage from Teotihuacán, as may be gathered from
the story of Topiltzín-Quetzalcóatl, it shows its own characteristics, which should not
be confused with those of other civilizations. The Toltec-Chichimec history unfolds between the years of A.D. 856 and 1250, in a geographical zone formed by the present states of Tlaxcala, Hidalgo, Morelos, Puebla and, outside the plateau, Sinaloa to the west,
and Yucatán and Chiapas in the Maya zone. The Toltec domination of the Mayas is one
of the most interesting and decisive events in Mesoamerican history.

The rise of Toltec civilization, its grandeur and decline, are narrowly connected with
the figure of Quetzalcóatl. History, myth and legend mix so freely in the Toltec phase
of this ancient god, that it is almost impossible to give a clear picture of this episode in
a few lines. The first difficulty is the different versions and interpretations which each
of the Mesoamerican peoples has given to the myth. Moreover the name of Quetzalcóatl
is used as a designation of the deity as well as of the high priest, who reigned in his
guise (a custom which lasted until the Aztec period). Finally, we find a historical Quetzalcóatl among the Toltecs. The following is the story of Topilztín-Quetzalcóatl, according to Jiménez Moreno and Guy Stresser-Péan: "The Toltecs are supposed to have invaded Central America around 900, when they were still relatively uncivilized. They
were led by a chief by name of Ce Tecpatl Mixcóatl, whose wife was supposed to have

come from the civilized nahua tribes, that had lived for a long time in the southern regions, such as Morelos and Guerrero. His son, the famous prince Ce Acatl Topiltzín-Quetzalcóatl, who was born around 935 (or 947) is said to have founded his capital at Tula in 968 (or 980). Having tried to introduce the cult of Quetzalcóatl and the gods who were worshipped by the old, long-established peoples of the south, he was forced to flee, and in 987 (or 999) he retired towards Yucatán with his adherents". — (Preface to the French edition of G. C. Vaillant: The Aztecs of Mexico 1951).

Here we thus have a historical Quetzalcóatl. In Tula, the capital of his realm, has been discovered a bas-relief with the date of 8 Tecpatl (980), a plausible date for his enthronement as king and high priest of Quetzalcóatl. The cause of his downfall is thought to have been a civil and religious war between the adherents of the cult of the plumed serpent, and those of Tezcatlipoca and the national gods of the Chichimec-Toltecs. This story is not without striking analogies with the myth, and particularly with the dualistic conception of the Mesoamericans. The struggle between princes and military leaders was mixed up with the mythical struggle between two rival and complementary cosmic principles. Quetzalcóatl is a nahuatl name composed of two words, quetzal (bird with beautiful feathers) and coatl (snake), a union of heaven and earth. The religious meaning was "precious thing" or "double thing", a reference to the principle of the twins who are adversaries. The new element in the Toltec version is the humanization of Quetzalcóatl or, if you prefer it, the deification of Topiltzín. This version was to have a decisive influence on the later history of Mesoamerica.

The first consequence of the humanization of Quetzalcóatl was ethico-religious. "The passion" of Quetzalcóatl contains numerous episodes: his childhood in exile; his descent into the lower world to dig up bones of his father, Mixcóatl, and bring maize to the humans; his return to his people to whom he reveals the arts, writing, the calendar, and ethics; his temptation and fall; the flight to Yucatán; the promise of his return. Seduced by the magical powers of Tezcatlipoca he sins against reason (he becomes intoxicated) and against the laws of the forbears (he commits incest with his sister). His flight, his wanderings and his final transformation into the planet of Venus, after having been consumed in the flames of the divine fire, indicate a ritual of penitence and purification. In this way Quetzalcóatl becomes god of the inner life, of self-sacrifice and penitence, and of redemption by self-immolation through the conflict between opposites.

Before the flames consume him, Quetzalcóatl promises to return and start a new era. The myth describes him as a white, bearded man. On his pilgrimage in the mountains he leaves as his seal, on the trees penetrated by his arrows, a quincunx, i.e. a five point cross, with reference to the four corners of the world, with a center. Finally, Cortés, by a strange coincidence, landed in the year of I Acatl (1519), a year consecrated to Quetzalcóatl. No wonder that Moctezuma II saw in Cortés a manifestation of Quetzalcóatl, coming to reconquer his realm.

In the year 1000 a new dynasty was founded. The Toltec dominion ended, when the groups still living in Culhuacan were conquered by the new *Chichimecs,* or barbarians, who arrived in 1246. Tula, which had been destroyed for the first time in 1186, was once more occupied by "mexica" tribes. In time it developed into an important power, thanks to the connections with the Aztec capital.

Unlike the classic centers (Teotihuacán, Monte Albán, El Tajín and the Maya towns), that were governed by a clerical caste, the Toltec-Chichimec society shows definite military characteristics. Everything goes to indicate that this was a warrior state. The Toltecs invaded the Maya country in the tenth century and forced a regime of the military type on them. Chichen Itza, an old Maya center of ceremonies, was transformed into a city whose architecture is reminiscent of Tula. On the walls at Uxmal and other centers the Toltecs left permanent traces. The Toltec character of the culture is reflected in the sculpture and the architecture of these Maya towns, as well as in Tula and other places on the plateau.

Tula (Tollan Xiccotitlan) is situated in the State of Hidalgo, not far from the barren region of Mezquital. Around the little square and the pelote grounds, are seen the Quetzalcóatl pyramid, the Coatepantli with the serpent rampart, and the Palace of Columns. The buildings were splendid, with a tendency to sumptuous decoration, rather than spiritual contents. Among the architectural elements invented by the Toltecs should be mentioned the columns (caryatid figures), representing warriors. They were made of several pieces, joined together by pegs, fitted into holes, and supported the roofs of temples or adorned arcades or facades. Noteworthy also are the sculptures *(Chac Mool)* of reclining persons, holding vessels for offerings on their stomachs, a new kind of representation of Quetzalcóatl, in his capacity of "he who was and shall one day rise and govern again". This image was to be found with increasing frequency in all the regions that were exposed to Toltec influence. No less outstanding are the caryatid figures that support the friezes of the altars, in the shape of carved, polychrome figures of warriors, the reliefs representing eagles, jaguars and coyotes, now and then consuming human hearts; the stelae, the standard-bearers, armed with the *atlatl* (spearthrower): procession-sedans with princes or priests usually traveling in opposite directions; calendar signs, sun disks, stellar signs and volutes, symbolizing the world. In sculpture the representations of animals and birds are more realistic. Hardly any objects of luxury have been found at Tula. Compared to the architecture of Teotihuacán, that of Tula seems almost "provincial", in spite of its forcefulness. It is an art which above all expresses temporal *power.*

**689. Atlantean colossal figure from Tula***

A caryatid that, with three others of the same dimension, and four square pillars, supported the roof of the main temple of the city of Tula. The temple was placed on a pyramid dedicated to Venus, the star of the morning. It is a notable example of the Mesoamerican column, the technical invention of the Toltecs. The colossus represented the planet of Venus, one of the manifestations of Quetzalcóatl, the most important deity of the Toltecs, here shown as a warrior fighting the darkness, to secure the rise of the sun. The figure is richly adorned. The headdress consists of a band with five rows of precious stones (chalchihuitl), crowned with plumes of eagles and red herons. The facial decoration consists of red and yellow stripes, the eyes and the mouth are perforated for the purpose of incrustation with semi-precious stones. The ear-ornaments are rectangular, and he wears a necklace of several rows of beads, and a breastplate decorated with a stylized butterfly, painted yellow, symbol of warriors that had been sacrificed or were dead in battle. It is tied around the neck by a band with bells. The figure is dressed in a *patio* (short triangular skirt) with a fringe, held up by a wide woven belt, that is closed at the back by a *teotezcacuit-lapilli*, a disk representing the sun in the shape of a human face, the rays represented by four fire serpents. The arms are encircled by four bracelets, the right hand holds an *atlatl*, an arrow thrower, and the left hand holds a bag of *copal* (a kind of incense) as an emblem of priesthood. The legs are painted with red vertical stripes and the sandals are decorated with serpents, the sides nude and with tassels of plumes at the upper part. The caryatid consists of four sections, joined with pegs. Basalt, with traces of red paint. $189 \times 53 \times 51''$. Toltec: A.D. 856-1168. (Tula, Hidalgo).

**690. Atlantean figure with raised arms***

Wearing a pyramid shaped diadem. The headdress, necklaces, bracelets and costume are of plumes. Like other similar statues he served to support a large stone table. Basalt with remnants of red, yellow, blue and white paint. $32^5/8 \times 16^1/2''$. Toltec: A.D. 856-1168. (Tula, Hgo.).

**691. Head of a wild boar***

The hide rendered by a mosaic of mother-of-pearl. In the open mouth is seen a bearded man, whose head is likewise covered by mosaic of mother-of-pearl. Terracotta, with plombyte, covered with mother-of-pearl. $5^3/8 \times 3^5/8''$. Toltec: A.D. 856-1168. (Tula, Hgo.).

**692-694. Small modelled sculptures**

a): *Tlaloc,* the god of Rain, seated and dressed in a mantle and a headdress of feathers, b): *Tezcatlipoca,* deity of the Night, with a crown and a crossed band, c): *Chicomecoatl,* goddess of the Maize, with headdress and a round breastplate. Ochre terracotta with fresco painting in blue, black, red and yellow. $7^5/8 \times 4^3/4''$, $6^1/8 \times 3^1/8''$, $5^7/8 \times 3^3/8''$. Toltec: A.D. 856-1168. (Ecatepec, Mex.).

**695. Snake's head**

With cleft tongue. Ochre terracotta with fresco painting in blue, black, pink and yellow. $5^3/8 \times 3^1/2''$. Toltec: A.D. 856-1168. (Ecatepec, Mex.).

**696. Standing warrior**

With outstretched arms; disguised as a tiger, with mask, necklace and belt. Ochre terracotta with fresco painting in blue, pink and black. $4^1/2 \times 3''$. Toltec: A.D. 856-1168. (Cerro del Gavilán, Ecatepec, Mex.).

**697-700. Four small modelled figures***

Representing standing women with flat bodies, probably goddesses. One carries a child on her left arm. Terracotta with traces of fresco paint in red, black, blue and yellow. $10^1/4 \times 2^1/4''$, $6^7/8 \times 4^3/4''$, $7^1/8 \times 4^3/4''$, $6^1/8 \times 2''$. Toltec: A.D. 856-1168. (Ecatepec, Mex.).

Pyramid and colossal atlantean in Tula. Toltec culture. Cat. 689.

Terracotta figurine. Toltec. Cat. 697-700.

Head of a wild boar. Toltec. Cat. 691.

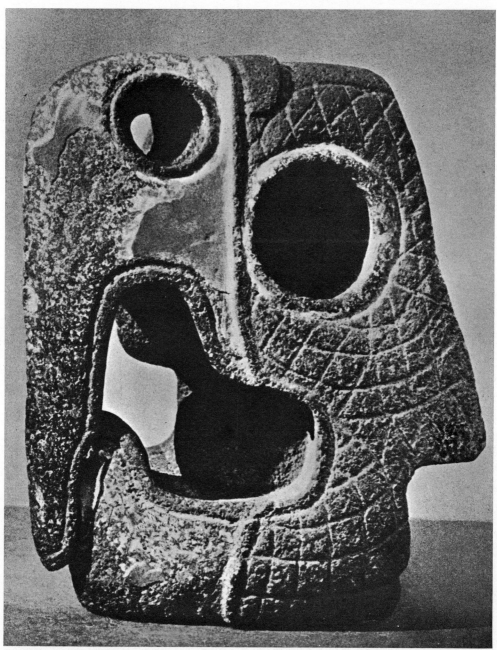

Head of Macaw. Basalt. Toltec. Cat. 701.

Atlantean figure with raised arms. Basalt. Toltec. Cat. 690.

**701. Head of macaw***

Notable example of a hieroglyphic sculpture, combining the features of man and bird, charged with significance. Eyes, nose and beak perforated. The head served as a goal in the pelote game, the sacred game, representing the eternal struggle between the sun and the darkness. The head of the macaw was placed on the wall of the pelote enclosure at about a 16 ft. height, and the players were to send the ball through the opening in the parrot's beak. Basalt. $22^{1}/_{2} \times 15''$. Toltec: A.D. 856-1168. (Xochicalco, Mor.).

# 10. The Maya Civilization

*1000 B.C.-A.D. 1697.*

*Formative period* (1000 B.C.-A.D. 300): Uaxactún (Petén, Honduras).

*Classic period* (A.D. 317-987): Palenque, Bonampak, Chinkultic, Tonina (the State of Chiapas); Labná, Sayil, Cabah, Chichén Viejo and Uxmal (the State of Yucatán); Jonuta (the State of Tabasco); Jaina, Rio Bec, Etzna, Cumpich (the State of Campeche); Copán (Honduras); Tikal, Uaxactún, Petén (Guatemala).

*Maya-Toltec period* (A.D. 987-1185): Chichén Itzá, Uxmal (the State of Yucatán); Las Palmas (the state of Campeche).

*Mayapan's supremacy* (A.D. 1200-1450): Mayapán (the State of Yucatán). Division into smaller states and the Spanish conquest (A.D. 1450-1697).

The ethnic group of the Mayas inhabited a very extensive area, including the states of Campeche, Yucatán, Chiapas, Tabasco and Quintana Roo in Mexico, all of the Belico territory and Guatemala, as well as certain parts of Honduras and El Salvador. The Maya linguistic group is the most homogeneous in all of Central America, and even to-day it constitutes a geographical unit.

The first documented information about the Mayas dates from the formative period (100 B.C.-A.D. 300). In this period the construction of low platforms as bases of small temples and houses was begun. Later appeared the first pyramids that served as bases for temples. The most remarkable construction of the preclassic Maya period is the open building in the town of Uaxactún, in the Petén region. It proves that the clerical hierarchy, which at a later date was to become the center of all forms of activity and the great promoter of all ideas and all progress, thereby guiding the Maya civilization towards a development stamped by ceremonialism, at the cost of all other forms of life, had begun to function already then.

Towards the end of this period the arts of writing and of the calendar arose. The classic period begins with the full development of the stelae on which are found the definitively formed hieroglyphs and calendar signs. This happened at the beginning of the fourth century, and of the most glorious period of the Maya civilization, the period of the innumerable monuments, the remains of which can be admired to-day at Copán, Tikal, Uaxactún, Piedras Negras, Yaxchilan and Palenque. The big cities in Yucatán, Uxmal, Labná, Sayil, Kabah, Chichén Itzá arose later. Their architecture is characterized by the false vault (the Maya arch) and by the abundant decorations in stone or stucco used in connection with a monumental sculpture, the most spectacular results of which are the altars and the hieroglyphic stelae. The purpose of these stelae was to commemorate the transitions from one period to another. The inscriptions refer to certain celestial phenomena: the conjunctions of Venus, sun eclipses, etc. The interpretation of these inscriptions, even when they are incomplete, have made it possible to establish an unbroken series of dates, extending over 600 years (more or less from 371 to

981). In these inscriptions appears the zero, thanks to which the Mayas were able to do what neither the Romans, nor the Europeans of the early Middle Ages could do, viz., enumerate successively, and thus describe enormous sums without any difficulty.

The erection of the stelae reached a remarkable stage of development in all the city-states until about A.D. 559. After this date, which coincides with the crisis which in a more marked fashion made itself felt about the same time in the other Mesoamerican cultures, the construction of stelae was arrested. But a century later (about 650) the construction of both stelae and large temples was recommenced. From the eighth century onwards sculpture reached an exceptional height both in the art of decoration and that of the stelae. In the year of 790 alone stelae were erected in 19 towns to celebrate this date. Independent of the stone sculpture, so richly developed in the Petén and Yucatán regions, the stucco technique for the decoration of buildings was applied by the Mayas. The best examples are undoubtedly Palenque and Comalcalco. At Palenque the fronts of the buildings are completely covered by figures and highly stylized motifs. The art of mural painting also reached a peak of development. Bonampak, which is not unique in this respect, offers a number of frescoes that are remarkable in their plastic force and dramatic composition. In the ninth century the construction of memorial stelae stops once more. One by one the Maya cities abandoned this ritual, which was no doubt inseparable from their conception of the world and signified their grandeur and civilization. The last stela at Copan shows the date of A.D. 800. The last one at Tikal A.D. 869. At the same time all construction stopped and the towns were abandoned. At Uaxactún, for instance, the walls of one of the buildings were never finished. There are numerous hypotheses to explain this abrupt fall of the city-state civilization; e.g., the exploitation of the rural communities, till a revolt of the peasants finished off the clerical caste, religious wars, etc. But the riddle has not yet been solved.

After fifty years of cultural decline (925-975) ethnic groups from the north invaded Yucatán and the higher regions of Guatemala. This was the beginning of the so-called "Mexican" period. The Itzas, a Toltec group, settled in the old Chichén, which now assumed the name of Chichén Itzá. They introduced there an art that is almost identical with the one found at Tula. It was, however, not merely a question of change on the artistic level, but of a change affecting life in all its ramifications. The cult of Quetzalcóatl and other Mexican gods replaced the worship of the old gods, bringing with it the custom of human sacrifice and the necessity of sacred wars in order to procure victims for the altars. The priesthood which had so far been the dominating caste, had to give up their position in favor of the military caste. This caused a complete change, not only of the political organization, but also of the forms of expression within the arts and architecture, for from now on the palaces where the warrior chiefs lived and assembled became more important than the temples. This Maya-Toltec art provided Chichén

Itzá with an architecture which, although showy, was artistically inferior to the classic architecture. There was a transition from religious to official art. The use of metallurgy, a technique that may have derived from South America, spread in this period, as did certain types of orange and gray ceramics. The Mayas also made turquoise mosaics in the Mexican taste, an art of which they had so far been ignorant.

Towards A.D. 1200 a strong reaction took place: the Mayas tried to liberate themselves from foreign dominion. After a series of upheavals Chichén Itzá fell, and thus ended the Toltec supremacy. In the following period the northern elements were absorbed, and a return to many aspects of the old Maya tradition took place. The cult centers became veritable cities. The best example of this new situation is the city of Mayapán, which became the capital of Yucatán, establishing an empire in the northern style with a tyrannical central government. In the fifteenth century occurred a number of rebellions against the tyrants of Mayapán, resulting in the establishment of a number of small independent princedoms. This new political situation could not, however, slow the decline of the Maya culture. On the contrary, this decline was precipitated by the constant wars that the local rulers conducted against each other. When the Spanish conquistadores reached Guatemala in 1525, and Yucatán in 1541, their conquest was facilitated by the local political weakness and the cultural decadence.

The Maya ceramics developed from simple forms and monochrome coloring. In the Famon phase, beginning about 850 B.C. dishes and bowls with flat bottoms were produced, as well as small and large jars with stripes reminiscent of the calabash, and clay seals and figurines with perforated eyes. In the Chikanal period that lasts until the beginning of the Christian era, appear bichrome jars with designs in negative and fresco painting. The forms became more end more varied. The following period, the so-called Matzanel period (till about A.D. 300) is not well known. The Tzakol phase (300-600) is characterized by polychrome earthenware with drawings of people, animals and ceremonial scenes, by jars with decorations in relief, by decorated dishes with crenellated supports and rims, and by clay figurines cast in moulds.

The modeling in stucco and clay renders not only the physical appearance of the Mayas, but also their social rank, their dress and their expressions. The noble posture of the princes, sitting on their thrones, the hieratic majesty of the priests, the arbiter at the pelote game, the priestesses, the deformed, and the common people were all subjects eagerly studied by the artists, as can be seen, in the innumerable variations, from the whistle and bell figurines and the dismountable puppets from the burial island of Jaina in Campeche. The fans, the copal-purses, the skirts, the sandals, the loincloths, the shields, the bracelets, the necklaces, the belts, inform us of the ways of dressing and of the personal ornaments; and the representations of animals in connection with these are of great documentary interest.

As already mentioned, the great technical invention of the Maya architecture was the false vault. We must here emphasize one of the special features of this purely Mayan style (notes on the Mexican period are found in the chapter on the Toltec civilization, and a note on mural painting appears in the description of the frescoes of Bonampak). Unlike the Teotihuacán architecture that simplifies the architectural lines and creates an entity in which the empty spaces and the truncated pyramids are arranged in a special order of spheric geometry, the Maya architecture surprises us with what might (at the risk of appearing inexact) call its "baroque" character. Right from the start, the Mayan art shows preference for complicated design, lines for volutes and spirals. It is unlike the movement in the Tajín art, a vegetation of symbols and elements that invade the very structure. Masks of Chac, the god of rain, and of other gods, cover the walls. It is an architecture destined for the eye; the walls are huge masks. In the reliefs the ornaments and attributes, particularly the headdresses, fill out the space, and the figures themselves obey the rhythm of the spiral. In architecture the facade is of primary importance. Consequently the open-work crest is an essential element in the religious architecture, though it does not have any functional character. This predilection for opulence and complication in form is combined with a striving towards the ascendant line (Paul Westheim: Arte antiguo de Mexico). The most remarkable examples are found in Palenque and Tikal. The upper galleries of the pyramid at Tikal were meant to be reached by help of ladders. At Monte Albán the Zapotecs created an architecture that seemed to emerge from the earth, ignoring the landscape. At Teotihuacán the horizontal conception of space dominates as geometrical sublimation of the landscape. The Mayas aspired to escape from the tyranny of geometry through an abundance of ornamentation, and suspended the weight of the materials by their impulse to reach towards the heights. In both cases they created an art that differs fundamentally from the art created by the other civilizations of Central Mexico. Their temples rise like gigantic, entangled trees. But it is not a matter of decorative art. There is no confusion in this abundance, no "aestheticism" in this profusion of ornaments. This opulence is impregnated with significance. Each element is a sign, and each monument is a combination of astronomical and religious symbols. The Mayan architecture reflects the complex nature of its creators' religion and metaphysical beliefs.

The Mayan religion differs from that of the other Mesoamerican peoples only in its perfection and complication. The mask of rain god Chac is found in all Meyan temples. Later, in the "Mexican" period, appears also the plumed serpent (the Quetzalcóatl of the plateau, called Kulkulkan by the Mayas). But their interest was primarily occupied by the question of time; the stelae erected every twenty years were covered with inscriptions in relation to the calendar and to astronomy. The codex of Dresden is an almanac serving divinatory purposes. The Chilam Balam, one of the few Mayan books we possess, contains prophecies based on the sacred caendar. Still the Mayas did not apply their remarkable mathematical knowledge to affairs of practical life, but reserved it for the study of celestial phenomena. They did not use their measurings of time to fix the dates of their own history, but to fix those of the heavenly bodies. They did not know from where they came, but they succeeded in calculating solar eclipses that had taken place centuries before their arrival in Petén and the woods of Chiapas. Their astronomer-priests watched the orbits of stars through generations, and they tried to discover the origin of time. One of their inscriptions registers a calculation of time of 90,000,000 years. Another arrives at 400,000,000 years. (J. E. S. Thompson: The Rise and Fall of Maya Civilization). These calculations were not disinterested. Science was subservient to divination. The astronomical knowledge was useful from a magic-religious point of view. The days *were* gods. Each god-day was, literally, a burden of time that could be propitious harmful or indifferent. But the days did not present themselves individually. They belonged to a month, a year, a century, a millennium. It was necessary to calculate and weigh all this time that merged or separated, and produced abundance or misery, according to the conjunction or separation. The extraordinary and complex perfection of this calendar corresponds to that of the religious system. In order to face this astronomical fatality it was necessary to have a great number of learned priests.

The cyclic conception of time corresponds to the circular structure of the calendar ("the wheel of time"). The description of this system is too technical to be treated here. Let us merely indicate that it was the question of a double calendar, as in the rest of Mesoamerica: a sacred calendar of 260 days, and a sun calendar of 365 days (the last five days were harmful, empty days, without names, during which time might stop). Even so the Mayas possessed a system that was superior to that of the other Mesoamerican peoples. Their "long count" enabled them to make notations as exact as those obtained by modern systems. The years were called *tunes*. Each twentieth year was a completed cyclus or Katun. Each 260 years a Katun repeated itself, and the corresponding deity reigned anew. Katun Arau meant battles and changes. It occurred again in 1696. The Mayas of Tayasol, who had so far successfully resisted the Spaniards, decided to stop defending their city. It seemed improbable to them that they would be able to surmount the adverse influence from the deity that ruled this gloomy period.

The mathematical knowledge and writing system of the Mayas are perfections of the discoveries of the Olmecs: the numeration, the zero, and the numerical system based on a unit of twenty. But the Mayas utilized these discoveries better than the other Meso-american civilizations, who had also inherited the Olmec knowledge. In their writing (that is not yet entirely deciphered) they used simple phonetic signs (pictograms) combined with ideographic hieroglyphs. The system was complicated by the fact that each individual ideographic sign can be altered by help of suffixes and prefixes. The Mayas possessed an important religious, magic and poetic literature. Apart from the fragmentary chronicles and other secondary texts, two works provoke our admiration: Popol Vuh (a kind of Mayan "Genesis") and the enigmatic Chilam Balam, a book of prophecies and riddles. It would be a historical contradiction to speak of Mayan science, but we can speak of their scientific discoveries. Numeration through position, the use of zero and a patient and careful observation of the heavenly bodies enabled them to realize certain intellectual feats that are more impressive considering the epoch and the modest equipment for observation. Among these feats are: the calculation of Venus' synodic revolution (their error was only 0,08th of a day per half century); the exact prediction of sun eclipses; the measuring of the tropic year. The astronomer-priests who made these calculations were the contemporaries of Charlemagne. When the Spaniards invaded the Maya country, this culture had been moribund for several centuries. To add to our confusion, their manuscripts and codices were burned in the sixteenth century by order from a bishop Landa.

**705. Tripod jar**
Almost spherical, with incised ornaments. Grayish ochre terracotta. $5^1/2 \times 5^1/2''$. Classic Maya, Tzakol: A.D. 300-600. (Yucatán).

**706. Tripod jar**
Representing an armadillo. Delicate orange terracotta. $8^1/4 \times 9''$. Classic Maya, Tzakol: A.D. 300-600. (Yucatán). Coll.: F. V. Field, Mexico.

**707. Tripod dish**
Polychrome, with representation of a seated person. Terracotta. $2^3/4 \times 11^3/8''$. Classic Maya, Tzakol: A.D. 300-600. (Yucatán). Coll.: K. Stavenhagen, Mexico.

**708. Dish**
Polychrome, with representation of a dancer, disguised as a bat. Terracotta. $2^3/4 \times 11''$. Classic Maya, Tzakol: A.D. 300-600. (Yucatán). Coll.: K. Stavenhagen, Mexico.

**709. Chinkultic disk***
Commemorating a game of pelote. In the center of the bas-relief is seen a pelote player with a sumptuous headdress of quetzal-plumes. Ear-

ornaments, necklace, wide belt of heavy material, apron of jaguar's hide, protective arm and knee-pads of leather for the right arm and the right knee. This figure is surrounded by a band of hieroglyphs and number signs. denoting a date in the year of 590 of our era. Limestone. $5^1/8 \times 22''$. Classic Maya: A.D. 590. (Chinkultic, Chis.).

**710. Stela**
With representation, in relief of a priest, richly adorned with a headdress of macaw-feathers, kneeling in a pious attitude and offering a vessel with birds. The bas-relief measures at the deepest place $1/8''$. Limestone. $40^1/2 \times 26''$. Classic Maya: A.D. 317-987. (Jonuta, Tab.).

**711. Stela**
With carefully engraved representation of Chac, the god of Rain. Polished limestone with traces of red and blue paint. $10^5/8 \times 7^5/8''$. Classic Maya: A.D. 600-987. (El Palacio, Palenque, Chis.).

**712. Cylindrical receptacle for offerings***
With representation in high relief of the face of

Seated female figure. Terracotta. Maya. Cat. 715.

Pyramid of Chichén-Itzá. Maya.

Chichén-Itzá (detail). Maya.

Nude male figure. Limestone. Maya. Cat. 714.

Chac-Mool, god of Rain. Limestone. Maya. Cat. 776.

Chinkultic disk. Limestone. Maya. Cat. 709.

Cylindrical vessel for offerings representing the god of Sun. Terracotta. Maya. Cat. 712.

The frescoes of Bonampak. Maya. Cat. 761.

The frescoes of Bonampak. Maya. Cat. 761.

"Venus of Jaina" (detail). Terracotta. Maya. Cat. 723.

Warrior. Terracotta. Maya. Cat. 751.

"The Queen of Uxmal". Limestone. Maya. Cat. 780.

Person embracing a jaguar. Terracotta. Maya. Cat. 722.

Stela representing a jaguar in low relief. Limestone. Maya. Cat. 778.

Ocarina, representing a fat person. Terracotta. Maya. Cat. 720.

Censer, representing Uija-Tai, "he who sees everything". Terracotta. Maya. Cat. 786.

Whistle, representing Ah Kin Koc, the god of Dance. Terracotta. Maya. Cat. 750.

the Sun god. Wide open eyes, surrounded by arched lines, aquiline nose and front-teeth filed in the shape of a T (an Olmec heritage), the hieroglyph for the god Ik, name of the days with the number twenty, which, in combination with the numbers 1 to 13, represent the ritual Maya year of 260 days. Ik also means breath, life, so that the conjunction of the sun and the air must be a symbol of life. The face of the god appears in the jaws of the earth monster, and his high elaborate headdress is decorated all over with motifs connected with water and sea birds. At the top a reclining figure. These representations are supposed to signify the process of creation. The face of the Sun and its headdress are seen against a rectangular plaque, decorated with signs for the sun, the earth and the water. This vessel, like others similar found in the Temple of the Cross at Palenque, were placed at either side of the entrance to the temple to receive offerings, consisting of precious feathers. Reddish terracotta with traces of red and blue paint. 37³/₈x19⁵/₈″. Classic Maya: A.D. 600-987. (Temple of the Cross, Palenque, Chis.).

### 714. Nude male figure*
Damaged. Represents the god of Virility in an attitude of ecstasy. Tattooed head, necklace of snakes with humming-bird, feathers, symbol of resurrection. Limestone. 25¹/₄x16¹/₂″. Classic Maya: A.D. 600-987. (Etzna, Camp.).

### 715. Seated female figure*
With a high headdress, tubular ear-ornaments, facial tattoo, and deformed head. The Maya artists used not only stucco to model the physical appearance of their contemporaries, but also clay, and they rendered very faithfully the social rank of their models, their garments and all their human expressions. The noble attitude of their chiefs sitting on their thrones, the solemn dignity of warriors and priests, pelote players, priestesses, the actor and the dancer, the deformed individual, the very fat, and the common

people, were all sources of observation for the Maya artists who used all their talent and inspiration in realizing these figurines – whistles and rattles, musical instruments with soft or penetrating sounds. Fans, copal-purses, short skirts, sandals, loin-cloths, shields, bracelets, necklaces, ear-ornaments, belts, high and complicated headdresses, all testify in a unique way to the dress and personal ornaments of the Mayas, as well as furnishing information about their domestic animals. There are representations of these, and of birds, felines and other animals from these regions. These statuettes, endowed with a fragile grace, are found as funeral gifts in tombs on the island of Jaina, off the coast of Campeche. Ochre terracotta with traces of blue paint. 13³/₈x6¹/₄″. Classic Maya: A.D. 600-950. (Cemetery, Isla de Jaina, Campeche). Coll.: Museo Regional de Michoacan, Morelia, Mich.

### 716. Whistle
Representing a seated male figure with crossed arms and legs. The head is deformed, the skin tattooed, and the nose is artificially enlarged to imitate the quetzal-bird. High headdress, ear-ornaments, necklaces, and rich feather mantle. Ochre terracotta, with traces of blue and orange paint. 8⁵/₈x3¹/₂‴ Classic Maya: A.D. 600-950. (Cemetery, Isla de Jaina, Campeche). Coll.: Museo Regional de Michoacan, Morelia, Mich.

### 717. Small seated male figure
(Fragment). Nude, with feather mantle. Ochre terracotta with traces of orange paint. 5¹/₂x1¹/₈″. Classic Maya: A.D. 600-950. (Cemetery, Isla de Jaina, Campeche).

### 718. Small seated female figure
High headdress, round ear-ornaments, necklace of seven beads and a blouse with round border cut low to the level of the breasts. Ochre terracotta. 7¹/₄x4¹/₂″. Classic Maya: A.D. 600-950. (Cemetery, Isla de Jaina, Camp.).

**719. Figurine**

Representing a seated person with his hands on his knees. Deformed head, moustache and beard, round ear-ornaments, necklace, bracelets, and large belt. Ochre terracotta. $6^1/2 \times 3^7/8''$. Classic Maya: A.D. 600-950. (Cemetery, Isla de Jaina, Camp.).

**720. Ocarina***

Shaped like a fat, heavy-jowled person, dressed in feathers; with fan. Ochre terracotta, with traces of blue and red paint. $5^7/8 \times 2^1/2''$. Classic Maya: A.D. 600-950. (Cemetery, Isla de Jaina, Camp.).

**721. Small female figure**

With high headdress and the hair indicated by transverse lines. Delicate and well-proportioned features. Ear-ornaments. Dressed in blouse, decorated with rhomboid pattern and fringes, and a small skirt. Ochre terracotta with traces of blue paint. $7^3/8 \times 3^3/8''$. Classic Maya: A.D. 600-950. (Cemetery, Isla de Jaina, Camp.).

**722. Whistle***

Shaped like a person, embracing a jaguar. Ochre terracotta. $5^3/8 \times 4^3/4''$. Classic Maya. A.D. 600-950. (Cemetery, Isla de Jaina, Camp.).

**723. Small female figure***

Called "Venus of Jaina", seated in a majestic attitude, with her bust high, dressed in simple garment, high headdress, hair indicated by transverse lines, forehead-ornament and necklace. Ochre terracotta with traces of blue paint. $8^5/8 \times 3^7/8''$. Classic Maya: A.D. 600-950. (Cemetery, Isla de Jaina, Camp.). Coll.: Museo Regional de Campeche, Camp.

**724. Figurine**

Representing an important priest with crossed arms and a very dignified attitude. High headdress, artificial nose, tattooed face, breastplate in the shape of a sea-shell. Ochre terracotta. $7^1/8 \times 2^7/8''$. Classic Maya: A.D. 600-950. (Cemetery, Isla de Jaina, Camp.). Coll.: Museo Regional de Campeche, Camp. (Courtesy of Museo Nacional de Antropología, Mexico).

**725. Figurine**

(Fragment of a breastplate). Representing an important figure, standing. Artificial nose, breastplate, ear-ornaments, large turban-like headdress. Terracotta. $11 \times 3^7/8''$. Classic Maya: A.D. 600-950. (Cemetery, Isla de Jaina, Camp.).

**726. Small male figure**

Nude, presumably a comic figure, with a swollen eye. Several versions of this figure have been found. Ochre terracotta. $6^1/2 \times 2''$. Classic Maya: A.D. 600-950. (Cemetery, Isla de Jaina, Camp.).

**727. Whistle**

In the shape of a fat, seated person, with his arms over his stomach. Ochre terracotta. $3^3/8 \times 2^3/4''$. Classic Maya: A.D. 600-950. (Cemetery, Isla de Jaina, Camp.).

**728. Whistle**

In the shape of a richly adorned person. High headdress of feathers, round ear-ornaments, necklaces, bracelets, belt, ankle-rings, and sandals. Ochre terracotta. $7^7/8 \times 4''$. Classic Maya: A.D. 600-950. (Cemetery, Isla de Jaina, Camp.).

**729. Whistle**

In the shape of a person sitting on a throne. High headdress of feathers, ear-ornaments, necklace with breastplate, and bracelets. Ochre terracotta with blue paint. $7^1/2 \times 2^1/2''$. Classic Maya: A.D. 600-950. (Cemetery, Isla de Jaina, Camp.).

**730. Whistle**

In the shape of an important person, standing in an attitude of command, with crossed arms. Artificial nose, high headdress, ear-ornaments, and necklace shaped like a serpent with humming-bird feathers. Ochre terracotta. $8^5/8 \times 3^3/4''$.

Classic Maya: A.D. 600-950. (Cemetery, Isla de Jaina, Camp.).

**731. Whistle**

In the shape of a seated person with arms crossed over his chest and a fan in his left hand. Covered head, bulbous nose, facial painting in transverse lines. Ochre terracotta with traces of orange paint. 4⁷/₈×2³/₈″. Classic Maya: A.D. 600-950. (Cemetery, Isla de Jaina, Camp.).

**732. Jaguar**

With open jaws. The front paws crossed, the hind legs stretched out. Ochre terracotta. 3⁷/₈× 7⁷/₈″. Classic Maya: A.D. 600-950. (Cemetery, Isla de Jaina, Camp.).

**733. Whistle**

In the shape of an important person with crossed arms. High headdress of strings of cotton, ear-ornaments, necklace, and short skirt. Gray terracotta. 5⁷/₈×2¹/₂″. Classic Maya: A.D. 600-950. (Cemetery, Isla de Jaina, Camp.).

**734. Ocarina**

In the shape of an actor, seated with his legs joined. High forehead, closed eyes and tattooed face; dressed in a garment of feathers. Ochre terracotta. 4¹/₈×2³/₈″. Classic Maya: A.D. 600-950. (Cemetery, Isla de Jaina, Camp.).

**735-739. Rattles**

In the shape of male and female persons: A) Dancer with mask, large headdress of feathers at the back of his head, and loincloth. 10⁷/₈× 6¹/₄″. B) Person in an attitude of command, with high headdress, painted face, necklace and cape. 9¹/₂×4³/₄″. C) Person in an attitude of command, with high, rectangular headdress, necklace, fan, purse, and cape over his shoulders. 7⁷/₈×3⁷/₈″. D) Pelote player with cylindrical headdress and belt; hands on hips. 7⁷/₈× 4³/₈″. E) Standing woman with outstretched hands, high headdress, ear-ornaments, necklace, "huipil", and skirt. 7¹/₈×4³/₄″. Ochre terracotta,

with traces of red and white paint. Classic Maya: A.D. 600-950. (Cemetery, Isla de Jaina, Camp.).

**740. Whistle**

In the shape of a sitting person, performing an autosacrificial act of a sexual kind. Ochre terracotta with traces of red and blue paint. 6³/₄× 3¹/₂″. Classic Maya: A.D. 600-950. (Cemetery, Isla de Jaina, Camp.). Coll.: K. Stavenhagen, Mexico.

**741. Whistle**

Shaped like two persons; a goddess with a large headdress, and a dignitary, whom she seems to protect. Terracotta, with traces of blue paint. 9×2³/₄″. Classic Maya: A.D. 600-950. (Cemetery, Isla de Jaina, Camp.). Coll.: K. Stavenhagen, Mexico.

**742. Figurine**

Representing a warrior, with incisions on the forehead, indicating a mask of an old man. High, round, pleated headdress, ear-plugs, breastplate of a conch, shield and sling. Terracotta. 8⁵/₈×4³/₈″. Classic Maya: A.D. 600-950. (Cemetery, Isla de Jaina, Camp.). Coll.: K. Stavenhagen, Mexico.

**743. Figurine**

Dancer; feather-headdress, collar, skirt and belt with a large brooch in the shape of a rabbit's head. Decorated with white paint. Terracotta: 7¹/₈×3¹/₈″. Classic Maya: A.D. 600-950. (Cemetery, Isla de Jaina, Camp.). Coll.: K. Stavenhagen, Mexico.

**744. Whistle**

Representing an old man, sitting on a young woman's lap. This representation is frequent among the Jaina sculptures. Ochre terracotta, with traces of yellow and blue paint. 4¹/₂×2³/₈″. Classic Maya: A.D. 600-950. (Cemetery, Isla de Jaina, Camp.). Coll.: K. Stavenhagen, Mexico.

**745. Whistle**
Representing a fat man, seated, with a large headdress in the shape of a deer's head. Ochre terracotta, with traces of yellow and blue paint. $5^7/8 \times 3''$. Classic Maya: A.D. 600-950. (Cemetery, Isla de Jaina, Camp.). Coll.: K. Stavenhagen, Mexico.

**746. Whistle**
In the shape of a seated woman, with crossed legs and her hands raised and open. Dressed in a short skirt. Terracotta. $3^1/8 \times 2''$. Classic Maya: A.D. 600-950. (Cemetery, Isla de Jaina, Camp.). Coll.: K. Stavenhagen, Mexico.

**747. Rattle**
Made in mould, representing a dignitary with a large round headdress, ear-plugs, necklace, and large collar over his shoulders. Ochre terracotta, with white and blue paint. $8^1/4 \times 9''$. Classic Maya: A.D. 600-950. (Cemetery, Isla de Jaina, Camp.). Coll.: K. Stavenhagen, Mexico.

**748. Rattle**
Made in mould, representing a dignitary with high headdress, decorated with a jaguar, serpents, and a monkey. Terracotta. $8^1/4 \times 4^3/8''$. Classic Maya: A.D. 600-950. (Cemetery, Isla de Jaina, Camp.). Coll.: K. Stavenhagen, Mexico.

**749. Whistle**
In the shape of an actor, disguised as a rabbit, painted dress with white spots. Ochre terracotta, with white paint. $5^1/8 \times 3^1/2''$. Classic Maya: A.D. 600-950. (Cemetery, Isla de Jaina, Camp.). Coll.: K. Stavenhagen, Mexico.

**750. Whistle***
(Fragment) representing *Ah Kin Koc,* the Maya god of Dance, in dancing position. High headdress, an ornament representing large bird's wings, ear-plugs, necklace. Ochre terracotta. $4^3/4 \times 3^7/8''$. Classic Maya: A.D. 600-950. (Ceme-

tery, Isla de Jaina, Camp.). Coll.: K. Stavenhagen, Mexico.

**751. Warrior***
Feather headdress, breastplate with skull, and buckler in his left hand. Light ochre terracotta. $1 \times 3^1/8''$. Classic Maya: A.D. 600-950. (Cemetery, Isla de Jaina, Camp.). Coll.: A. Carrillo Gil, Mexico.

**752. Standing male figure**
High headdress in the shape of a hat. Ochre terracotta, with traces of blue, red and white paint. $11 \times 2^3/4''$. Classic Maya: A.D. 600-950. (Cemetery, Isla de Jaina, Camp.).

**753. Seated female figure**
High headgear, simple dress. Ochre terracotta, with traces of blue paint. $5^1/2 \times 2^3/4''$. Classic Maya: A.D. 600-950. (Cemetery, Isla de Jaina, Camp.). Coll.: A. Carrillo Gil, Mexico.

**754. Warrior**
Luxuriously adorned, with removable helmet decorated with feathers, necklaces, belt, pendants. Light ochre terracotta. $5^7/8 \times 2^3/4''$. Classic Maya: A.D. 600-950. (Cemetery, Isla de Jaina, Camp.). Coll.: A. Carrillo Gil, Mexico.

**755. Seated male figure**
(Fragment). High headdress, triangular mantle and necklace. Ochre terracotta. $5^7/8 \times 2^3/4''$. Classic Maya: A.D. 600-950. (Cemetery, Isla de Jaina, Camp.). Coll.: A. Carrillo Gil, Mexico.

**756. Rattle**
In the shape of a woman, standing with outstretched hands. Large headdress with head of a nocturnal bird. Ochre terracotta, with traces of blue paint. $5^7/8 \times 3^1/8''$. Classic Maya: A.D. 600-950. (Cemetery, Isla de Jaina, Camp.). Coll.: A. Carrillo Gil, Mexico.

**757. Whistle**
In the shape of a standing warrior, with very

high headdress, ear-plugs, necklace and mantle that goes down to his feet. Ochre terracotta. $5^7/_8 \times 2^3/_4''$. Classic Maya: A.D. 600-950. (Cemetery, Isla de Jaina, Camp.). Private collection, Mexico.

**758-760. Cephalomorphic whistles**
(Fragments). A) Woman with high headdress. B) Man with headdress with left side ornament and tattoo. C) Head of an old man with large nose and wrinkles. Terracotta. $3^7/_8 \times 1^5/_8''$, $3^3/_4 \times 1^5/_8''$, $2^3/_8 \times 2^3/_8''$. Classic Maya: A.D. 600-950. (Cemetery, Isla de Jaina, Camp.).

**761. The painted rooms of Bonampak***
In the heart of the tropical forests of Chiapas, in Southern Mexico, lies the town Bonampak, which was discovered in 1945, and whose name, in the Mayan language, means "painted walls". In the midst of the ruins looms a pyramid, on the top of which "the Temple of Paintings" is found. This temple is decorated on the outside with stucco figures in high relief, and contains three rooms, richly decorated with frescoes. The rooms here exhibited are a life size copy of the real ones, with their so-called "false Mayan vault", i.e. a step vault, and tracings of the frescoes, covering the walls from floor to ceiling. The "Temple of Paintings" was a commemorative monument for a military victory. The paintings of the first room represent ceremonies in connection with the dressing of "Ahua Balam" and the introduction to the nobles of a young prince. Also ceremonies of a propitiatory nature to ensure victory, with dances and procession of musicians. In the second room the paintings represent sacrificial rituals to ensure victory, the fury of the battle, and the punishment of the prisoners. Finally, in the third room, we see ceremonies with dancers, adorned with feathers, on a terraced pyramid, celebrating victory. These frescoes are, with those of Teotihuacán the oldest and most handsome in precolombian America. They were executed in the 8th century. The paintings have historical

themes, and in strict terms they are not, like those of Teotihuacán, of religious significance. The detailed representation of the splendid and highly varied garments, and of the various persons of different ranks, of the rich headdresses, none of which is like another, of the uniform-like equipment of the warriors, of the movement of the dancers, disguised as birds, and representing Ah Kin Koc, the supreme deity of the Dance – all this has no other purpose than exact historical record.

*Room I*. Part of the second and third upper panel on each side of and opposite the entrance represents persons of high rank, waiting in the rooms of the palace close to the throne, for the "Halach Huinic", the king-ruler, to finish dressing. To the right stands the queen, and the young prince, who is to be introduced to the court, is being carried in the arms of a person of the court. The king has already donned a headdress of quetzal-feathers, a mantle of jaguar hides, that covers him to the feet, ear-plugs, a large breastplate of jade beads, and bracelets also of jade. He is surrounded by his servants and his family, and a dignitary is preparing to paint his body. The four bottom panels represent a procession of musicians with large trumpets, turtle-shells, snails, drums, and other musical instruments as an adequate framework for the dancers, whose masks and clothes are reminiscent of mythological creatures. The retinue outside the palace is starting a procession to prepare the spirits for the fight and implore the gods to lend victory. The vault of this room, like those of the others, is decorated with glyphs of calendar dates in connection with this event.

*Room II*. The paintings of this room, with their many persons of lively appearance, show, on the wall across from the entrance, and on the side-walls, the clash of the battle in the dense tropical forest. The enemies have been surprised by the warriors of Bonampak. The rich garments, the disguises as animals or dead, or as the

Maleficent God, or the Black Lord of War, the arms, and the bellicose musical instruments, all contrast strongly to the poverty of the enemy group. On the entrance wall, which is divided into two parts, is seen a stepped pyramid, on which are placed a lot of prisoners of war. One of them is already dead, the others are wounded and implore the "Halach Huinic" to show mercy. He is surrounded by the "Batab" (priest), the queen, the captains of war, and his most important servants. On the bottom panel two rows of victorious warriors from Bonampak are to be seen.

*Room III.* After the representation of the battle and the punishment of the prisoners, this room shows on the entrance wall, and at the top, a row of nobles and dignitaries, accompanying the "Halach Huinic", moving towards the place where the victory is to be celebrated outside the palace. On the left side of the left wall a group of nobles, including the queen and other women, and the young heir prince, perform autosacrificial acts, as part of the rituals. They are seen perforating their lips to make drops of blood spurt out. On the opposite wall, on the upper part, the "Batab" moves towards the festivities on a litter, carried on the shoulders of his servants. On the wall opposite the entrance, and on the bottom part of the other three walls, a number of musicians, acrobats, and dancers, abundantly adorned with birds' feathers to resemble wings after the image of the god Ah Kin Koc, dance on the steps of a stepped pyramid. Dimensions 16¹/₂×11¹/₂×46 ft. Classic Maya: A.D. 600-800. (Bonampak, Chis.). This copy is the work of the archaeologist and painter Augustín Villagra Caleti.

### 762. Head of a symbolically sacrificed warrior
Moulded. High headdress of feathers and flowers. The nose artificially enlarged to make the human profile more like the aesthetic ideal which was inspired by the profile of the quetzal-bird. This head, which was part of a rich offer-ing, was discovered on the tomb of a Maya chief, in the so-called "Temple of Inscriptions" at Palenque, (Chis.). It is assumed that this head, like another found in the same place, was cut off a whole figure, in order to be offered as symbolical decapitation. Sacrifice by decapita-tion, a very old pre-colombian rite, that was, however, rarely performed, secured the sacrificed person at the same time an apotheosis and a transformation into a star. The Temple of In-scriptions is an impressive building, visible from a distance of 6 miles. It rises to a height of 23 yds. on a high pyramid consisting of 8 levels, and the main front is abundantly decorated with stucco figures. The building corresponds to the year of A.D. 692. In 1949 a secret staircase was discovered, and after three years work, this was found to lead to a hollow crypt 5 ft. under the surface of the earth, and 27 yds. under the floor of the temple. The crypt measures 10 yds. by four, and its walls are decorated with high reliefs in stucco, representing nine priests who symbolize the "Lords of the Height". The larger part of the crypt is taken up by a monolithic sarcophagus, covered by a heavy, carved stone. It contains the skeleton of a man, between 40 and 50 years of age, covered with jade orna-ments and wearing a mask of jade mosaic. From an archaeological point of wiev this dis-covery was of the greatest importance, since it proved the fact that the mexican pyramids were also tombs, and not merely bases of tem-ples. This pyramid was built on top of the tomb of this priest-king, who was probably deified by his people in the hope that he would, from his grave, continue to keep watch for them and secure their protection from the gods. Stucco. 15³/₄×7⁷/₈". Classic Maya: A.D. 692. (Temple of Inscriptions, Palenque, Chis.).

### 763. Small head in profile
(Fragment). Stucco with traces of red and pink paint. 6¹/₄×4³/₈". Classic Maya: A.D. 600-950. (Palenque, Chis.).

**764. Head**

(Fragment of a larger figure, probably from some high relief at Palenque). Stucco. 11×7⅞″. Classic Maya: A.D. 600-950. (Unknown place of discovery).

**765. Glyph**

Indicating a chronological period, represented by a human head in profile. To the right the number 3 decorated with an animal profile. Stucco. 7½×8⅝″. Classic Maya: A.D. 600-950. (Templo Olvidado, Palenque, Chis.).

**766. Glyph**

Indicating a chronological period, represented by two profiles, one of an old man's head, the other a fleshless animal's skull. Stucco. 7¼×8⅝″. Classic Maya: A.D. 600-950. (Templo Olvidado, Palenque, Chis.).

**767. Glyph**

Indicating a chronological period, represented by a human head in profile, a hand, and a number with stylized fleshless animal's skull. Stucco 7⅛×8¼″. Classic Maya: A.D. 600-950. (Templo Olvidado, Palenque, Chis.).

**768. Double mask**

Representing old man, with small high reliefs. Using part of the features of the main mask, another mask is superposed, representing the same old person. The system is the same as that used in the figure of a warrior from Jaina, no. 742. Ochre terracotta. 6¾×5½″. Classic Maya; Tepeu: A.D. 600-950. (Yucatán). Coll.: K. Stavenhagen, Mexico.

**769-770. Vases**

With slightly concave bottoms, divergent rims, ring-shaped bases. One has four bulbous supports, the other three cylindrical supports. Polychrome terracotta. 5½×11⅜″, 6¼×7½″. Classic Maya, Tepeu: A.D. 600-950. (Tabasco).

**771. Vase**

Cylindrical, with flat bottom. Polychrome decoration, representing two persons and two glyphs. Ochre terracotta. 4¾×7⅞″. Classic Maya, Tepeu: A.D. 600-950. (Lago de Atitlán, Guatemala).

**772-773. Vases**

With flat bottoms. Engraved representations of richly adorned persons and hieroglyphs. Ochre terracotta. 5⅞×5⅛″, 4⅝×5⅜″. Classic Maya, Tepeu: A.D. 600-950. (Yucatán).

**774. Jar**

High, cylindrical, with truncated cone base. Engraved decoration: white figure. Delicate orange terraeotta. 9¼×5⅛″. Classic Maya, Hepeu: A.D. 600-950. (Campeche).

**775. Tripod jar**

Pearshaped, three bulbous supports and incised pattern. Ochre terracotta. 8⅝×5⅞″. Classic Maya, Tepeu: A.D. 600-950. (Yucatán).

**776. Chac-Mool***

God of the beneficient Rain, but also endowed with a demoniac power, like all the gods. Ruler of Thunder and Lighting and Floods. Represented as a nude, reclining figure, leaning on his elbows, in a position as if he were on the point of getting up. The hands, resting on his stomach, hold a round bowl for offerings. Headdress with feathers and several rows of beads. Rectangular ear-plugs with snakes, rings on arms and legs, and sandals. Wears a breastplate in the shape of a stylized butterfly, symbol of warriors who died in battle or who have been sacrificed and were transformed into stars, and whose blood the sun had drunk to be able to continue its course. At Tula and Chichén Itzá these figures were placed in the center of ceremonial rooms or sacred cloisters to receive offerings. They were considered representations of Quetzalcóatl (the god who has gone and is absent) in the state of sleep, from which he will one day return to rule anew. Limestone. $41^3/_8\times$ $58^1/_4''$. Maya-Toltec: A.D. 987-1185. (Chichén Itzá, Yuc.).

**777. Atlantean figure**
Richly dressed person, with the attributes of Chac. The hands raised to support an altar or table, made of a large stone plate. Limestone. $35\times19^1/_8''$. Maya-Toltec: A.D. 987-1185. (Chichén Itzá, Yuc.).

**778. Stela***
With low relief, representing a jaguar that makes a florid speech before devouring a human heart, according to the hieroglyphs surrounding its top part. The spots on the hide of this animal represent warriors, dead in battle or on the sacrificial altar, and transformed into stars, whose blood and light enable the sun to run its course. Limestone with traces of fresco painting in red and blue. $44^1/_8\times35^3/_8''$. Maya-Toltec: A.D. 987-1185. (Chichén Itzá, Yuc.).

**779. Fantastic ceremonial knife**
With representation in profile of four persons with large headdresses of feathers. Flint. $12^3/_8\times$ $10^1/_2''$. Maya-Toltec: A.D. 987-1185. (El Palmar, Camp.).

**780. »The Queen of Uxmal«***
This figure, known under this name, may represent *Kukulkan*, the god of Life, and of the planet of Venus. A warrior's head with a handsome tattoo on the right cheek, is placed in the jaws of a highly stylized snake, whose head is equipped with a peg, so that it can be joined to some other monument, serving as architectural ornament in the interior of the Temple of the Soothsayer, at Uxmal. Limestone. $31^7/_8\times39''$. Maya-Toltec: A.D. 987-1185. (Pyramid of the Soothsayer, Uxmal, Yuc.).

**781. Teotezcacuitlapilli**
or buckle, worn by the Mayan dignitaries. Mosaic of turquoise, (fragment) representing the sun with four fire serpents, on a disk, rimmed with 16 undulating lines. Wood, turquoise, and pyrites. $9^5/_8''$ in diameter. Maya-Toltec: A.D. 987-1185. (El Castillo, Chichén Itzá, Yuc.).

**782. Jar**
Representing a bird, decorated with a necklace of eight skulls, and holding a skull in its beak. Terracotta with plumbyte (graphite) $6^3/_4\times6^3/_4''$. Maya-Toltec: A.D. 987-1185. (Yucatán).

**783. Jar**
Almost spherical, with a long engraved neck and three rattle-supports. Terracotta, with plumbyte (graphite). $7^1/_8\times5^1/_2''$. Maya-Toltec: A.D. 987-1185. (Yucatán).

**784. Jar**
Cylindrical, with a truncated cone as base. Decorated with figure, representing the god of Rain. Terracotta with plumbyte (graphite). $7^1/_8\times7^1/_8''$. Maya-Toltec: A.D. 987-1185. (Yucatán).

**785. Tripod jar**
Almost spherical, adorned with a figure, with high headdress, and arms folded over his knees. Terracotta with plumbyte (graphite). $7^1/_8\times$ $10^1/_4''$. Maya-Toltec: A.D. 987-1185. (Yucatán). Coll.: Dolores Olmedo de Olvera, Mexico.

**786. Censer***
With representation of UIJA-TAI "he who sees everything and is the supreme judge". The priest wears a complicated headdress of feathers and snakes, and a mask of Chac, with large nose and large snake's fangs. On each arm hangs a purse for copal (incense of resin), the emblem of priesthood, and in his hands he holds symbols of maize and a bowl. Copal was not merely burnt in large quantities as incense in the tem-

ples, it was also burnt on mountain tops to make the rain come down, not unlike modern methods of provoking rain by spreading soot over the clouds. Terracotta, with fresco painting. $21^5/8 \times 12^1/4''$. Maya, Sovereignty of Mayapán: A.D. 1200-1450. (Mayapán, Yuc.).

# 11. The Aztec Civilization

*A.D. 1324-1521*
*Sites*

Mexico, Colhuacán (D.F.); Texcoco, Tlacopán, Chalco, Tlalmanalco, Calixtlahuaca, Malinalco, Tenayuca (the State of Mexico); Cozcatlán (the State of Puebla); Zempoala, and Castillo de Teayo (the State of Veracruz).

The Mexican-Aztec people's history is rich in dramatic vicissitudes. The arrival of the Mexicans on the central plateau coincided with a state of deep dissension between the principalities that had been established in the Valley of Mexico, after the fall of the Toltecs. In less than two hundred years they succeeded with a belligerence and a will to power, seldom matched in history, in incorporating a large number of tribes in their sphere of influence. During their vertiginous ascent they appropriated cultural, artistic and religious elements from all the conquered tribes, and from their predecessors, the builders of Teotihuacán, and the Toltecs, from whom their artistic style — mixed with Mixtec refinement — basically derived, though they endowed it with a grandiose, violent, and dramatic expression.

The Aztecs were a tribe of nomads from the North. It is not known exactly where they came from. They were Nahuas and believed themselves that they had sprung from a mythical Aztlán (the Place of Herons). Before they penetrated into the Valley of Mexico, they had led a migratory existence through lowlands and mountains for about 200 years, in the beginning led by Huitzilopochtli, a priest, whom they later made into a tribal god, and who eventually developed into a sun deity, the only one invented by the Aztecs. The oracle of the god had predicted that the seat of the Aztec culture was to be a place where an eagle, sitting on a nopal cactus, was devouring a snake. This also meant that it would be a propitious place for harmony between the principle of the sun (the eagle), and that of the earth (the snake), a point of union for magic forces that were to secure the life and fertility of the tribe, and at the same time a symbol of the sacred war, struggle and synthesis of opposite elements. The Aztecs felt a vocation for war as well as for religion. In 1324 the prophecy of the oracle was fulfilled, and the Aztecs founded Mexico-Tenochtitlan, the capital of their future empire.

The first Mexican chiefs were "caciques" who were subordinated to the prince of Atzcapotzalco. The first king was Acamapichtli (1376-1396), who until 1440, was followed by Huitzilihuitl, Chimalpopoca, and Izcóatl. The latter, being a great statesman and organizer, decided to make Tenochtitlán independent of Atzcapotzalco. He joined forces with the Texcoco prince, Netzahualcóyotl, beat the warriors of Atzcapotzalco, and established a triple alliance between Tenochtitlán, Texcoco, and Tlacopán (the latter being the kingdom of the Tepanecas. From 1440 to 1525 Moctezuma I, Axayacatl, Tizoc, Ahuitzotl, Moctezuma II, Cuitlahuac and Cuauhtémoc, succeeded each other; the last of them was executed by Cortés. To this day the descendants of the old Mexicans have preserved the physical features of their forbears, their language and a number of their customs.

Society was divided into clans. Each district or village (calpulli) owned the soil collectively. Apart from this horizontal division there was a vertical one: priests, warriors, tradesmen, common people, and slaves. As the wealth of the city increased, society grew more complex, and the number of functionaries and hierarchies grew. The common ownership of the soil, the strong clan- and family ties, the lack of hereditary classes, and the supremacy of religion no doubt strengthened the social cohesion. At the arrival of the Spaniards, the theocratic-military State showed symptoms that suggested a transition from the sacred to the political life. The Aztec society was a firmly built unit. The collective life was the all-important thing. War was a religion, a reflection of the cosmic struggle on the human level. This very literal interpretation of the old Mesoamerican religions suited the Aztec expansion perfectly. The purpose of war was to subdue other peoples, but more important than the territorial expansion was the procuring of tributes and prisoners for the sacrifices. Thus arose the institution called "the flowery war" (not unlike the tournaments of the Middle Ages). This explains the fact that the Aztecs left certain neighboring tribes, e.g. the Tlaxcalas, independent. The sacrifices were a permanent feature of the Mesoamerican civilization, like the cultivation of Maize, the pelote game, the numerical system based on twenty, the sacred calendar of 260 days, and the highly developed cosmogenic concepts. But with the Aztecs the sacrifice developed into an obsession, reflecting their physically and historically unstable situation.

Together with these features we find highly refined manifestations. The Spaniards were amazed at the high public morals of Tenochtitlán, and at the gentleness of the human relations, in contrast to the ferocity of the sacrifices and punishments. The ethical codex of the Mexicans was strict, but human. In this collective world family was the social cell. Education was the task of the parents, and it was later continued at the *telpuchcalli* (college for social relations) and the *calmecac* (clerical college). The merchants, who were also used as ambassadors and spies, traveled all over the Mesoamerican territory. Tenochtitlán, which was a great political and military center, was a big city also in the economic and cultural sense. Alfonso Caso points out that the priests had begun a very complicated elaboration of the cosmogenic and religious ideas. The purpose of theological speculation was to adapt Aztec beliefs, which reflected the recent nomadic past of the people, to the more elevated and complicated conceptions of the Teotihuacáns and the Toltecs. The Aztecs were a people of warriors and priests, but also of poets. We know next to nothing of Mayan literature, and have very few preserved remains of the literature of the other tribes (apart from some Otomi songs). But we possess a very large collection of Aztec songs and anthems, that miraculously have survived the destruction of the Conquest. It is no exaggeration to say that these poems are among the purest verbal works of art of the human race. In its general structure Aztec culture did not differ much from that of the other Mesoamerican peoples: cosmogeny, rites, plays, astronomy, mathematics, all this is common patrimony. Still, few peoples have ever had more definite or stronger personality.

The different types of ceramics throw light on the development of styles from the years of nomadic life in the Valley of Mexico to the definitive establishment of Tenochtitlán. There are four phases: Culhuacán, with realistic motifs, animals and flowers; Tenayuca, with geometrical designs, hooks, frets, parallel lines, drawn with a coarse brush that sometimes wavers a bit; Texcoco, a continuation of the preceding period, but with perfection of line, which is finer now and more secure; Tenochtitlán, where there is a reversion to renderings of flora and fauna: birds, snakes, fish, plants. Notable products are the dishes, urns, coniform cups for *pulque* (an alcoholic beverage), seals, (to paint materials and the human skin), pipes, and figurines of gods, temples and warriors.

Aztec sculpture expresses with great force the Aztec temperament, the concentrated passion, the magic-heroic conception of life, the preoccupation with cosmogeny, and the dominating role of analogical thought. What surprises one above all is the accumulation of elements, which is, however, not an empty one: each sculpture is an entity of symbols, each element has a double or triple sense, each sense has a hidden or open connection with other elements. It is a maze of symbols, but a coherent maze. Religious syncretism and accumulation of attributes join hands. Then there is the sense of material: forms merge with stone or wood, so that they constitute one body, become stone or woodsculptures rather than being sculptures in stone or wood. The Aztec sculptor conceived of his work as one perfect object, in which all planes present themselves simultaneously, outside and inside. Such a conception sometimes bears a certain resemblance to cubism, just as the accumulation of symbols is reminiscent of surrealistic inspirations. It is an art in which the delirium is guided by a kind of implacable rigor.

Tenochtitlán was built on a small island, which fact necessitated construction of a network of embankments and canals, like that of Venice. When the Spaniard arrived at the Aztec capital, consisting then of Tenochtitlán and Tlatelolco, it was a huge square about two by two miles, and covering about 2500 acres. In the center rose the Great Temple, dedicated to Huitzilopochtli and Tlaloc. It consisted of a pyramidical base for two twin buildings one painted blue and white (that of Tlaloc), the other adorned with white cranes on red ground (that of Huitzilopochtli). In front of it were numerous braziers, sculptures serving as standard-bearers, and sacrificial altars. Other important structures were the temples of Tezcatlipoca, Quetzalcóatl and Cihuacóatl (the Snake Temple), where the gods of the conquered peoples were placed. Within the walls (coatepantli) were pelote grounds, arsenals, the *calmecac* and the music school, or *mecatlan*.

Aztec architecture is distinguished by its severity, its grandiosity, and the impressive character of the buildings. The most important buildingmaterials were volcanic rock, called *"tezontle"*, or bloodstone, *adobe,* or unburnt clay, wood and mortar. The walls were usually covered with a coat of brick red paint. The roofs were flat on the inside and slanting on the outside, and the facades were adorned with tall vertical battlements, particularly on the palaces. Among the architectural elements we find pillars, columns and corniches. There were decorative friezes, and the floors were covered with flagstones. The stairs were wide and majestic, with smooth or ornamental banisters. Curtains were used instead of doors. There are few remnants left of this architecture, with the exception of the ruins of the Great Temple (Mexico), Tenayuca, Texcutzingo, Teopanzolco, and Tepotzteco (the State of Morelos), Huexotla, famous for its ramparts, Malinalco with its monolithic structures, Calixtlahuaca, near Toluca, and the great pyramid of Cholula.

There were celebrations on certain days, according to the calendar, when music, dancing, singing, poetry, oratory, soothsaying, sacrifices, and theatrical performances were combined in a *fiesta.* The music was pentatonal, and rather monotonous, since the scale was short. Apart from two kinds of drums, there were flutes, snails, turtle shells, bones with grooves to blow on, ocarinas, and whistles. The dance was usually group dancing. Composers created songs and ballets for important occasions, and sometimes staged big general dances, in which most of the population participated.

Like all other pre-colombian peoples the Mexicans developed their culture in total isolation from the rest of the world, ignorant of other countries and other people. When the Spaniards landed at Veracruz, in 1519, the Aztec empire was at its peak. The clash between the two cultures was terrible. Two circumstances contributed to the victory of the invaders, apart from their technical superiority (armour, fire weapons, horses), viz.: the cyclic conception of time (Moctezuma thought that a cosmic era was over, and that Cortés was Quetzalcóatl), and the political competence, with which the Spanish captain played on the justified complaints of the Mesoamerican peoples against the Aztec supremacy. Through an irony of fate Cortés appeared as a liberator in the eyes of the Indians. The fight of the Aztecs ended with the fall of Tenochtitlán, of which the enemies, literally, did not leave one stone upon another.

# The Mexican Religion

One of the basic elements of the primitive Mesoamerican religion is the belief that the origin of all things can be ascribed to one dual principle. The gods, the world, and man are its work. Apart from this, certain people, like Netzahualcóyotl, the king of Texcoco, propagated the idea of an invisible god, who cannot be depicted, and who was called "Tloque-Nahuaque" or "Ipalnemohuani", i.e. "the god who is close to us", or "he by whom all things live". They placed him above all the gods. Among the Aztecs the names of the double god, the masculine and feminine creative principle, are: Ometecuhtli (2 Lord) and Omecíhuatl (2 Our Lady). Both live in Omeyocan (the Place 2). They were also called "the Lord and Lady of our flesh and sustenance", and they were represented by fertility-symbols and adorned with maize seeds. Both these gods and the poet, Netzahualcóyotl's invisible god, whose cult was close to monotheism, were, however, a bit vague for the public mind that preferred the lower gods of agriculture as safer and more concrete.

The Mesoamerican religion grouped all living beings according to the corners of the world. Each corner of the World is governed by one of the four Tezcatlipoca. The "official" Aztec version of this horizontal division of the world is the following: In the center, the old god of fire, Huehueteotl; to the east, Tlaloc, the god of rain; to the south Xipe, the god of maize; to the west Quetzalcóatl, the planet of Venus; to the north Mitlantecuhtli, the god of death. Apart from the gods, the colors, the animals, the trees, the days, and men were divided in this way. Red thus corresponded to the east, black to the north, blue to the south, and white to the west. Men were named by the day on which they were born, according to the sacred calendar of 260 days, divided into four periods of 65 days each, corresponding to the four corners of the world. The form and function of the pyramid is a kind of materialization of these concepts.

A vertical division of the cosmos corresponds to this horizontal one. There are thirteen "floors", or worlds, that, by their position, and without implying moral signification, were lower or higher. Still the horizontal division, that may be the older one, has lent each of these worlds a special shade of meaning. The "Western sky" was reserved for the warriors, the Eastern for women dead in childbirth. Tlaloc's water paradise lies to the west. Mictlan is the place where common mortals go: neither heaven, nor hell, but the ultimate destination of man, which the dead person arrives at after passing numerous tests.

To the ancient Mexicans time was no abstract entity, nor was space a mere extension. The two concepts merged and constituted one substance, that was born, grew, died away and was reborn. According to this cyclic conception of time, the world and men had been created several times. The creation of the world and its destruction were phases in the cosmic movement and therefore closely connected with the sacred calendar (which was its highest manifestation). The movement was the result of the incessant opposition and union of the dual principle, embodied in a divine couple and a number of gods that were simply attributes or manifestations of the cosmic movement. For the Aztecs the two principles were incarnate in Tezcalipoca (in his black, destructive aspect) and Quetzalcóatl. The struggle between these gods is the very history of the universe, which consists of five eras (suns), which four times has been terminated by cataclysms. The fifth era is that of man. The sign of the first sun is 4-jaguar, that of the second 4-wind, that of the third 4-rain, that of the fourth 4-fire. The catastrophe that put an end to the fourth era, was a flood which changed men to fishes. After that Tezcatlipoca and Quetzalcóatl united a fifth time to recreate the world and begin a new era, a new sun. This happened at Teotihuacán, in the presence of the other gods. One of them had to sacrifice himself. The first one that offered to do so was the noble and rich Pantecatl, followed by Nanahuatzin, who was poor and covered with pustules. At the last moment Pantecatl hesitated before the flames. It was Nanahuatzin who sacrificed himself and thus inaugurated a new era, the sign of which was 4-movement. Nanahuatzin was transformed into the sun and Pantecatl into the moon. Thus began the fifth era, which is to end in an earthquake.

Nanahuatzin and Pantecatl are simply manifestations of the dual principle, and in this capacity, they are probably mere personifications of Quetzalcóatl. In the second part of the myth, Quetzalcóatl, in his own person or in that of Xolotl (the lord of metamorphosis and duality), sets the world in motion, descends into the realm of the dead, disinters the bones of his ancestors, fertilizes them with his blood, and creates the present human kind. Quetzalcóatl thus functions as a creative god, but the creation is the fruit of his self-sacrifice. Ideas of sin, penitence, purification, self-sacrifice, and inner life, are closely connected with the image of Quetzalcóatl. Asceticism was one of the essential elements of Mexican religiosity. It is a matter of cosmic asceticism, so to speak, since it demands not only sacrifice of others and of oneself, but sees the whole natural process as one immense sacrifice. Everything from the stars to man is subjected to the law of sacrifice. In the Aztec interpretation such a concept must lead to a series of hallucinatory, sanguine rituals. In a literal sense, all creation must be nourished by the magic food, the substance of sacrifice. The blood was the "precious water", the heart was the flower. The flowery war, the harvest of hearts.

Both the Mexican pantheon and their cosmogenic ideas were the result of the syncretic elaboration undertaken by the clerical caste. The synthesis had not been completed when the Spaniards arrived. Side by side with the solar religion, in which the celestial bodies dominate (perhaps echoing the nomadic life), we thus find another older religious tradition in which the most important figures were the gods of vegetation and procreation. A very old god is the old god of fire who had been worshipped at Tlatilco for over 2000 years, Huehueteotl. He was called the Lord of the Year when he was disguised as Xiucoatl, the fire serpent. Quetzalcóatl was, as already mentioned, identified with Venus, the planet in its dual aspect of morning and evening star. In the latter guise he is his twin brother, Xolotl, the god of metamorphosis, and so connected with a Mexican amphibian, the "axolotl", which had esoteric significances as astonishing as the European salamander. Tezcatlipoca represents the evening star and the nocturnal sky, and is connected with everything deadly and destructive. In his capacity of warrior from the north, he is called Huitzilopochtli; in his capacity of protector of warriors he is Yaotl. He was also called the "Mirror of Obsidian" or the "Fuming Mirror". He was the god who protected Texcoco and symbolized the nocturnal mist of evaporated water from the large lake. Tonatiuh was the sun, in the shape of an eagle that rose on the firmament every morning and returned in the evening. In a certain sense Huitzilopochtli was also an incarnation, according to the cult of him at Tenochtitlán.

The oldest among the fertility gods (appearing under different names among all the Mesoamerican tribes) is Tlaloc, the god of rain. Another deity from the coastal region is Xipe-Totec, worshipped already by the Huaxtecs and the Totonacs. Xipe ("Our Lord of the Flayed Skin") is a maize god and must wear a golden mantle, as the corn cobs are wrapped in silken husks. For this reason he is wrapped in the flayed skin of a victim, and this may explain why he, like Quetzalcóatl, is the god of penitence and asceticism. As the virile god, ploughing the field, he was on the coast before being adopted on the plateau in connection with Tlazolteotl, the life-creating soil. This enigmatic Huaxtec goddess, the protector of births and harvests, was the mother of all gods and presided at steam baths and at sensual pleasures. As the goddess of filth, she was a purifying force, "eating the sins of men". In Tlazolteotl we find again the Mesoamerican dualism; she is the goddess of both confession and of physical love. Xochipilli, a young god of maize, poetry and song, is probably of Totonac origin, like Xochiquetzal. This enumeration would be incomplete without mention of the mighty Coatlicue, whose image is a veritable constellation of symbols and significances. She is primarily Earth, in its double sense of grave and womb, but she is also the creation, in all its manifestations and phases. In a perpetual fight with herself, she ceaselessly creates and destroys herself.

All these and many other deities are connected with a given space and time (the Mexican pantheon surprises not only by its number of gods, but also by the variety and complication of their attributes). It would be inexact to say that they are representations of the cosmic movement, or that their apparition and disappearance is determined by the cycle of the calendar. They are time itself, the smiling or frightening, fatal or beneficial face of the day, the year, or the cycle (52 years). They are the rhythm of the seasons, the course of the stars. Nothing is permanent, for all is change and movement.

Tenochtitlán, Aztec capital. A.D. 1519.

Xochipilli, "the Lord of Flowers". Volcanic rock. Aztec. Cat. 798.

Coatlicue, goddess of the Earth, Life and Death. Basalt. Aztec. Cat. 787.

Large ceremonial brazier. Terracotta. Aztec. Cat. 840.

Ceremonial brazier representing a Maize deity. Terracotta. Aztec. Cat. 837.

Xipe-Totec,
god of Spring. Basalt
Aztec. Cat. 797.

Monkey, god af Dance. Basalt. Aztec. Cat. 829.

Reclining jaguar. Andesite. Aztec. Cat. 834.

Plumed coyote. Basalt. Aztec. Cat. 830.

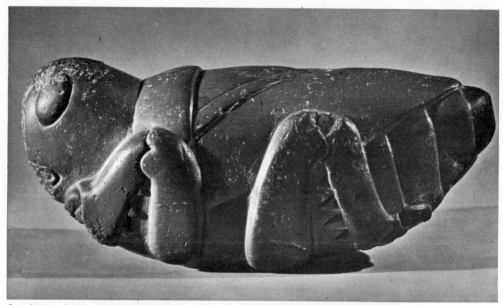

Grasshopper. Red stone. Aztec. Cat. 833.

Coiled snake. Granite-like stone. Aztec. Cat. 819.

Coiled snake. Granite-like stone. Aztec. Cat. 819.

Plumed serpent. Basalt. Aztec. Cat. 817.

Tlapanhuehuetl, large war-drum. Wood. Aztec. Cat. 842.

Head of a dead man. Basalt. Aztec. Cat. 808.

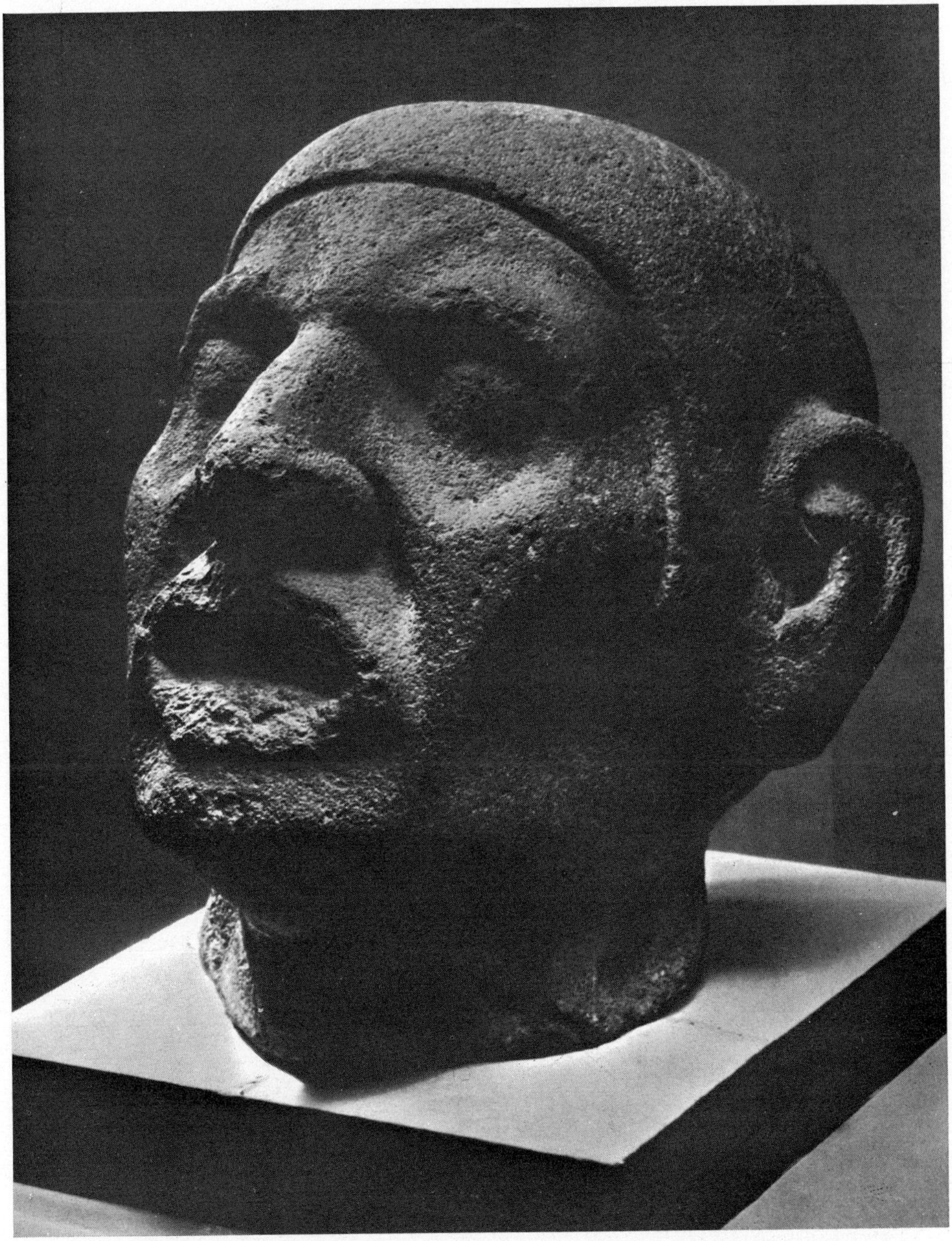

Coatlicue, goddess of the Earth, Life and Death. Basalt. Aztec. Cat. 788.

Coiled snake. Granite-like stone. Aztec. Cat. 820.

Teponaztli. Wooden drum. Aztec. Cat. 843.

Teponaztli. Drum. Stone. Aztec. Cat. 844.

Plumed serpent, Quetzalcóatl. Basalt. Aztec. Cat. 821.

Head of Eagle Knight. Andesite. Aztec. Cat. 811.

Cuauhxicalli, monumental receptacle for offerings. Basalt. Aztec. Cat. 803.

But everything repeats itself, and every 260 days, after the period of the sacred calendar (Tonalpohualli), a kind of cosmic return occurs. Every 52nd year the ceremony of the new fire was repeated, and this rite was, according to George C. Vaillant, to the Aztecs "something like the death of one existence and the birth of another. The thought that nature might well interrupt the course of their own life lent these rites a profound solemnity". This, though, also explains the obsession with sacrifice. Every day man had to ward off the catastrophe with his blood. No wonder that the ritual absorbed all public life and stamped all activities. War was one ritual, dance another, in a society where all was subject to the cosmic rhythm, and in which the ritual was the only possible form of participation, whether in order to profit from the positive influence, or neutralize the harmful ones, celebrations and ceremonies succeeded each other all year.

Like all the other Mesoamerican tribes, the Aztecs had two calendars: the sacred one (260 days) and the solar calendar (365 days). The former was divided into 13 "weeks" of 20 days each. The latter had eighteen "months", also of 20 days, plus five fateful days (nemotemi). The rituals were celebrated according to the solar calendar. Each of these celebrations that so impressed the Spaniards, was in effect a representation of the cosmic movement in each of its phases. As a people of warriors, the Aztecs could only conceive of the god as a hero. To see him radiant in the sky, spreading light and life, was like participating every day in his victory.

### 787. Coatlicue*

"She of the Snake Skirt", goddess of Earth, Life and Death, represented as a very old, bent woman with sunken breasts and fleshless skull. The cheeks encrusted with turquoise, and the teeth with mother-of-pearl. Skirt of entwined snakes, belt of snakes, hands and feet equipped with jaguar's claws. The claws of the hands prepare to take life, the claws of the feet to till the ground and affirm life. On the shoulder the date "8 malinalli" (grass). Basalt 46×15³/₈". Aztec: A.D. 1324-1521. (Cozcatlan, Pue.).

### 788. Coatlicue*

In the shape of a young woman. Tangled hair. Diadem of skulls, round ear-plugs, skirt decorated with feathers, necklace adorned with hands and a skull. Represented in an attitude of attacking the dead. Placed on a pedestal, decorated with skulls. Basalt. 29⁷/₈×19¹/₄". Aztec: A.D. 1324-1521. (Calixtlahuaca, Mex.).

### 789. Coatlicue, deity of the earth

Dressed in a "quexquemitl" (short shoulder-cape), a skirt with embroidered ornaments imitating the skin of a snake, and with a rattlesnake for belt. High headdress with a diadem of chalchihuites (green stones) and large pendants of strings of cotton. She also wears the attributes of the deities of maize and water, symbols of fertility. The earth was considered as the mother, who, when fertilized, would yield the fruits that preserve life. The significance of this representation is clear: the earth is at the same time the mother and tomb of humanity. Basalt. 32⁵/₈×15³/₄". Aztec: A.D. 1324-1521. (Valley of Mexico).

### 790. Xiuhtecuhtli

The god of fire and hearths. Also the lord of the

native rulers and the officials of the government. Head drilled for insertion of ornaments, eyes and teeth encrusted with pyrites and mother-of-pearl, round ear-plugs, dressed in a short, round skirt and sandals. His right hand he probably used to hold a finely wrought "atlatl" (spear-thrower), carved in gilt wood. The shoulder adorned with a tail of "Xiuhcóatl", the fire serpent, and the date: 4 Cipactli (crocodile), which is the calendar sign of this god. Basalt. $45^{1}/_{4}\times15''$. Aztec: A.D. 1324-1521. (Cozcatlán, Pue.).

### 791. Centeociuatl

Goddess of Maize and Agriculture. Dressed in a sumptuous mantle covered with flowers in bas-relief. Jade necklace and skirt adorned with a fret symbolizing the serpent. On the back part of her cape is a maize-plant whose root is a jaguar's claw. In her right hand she holds a rattle snake and in her left hand an ear of maize. This deity, like Xochiquetzal, another deity with similar functions, lived at the top of heaven and kept a court of dwarfs, hunchbacks and fools. Pink Basalt. $31^{1}/_{2}\times13^{3}/_{4}''$. Aztec: A.D. 1324-1521. (Valley of Mexico).

### 792. Centeociuatl

With a high geometrical headdress and snake-belt. A hole in her hand is meant to hold a sceptre, symbol of fertility. Pink stone. $22\times8^{5}/_{8}''$. Aztec: A.D. 1324-1521. (Veracruz).

### 793. Quetzalcóatl

The plumed serpent, representing the union of earth and sky. The feathers of the quetzal bird symbolize the sky, which is light and life, while the snake symbolizes earth, i.e. death and darkness. He also represents the planet of Venus, in its diurnal and nocturnal phases, and in the night assumes the name of Tezcatlipoca, the god of civilization, the benefactor of man, and the creator of art and knowledge. The identification with Venus, the study of which planet is the basis of astronomy and of the calendar, makes

Quetzalcóatl the zodiacal god of Mexico. His greatest importance to mankind is that he has given it the sense of spiritual life, in his capacity of god of knowledge. The attraction of Quetzalcóatl as the savior, who burned himself as an act of penitence, grew in time to such an extent that later all priest-kings took his name and claimed to be his vicar. The cult of Quetzalcóatl may have originated on the coast among the Huaxtecs. In Teotihuacán he was the god of rain. Among the Toltecs he achieved the greatest importance, first being honored as a person, and later being worshipped as a god. As an old priest-king, ruling at Tula, he sacrificed himself by throwing himself into a fire in order to purify his people. He rose again from the stake as the brilliant planet of Venus, having promised that he would one day return as a person, coming from the east to liberate his adherents. The myth of Quetzalcóatl represented as a blond and bearded man caused the sad error of the Aztecs, when they thought that Cortés was the god returning to them. The Aztec monolith is shaped like a pyramid with a round base. In the jaws of a snake, coiled in a position to strike is seen a man who wears on his chest the hieroglyphs of water and fire, "burnt water", or the union of contrary elements, symbol of the inner fight and the union of opposites. Basalt. $51\times75''$. Aztec: A.D. 1324-1521. (Mexico). Copy.

### 794. Ehecatl-Quetzalcóatl

The god of Wind. Between this god and Quetzalcóatl the plumed serpent, there was a close connection, and Ehecatl can be considered as a special manifestation of Quetzalcóatl. One representation of the god of wind is a sectional cut of a conch, i.e. a spiral, the symbol of wind as precursor of beneficent rain. Here he is represented as a standing man, dressed only in a "maxtlatl" the garment of the common man, wearing a mouth mask in the shape of a beak, through which he blows at the clouds heavy with rainwater. He was regarded as the ruler of air. The pyramids built for the god of wind, were circular. Basalt. $75^{1}/_{4} \times 23^{5}/_{8}''$. Aztec, Maltazinca: A.D. 1324-1521. (Calixtlahuaca, Toluca, Mex.). Copy.

### 795. Tezcatlipoca

The god of Night. Representation of the planet of Venus, as the evening star, brother and antipode of Quetzalcóatl, the morning star, who rules the dawn. The two gods symbolize the struggle between day and night, summer and winter, life and death – obsession in the old Mexican world. Tezcatlipoca is also god of Providence and of Destruction. Basalt, with traces of paint. $33^{7}/_{8} \times 10^{5}/_{8}''$. Aztec: A.D. 1324-1521. (Mexico).

### 796. Xipe-Totec

"Our Lord the Flayed", seated with his hands on his knees. This god entered in the Aztec pantheon between 1469 and 1483, during the reign of a great chief who introduced this cult from Oaxaca, though the god had been worshipped for centuries by numerous tribes, thus by the Teotihuacáns, the Zapotecs, and the Huaxtecs. Among these he not only represented the idea of renewal, spring and harvest, but was also the god of sacrifices, penitence, and repentance, i.e. of the purification of the soul. Among the Aztecs he was often represented as a priest who served as intermediary between the people and the god, and who was dressed in a flayed child's skin, the symbol of renewal. In the civilizations of the south, as later among the Aztecs, Xipe-Totec was the protector of the jewellers, because he was also the god of Maize, and the ears of maize are covered with husks in the color of gold. Basalt. $15^{3}/_{4} \times 9^{7}/_{8}''$. Aztec: A.D. 1324-1521. (Mexico). Coll.: Museo de Arqueología e Historia del Estado de Mexico, Toluca, Mex.

### 797. Xipe-Totec*

Deity of Spring and Renewal. Standing, with a child's mask, and clad in a human skin, from which hands hang down. Seams are seen on chest and back. Basalt. $22^{1}/_{4} \times 8^{5}/_{8}''$. Aztec: A.D. 1324-1521. (Valley of Mexico). Coll.: S. Hale, Mexico.

### 798. Xochipilli*

"Lord of the Flowers", a male figure, sitting on a throne with crossed legs, and the hands half open to receive offerings of feathers and flowers and to hold a banner, called "The Flowery Heart". He was also the god of Joy and Play, of Poetry and Music, Acting and Dance, and of Love and already from his beginning among the Huaxtecs and Zapotecs, he was the god of Procreation and the new Maize. Wearing mask, necklace, anklerings, adorned with jaguar's claws. The body wears a dress decorated with symbols representing flowers and the heat of the sun in its spiritual sense. The head is adorned with feathers of the red heron, the face is covered with an actor's mask that seems to express ecstacy. The throne, on which he is sitting, is decorated with hieroglyphs that symbolize movements of wings and petals of flowers, and with the hieroglyph called "Tonalo", which is special for this god and consists of four joined plates. The significance of this god, who is also called "The Lord of Souls", was both material and spiritual, and, like flowers, he symbolized both spiritual and secular values at the same time: poetry and music, as well as real flowers with splendid colors and refined perfumes, and the human heart of the sacrificed. Andesite. $31^{1}/_{8} \times 15^{3}/_{4}''$. Aztec: A.D. 1324-1521. (Tlalmanalco, Mex.).

### 799. Xochiquetzal

Young goddess of flowers and vegetation, wife of Macuilxochitl, represented as seated with her hands on her knees. Wears a diadem of flowers, feathers and ears of maize, and ear-plugs, necklace, and triangular garment. She was also goddess of women's work, like weaving, and of married love. Through the quetzal-feathers she was connected with the sun cult, which was symbolized by this bird. Basalt. $13^3/4 \times 5^7/8''$. Aztec: A.D. 1324-1521. (Mexico).

### 800. Macehual

Man of the people, represented as a semi-nude man, dressed in a loincloth, the one garment the common man had the right to wear. One hand rests on the chest, the other seems to grasp for something, probably a standard. Andesite. $33^7/8 \times 10^5/8''$. Aztec: A.D. 1324-1521. (Mexico).

### 801. Macehual

Seated figure, dressed in a maxtlatl (loincloth), the common man's garment. Diorite. $11^3/4 \times 7^7/8''$. Aztec: A.D. 1324-1521. (Mexico City). Coll.: K. Stavenhagen, Mexico.

### 802. Atlantean figure

Representing Quetzalcóatl, in the shape of a warrior, with headdress, and a breastplate in the shape of a butterfly. Holds arrows and an "atlatl", the old Mexican arrow-thrower. He has all the attributes of the colossus from Tula (no. 689), which demonstrates the religious and artistic identification of the Aztecs with their immediate predecessors, the Toltecs. Basalt. $46 \times 11''$. Aztec: A.D. 1324-1521. (Mexico).

### 803. Cuauhxicalli*

Monumental vase for offerings from the main temple of Mexico, in the shape of a jaguar, lying down and ready to pounce, with menacing claws and jaws. On its back a cavity to receive offerings. Its bottom is adorned with the Death god in relief and eagle feathers on the sides. Hence the name of Cuauhxicalli (eagle's house). The jaguar-eagle was the symbol of brave warriors who distinguished themselves in battles fought to procure prisoners for the sacrifices. The jaguar is the symbol of Night and Death, and the disguise of the terrible Tezcatlipoca. This impressive monolith is a dramatic expression of the Aztec view of life, according to which life is only possible through death.

Basalt. $36^5/8 \times 47^1/4 \times 88^5/8''$. Aztec: A.D. 1324-1521. (Valley of Mexico).

### 804. Jaguar-knight

Warrior of high rank in the Aztec military order. Sitting on a round pedestal, richly adorned, with his hands on his knees. Helmet in the shape of a jaguar's head, in whose open mouth the warrior's face is seen. Round earplugs, ornament at the back of the head, of pleated paper, representing the rays of the sun. Jade necklace, bracelets, ankle-rings, sandals and nicely fastened maxtlatl. Basalt. $31^1/2 \times 17^3/4''$. Aztec: A.D. 1324-1521. (Mexico).

### 805. Seated male figure

Pendant of necklace. In his mouth and in one eye he has the hieroglyph "Tlaloc". On his chest is engraved the date "4 Acatl". Green Jade. $3^3/4 \times 3''$. Aztec: A.D. 1324-1521. (Mexico).

### 806. Small seated warrior

With shield and coat of arms. On the headdress the date "1 dead". Granitelike black stone. $4^7/8 \times 3^3/4''$. Aztec: A.D. 1324-1521. (Mexico).

### 807. Breastplate

In the shape of a human head. Headdress consisting of a band with two circles and feathers. Eyes and mouth perforated for encrustations. Green jadeite. $2^7/8 \times 1^3/4''$. Aztec: A.D. 1324-1521. (Texcoco, Mex.).

### 808. Head of a dead man*

Realistic features. Basalt. $12^1/4 \times 11''$. Aztec: A.D. 1324-1521. (Veracruz, Ver.).

### 809. Head of a man

Eyes and mouth perforated for encrustation with mother-of-pearl. Basalt $11^1/8 \times 9''$. Aztec, Matlazinca: A.D. 1324-1521. (Mexico). Coll.: Museo de Arqueología e Historia del Estado de Mexico, Toluca, Mex.

**810. Human head**

Eyes encrusted with mother-of-pearl and circles of pyrites, teeth of mother-of-pearl. Basalt. $7^{1}/8 \times 5^{7}/8''$. Aztec: A.D. 1324-1521. (Mexico).

**811. Head of an eagle knight***

One of the two military orders. Ornaments reserved for the dignitaries and the great army leaders. Represents a person with a headdress in the shape of an eagle, and with decoration at the back of the head of pleated paper, representing sunrays. Andesite. $15 \times 12^{1}/4''$. Aztec: A.D. 1324-1521. (Mexico).

**812. Mask of a female deity**

Connected with the cult of maize. Stylized features. Round, high headdress with feathers. The cheeks have two square cavities for encrustations. Granite-like green stone. $12^{5}/8 \times 6^{1}/2''$. Aztec: A.D. 1324-1521. (Valley of Mexico).

**813. Breastplate**

Representing a male mask. Eyes and mouth perforated for encrustations. Polished obsidian. $7^{7}/8 \times 6^{3}/4''$. Aztec: A.D. 1324-1521. (Mexico).

**814. Mask**

Of a man, with hair emphasized, finely modeled features, half-open mouth. Ochre terracotta. $8^{1}/4 \times 7^{1}/8''$. Aztec: A.D. 1324-1521. (Valley of Mexico).

**815. Mask**

Hair emphasized, open mouth, deep-set eyes. Green onyx. $7^{7}/8 \times 8^{5}/8''$. Aztec: A.D. 1324-1521. (Atzcapotzalco, Mexico D.F.).

**816. Small coiled plumed serpent**

Of irregular shape. Strongly marked scales, and cleft tongue. Gray porphyry. $5^{1}/2 \times 11^{3}/8''$. Aztec: A.D. 1324-1521. (Mexico).

**817. Plumed serpent***

Poised to strike, with open mouth. Representation of Quetzalcóatl. This *nahuatl* word means both plumed serpent, and erect serpent. This animal acquired a mythical character among the Toltecs, whom the Aztecs regarded as their forbears, and achieved the greatest importance in the Aztec culture as the union of day and night, of life and knowledge, the god of love among the humans, the protector and benefactor of men. Basalt. $13^{3}/4 \times 3^{7}/8''$. Aztec: A.D. 1324-1521. (Mexico).

**818. Coiled plumed serpent**

With jaws open, cleft tongue representing a stone knife for sacrificial purposes. The rings on the back realistically designed. Granite-like stone. $11^{3}/8 \times 29^{1}/8''$. Aztec: A.D. 1324-1521. Valley of Mexico).

**819. Coiled snake***

With smooth skin, representing the earth. Eyes hollowed for encrustations, cleft tongue and rings marked. Granite-like black, polished stone. $16^{7}/8 \times 9''$. Aztec: A.D. 1324-1521. (Valley of Mexico).

**820. Coiled snake***

With smooth skin, representing the forces of the earth. With open jaws and cleft tongue. Granite-like green stone. $29^{1}/2 \times 39^{1}/2''$. Aztec: A.D. 1324-1521. (Valley of Mexico).

**821. Plumed serpent***

Representing Quetzalcóatl, the union of heaven and earth. Basalt $9^{7}/8 \times 15^{3}/4''$. Aztec: A.D. 1324-1521. (Valley of Mexico).

**822. Coiled plumed serpent**

Representing the earth. Basalt. $5^{7}/8 \times 14^{5}/8''$. Aztec: A.D. 1324-1521. (Valley of Mexico).

**823-824. Plumed jaguar-serpents**

Architectural elements from a staircase, with pegs for fastening. In the bottom part the date "2 Acatl" (number 8 referring to the eighth fire, and corresponding exactly to A.D. 1507). It is made according to the same technique as is used for the strange image of the serpent-jaguar-eagle. These architectural elements were probably part of a temple, consecrated to commemoration of the Aztec "century" of 52 years. The transition from one cyclus to the next was celebrated by a great ceremony, called the New Fire (the rebirth of fire), which in the particular case was the last fire lit by the Aztecs, who were conquered in 1521. Basalt, with traces of fresco painting. 31¹/₂×27¹/₂". Aztec: A.D. 1507. (Mexico).

#### 825. Serpent-jaguar-eagle
Architectural element. Block of stone, in which the three animal elements are mixed in a fantastic way, as incarnation of a metaphysical concept. Basalt: 23¹/₄×21⁵/₈". Aztec: A.D. 1324-1521. (Valley of Mexico).

#### 826. Serpent
Representing the earth. Coiled inside out to give the illusion of an endless spiral. Gray basalt: 29¹/₂×39¹/₂". Aztec: A.D. 1324-1521. (Mexico D.F.).

#### 827. Monkey
Seated, hunchbacked, bearded and potbellied. Deity of the dance. Supports his belly with both his hands. Ear-plugs of snail's shell. Basalt. 11³/₄×9". Aztec: A.D. 1324-1521. (Valley of Mexico).

#### 828. Jumping rabbit
One of the deities of the moon, connected with the cult of agriculture and the cults of intoxicating drinks. The Aztecs associated this animal with the images of the moon and the influence of the four lunar phases on the vegetation. It was also regarded as a disguise of Tepoztecatl, the god of Wine, no doubt because of the rabbit's predilection for "aguamiel" (juice of maguey-plant). Basalt. 11³/₄×16¹/₂". Aztec: A.D. 1324-1521. (Mexico).

#### 829. Monkey*
Deity of the dance. It is seated, leaning its head on its hand. On its breast the hieroglyph of the god of Wind, Ehécatl, represented by a sea shell of spiral form, symbolizing the wind as precursor of the rain. Basalt: 11³/₄×7⁷/₈". Aztec: A.D. 1324-1521. (Mexico D.F.).

#### 830. Plumed coyote*
(Species of American wolf). Animal connected with the night and the shooting stars. When it is represented with plumes, it was associated with Xolotl-Quetzalcóatl on his journey through the subterranean regions, before he begins to light up the day. Basalt: 21⁵/₈×9". Aztec: A.D. 1324-1521. (Valley of Mexico).

#### 833. Grasshopper*
With folded wings, the front limbs bent, and the back limbs folded close to the body. Carneolite. 18¹/₂×6³/₄". Aztec: A.D. 1324-1521. (Chalpultepec, Mexico D.F.).

#### 834. Reclining jaguar*
In repose. Symbolizes the jaguar knights. At the back of the head the emblem of the warrior, consisting of down and a few magpie feathers. The spots on the hide are skilfully rendered by help of indentures. Andesite. 9¹/₂×17³/₈". Aztec: A.D. 1324-1521. (Valley of Mexico).

#### 835. Small seated coyote
Basalt. 13³/₈×6³/₄". Aztec: A.D. 1324-1521. (Mexico). Coll.: K. Stavenhagen, Mexico.

#### 836. Calabash
With flower. Realistic representation of this fruit, which seems to lack religious significance – a rare phenomeon in Aztec art. Green, polished stone. 11³/₄×7¹/₈". Aztec: A.D. 1324-1521. (Valley of Mexico).

#### 837. Ceremonial Brazier*
For copal (incense of resin), representing a deity of maize. Adorned with pleated paper, repre-

senting sun rays, at the back of the head, and necklace of ears of corn and dahlias. Ochre terracotta, with traces of fresco painting in blue and red. 21¼x23¼". Aztec: A.D. 1324-1521. (Mexico D.F.).

### 838. Ceremonial brazier

For copal. Fluted on the outside. Three cylindrical, hollow supports. The bottom part decorated with cones. Ochre terracotta, with traces of paint. 16⁷/₈x15". Aztec: A.D. 1324-1521. (Mexico D.F.).

### 839. Small brazier

for funeral purposes. Spherical, with wide rim and three hollow legs in the shape of eagle's heads. Pierced decorations. Red and ochre polished terracotta. 3¹/₂x3¹/₂". Aztec: A.D. 1324-1521. (Tenayuca, Mex.).

### 840. Large ceremonial brazier*

For copal; tubular form. Represents a person with a mask of Tlaloc, the god of Rain, with snakes on the forehead; the nose, the mouth and the eyes are round, symbolizing rain clouds, the hair put up at the back of the head and a diadem of turquoises. Breastplate of tubular jade beads, and a solar disk of gold, with two pendants. At the sides two small wings with snake motifs, the sign of water. The brazier for the burning of copal was equipped with a tubular lid that let the incense smoke escape. Red terracotta with traces of red and blue paint. 45⁵/₈x16¹/₈". Aztec: A.D. 1324-1521. (Atzcapotzalco, Mexico D.F.).

### 841. Large round ceremonial brazier

for copal. Decorated with spherical ornaments. Representing symbols of numbers and a band with the sign *ollin* (movement). Terracotta, painted black and red. 18¹/₈x15³/₄". Aztec: A.D. 1324-1521. (Valley of Mexico).

### 842. Tlapanhuehuetl*

Large drum of war. The bas-relief is divided into two parts by a band of entwined serpents. The top part has two main motifs: *Nahui – Ollin*, "the sun of movement" (cf. introduction), and an important person, possibly the sun, disguised as an eagle. On the sides are seen two warriors: one disguised as an eagle with a knife of flint, and the other as a jaguar. The eagle and the jaguar represented the two great military orders of the Aztecs. Each of the warriors had a headdress of feathers, and from the mouths of both issues the war-cry: "Atl-Tlachinolli", i.e. "burnt water", symbolizing the material and spiritual conflict, the dynamic union of the two opposites. The bottom part consists of three stepped supports and is decorated with an eagle and two jaguars, emitting the same war-cry. Carved out of a trunk. 38⁵/₈x19¹/₄". Aztec, Matlazinca: A.D. 1324-1521. (Malinalco, Mex.). Coll.: Museo de Arqueología e Historia del Estado de Mexico, Toluca, Mex.

### 843. Teponaztli*

Drum, with tongues, in the shape of a coyote. Teeth of bone. On the back two tongues that produce different sounds, when beaten. The coyote was regarded as one of the gods of the mountains, and in this capacity it evoked feelings of mystery and fear of the unknown. It is also associated with trees, and falling stars, and, as malevolent god, with the mysteries of the night. Carved in a trunk. 24¹/₄x9⁷/₈". Aztec: A.D. 1324-1521. (Mexico D.F.).

### 844. Teponatzli*

Drum with tongues, represented in stone, consecrated to Macuilxóchitl, tutelary god of Music, Song and Dance of the court, another manifestation of Xochipilli. He also has the attributes of the Earth god in the shape of jaguar's hide at the extremities and a round base, shaped as a coiled serpent. The plastic conception of the subject presents analogies with the cubistic figures, and the symbols are treated, as they were much later treated by the surrealists: wounded hands are the eyes of a mask with Xipe-mouth, the ears are hearts pierced by flint knives, and the face at the back part shows a flowering branch, whose pistils constitute the nose of the mask. Basalt. 11³/₈x28″. Aztec: A.D. 1324-1521. (Valley of Mexico).

### 845. Teponaztli
Drum with tongues, decorated in high relief with an arm, holding flowers, emblems of Macuilxóchitl, deity of the feasts of the court. Carved in a trunk. 9x30³/₈″. Aztec: A.D. 1324-1521. (Unknown place of discovery).

### 846. Stone stela
Showing sign of the year in relief, with hieroglyphs of the sun and the moon, and a rabbit. Basalt with traces of white paint. 15x12⁵/₈″. Aztec: A.D. 1324-1521. Coll.: K. Stavenhagen, Mexico.

### 847. Stone stela
Showing the image of king Ahuizotl in bas-relief. The hieroglyph of this ruler is a dog with a woolly hide, generally called "the dog of waters". Basalt. 24³/₈x23⁵/₈″. Aztec: A.D. 1324-1521. (Mexico D.F.).

### 848. Teocalli of the sacred war
Or the commemorative stone of the temple dedicated to the sun in 1507. Monolith in the shape of a truncated pyramid, completely adorned with reliefs. On the top part two gods are conversing: left Huitzilopochtli, god of the Sun and of War, the most important deity in Tenochtitlán, and right Tezcatlipoca, the god who illuminates the night, symbol of the Evening Star and of Death. The two support a large sun disk that shows the sign "ollin", which designates the cosmic movements, the halt of which will mean the end of all things. At the root of the large stairs, and on both sides, can be seen signs of the calendar that establish the date of 1507. On the top part jars for offerings. To the right we see Xiuhtecuhtli, the god of Fire and Xochipilli, the god of Flowers, Music and Dance. Above those, as if the temple had stairs, the date "one death's skull". On the left the god Tlahuizcalpantecuhtli, ruler of the "house of dawn", god of the planet Venus shining in the dusk and in the early dawn, and Tlaloc, the god of Rain. Above these a sign for the date "one flintstone". On the top of the staircase stands Coatlicue, goddess of the Earth and of Death. On the top part of the monolith, representing the roof of the temple are the signs of penitence (hay), in which have been stuck thorns of magey, with which the worshipers pierced their lips, their tongues, and the lobes of their ears as a kind of self-sacrifice. At the top is shown horizontally a ball of hay, with the sign "two houses". At the back of the monolith is shown in relief the foundation of the city of Tenochtitlán: an eagle (the sun) sitting on a nopal-cactus, consuming a snake (the earth), a symbol of the dynamic union of opposites, and, in the material world, a promise of good harvests. This scene, with another symbolical sense, is to-day found in the coat of arms of Mexico. The nopal-cactus bears fruits that symbolize human hearts. At the foot of the cactus is seen a reclining figure, symbolizing the goddess of Rivers. From the mouth of the persons issues the sign "Atl-Tlachinolli", "burnt water", (water and fire), the hieroglyph of the sacred war, the eternal struggle between opposites in nature. Basalt. 48⁷/₈x34⁵/₈″. Aztec: A.D. 1507. (Valley of Mexico).

### 849. Arrow
Symbol of war, made of rings and terminated with a rattlesnake's tail. Basalt. 49¹/₄x9⁷/₈″. Aztec, Matlazinca: A.D. 1324-1521. (The State of Mexico). Coll.: Museo de Arqueología e Historia del Estado de Mexico, Toluca, Mex.

### 850. Shield
Made of a feather-mosaic, representing the head of a deity. The makers of feather-mosaics ("amantecas"), fastened the highly valued tropical bird's feathers to each other with cotton-

thread, or put them on canvas or on paper in mosaic patterns, thus obtaining beautiful color-effects. The colors always had a specific significance to the old Mexicans, and were never chosen accidentally or for mere decorative effect. Like all other artistic manifestations, they contributed to express the beliefs of the age. The message of the colors, that were connected with myths and rituals, varied from one culture to another. In some of them red signified the east, life and light, white signified west and the setting sun, yellow was the north, the region of cold and dark, while black was the south. Blue when placed in the middle, meant heaven. In other cultures red was also light, while blue signified night and darkness, and green the renewal of the earth, turning green after rain. Diam: 7¹/₈″. Aztec: A.D. 1324-1521. (Mexico D.F.).

**851. Mirror**

Circular, probably used for divinatory ends, and connected with the cult of Tezcatlipoca, the terrible god of Night and Fog. Polished obsidian. 1¹/₈x10⁵/₈″. Aztec, Matlazinca: A.D. 1324-1521. (The State of Mexico). Coll.: Museo de Arqueología e Historia del Estado de Mexico, Toluca, Mex.

**852-853. Vases**

Widening towards edge, flat bottoms, one decorated with geometrical designs, the other with skulls. Ochre terracotta, with red and brown paint. 3¹/₂x9¹/₂″, 2x5³/₄″. Aztec: A.D. 1324-1521. (Mexico D.F.).

**854-855. Dishes**

With flat bottoms, polychrome decoration, black and white on red, polished ground. Ochre terracotta. 2³/₄x3¹/₈″, 1⁵/₈x3⁷/₈″. Aztec: A.D. 1324-1521. (Texcoco, Mex.).

**856. Cup**

With effigy of the god Xipe, base in the shape of truncated cone. Ochre terracotta, decorated with black paint on red polished ground. 6¹/₈x4³/₄″. Aztec: A.D. 1324-1521. (Valley of Mexico).

**857-859. Cups**

For "pulque" with widening sides and base in the shape of a truncated cone. Pulque was extracted from the magey-plant (agave), and was a sacred drink, reserved for priests and old people. Ordinary natives also drank pulque, but were seriously punished if abuse of the drink made them intoxicated. Ochre polished terracotta. 7¹/₈x9¹/₂″, 4³/₄x5⁷/₈″, 4³/₈x5³/₈″. Aztec: A.D. 1324-1521. (El Volador, Mex.).

**860-861. Cups**

for pulque. Ochre terracotta with dark brown decorations. Aztec: A.D. 1324-1521. (El Volador, Mex.). Coll.: F. Feuchtwanger, Mexico.

**862. Jar**

With wide spout and handle. Red polished terracotta. 7¹/₂x8⁵/₈″. Aztec: A.D. 1324-1521. (El Volador, Mex.).

**863. Jar**

Round, truncated spout and handle. Red polished terracotta with geometric motifs in black. 11³/₈x7¹/₈″. Aztec: A.D. 1324-1521. (Valley of Mexico).

**864. Pipe**

for tobacco. High bowl and wide stem, inspired by a duck's head, with decoration incised on red polished surface. Tobacco derives from Mexico. To smoke a pipe was a privilege reserved for the priests and dignitaries. Red polished terracotta. 3¹/₂x2³/₈″. Aztec: A.D. 1324-1521. (Valley of Mexico).

**865-866. Seals**

A) With flowers and fret motifs, 3⁷/₈x6³/₄″; B) With flowers and fret motifs, 4⁷/₈x4³/₈″. Ochre terracotta. Aztec: A.D. 1324-1521. (Mexico).

# 12. The Art of New Spain

A new society arose on the ruins of the indigenous cultures. The Spaniards called it New Spain, thus expressing their wish to create a world in their own image. For three centuries Mexico was governed by a viceroy. This society, founded on the double principle of the universal character of the Catholic Church and of the Spanish monarchy, became a firmly united realm. But it would be a mistake to consider it merely a satellite of the Spanish sun. Right from the start New Spain showed special features that became increasingly accentuated as time went by. The originality of New Spain was primarily due to the native population. Unlike what was the case in the British colonies, the native population of New Spain was an integrated part of the colonial society. The local traditions mixed with European ones and influenced them. The Spanish heritage was no less rich or original. Sixteenth Century Spain was, after having been successively Carthagenian, Roman, Visigothic, and Arabic, a nation which offered side by side with Renaissance features, purely Medieval forms of art and life. The co-existence of different periods and cultures is typical of the Spanish spirit. In this way Mexico became the meeting place of a number of contradictory influences. Behind the external (political and religious) unity New Spain contained a world of heterogenuous elements. The art of New Spain reflects this diversity, and at its greatest moments, — particularly the baroque — combines them in a felicitous synthesis.

One of the two axes of the life of New Spain was religion, the other was the power of the viceroy. All other activities turned on these two axes. Two aristocracies, sometimes opposed to each other, shone, each with its own light: the class of the feudal lords, consisting of the descendants of the "Conquistadores", and of the great landowners, and the clergy. The arts reflected this situation; on the "plaza", which was the heart in every town, the cathedral and the government house faced each other. The three centuries of Spanish dominion were rich in works of art: sculpture, painting, architecture, to say nothing of literature. The history of the art of New Spain falls into three periods: the first is characterized by a singular architecture, combining the Renaissance forms with Gothic, Romanesque and "Mudejar" elements. Then followed the Baroque that carried the audacity and complication of the Spanish models to an extreme, creating a variant that may, without exaggeration be called a special "Mexican Baroque", and finally Neo-Classicism. To round off this summary description, let us mention two characteristics of colonial art in New Spain: the influence of the native artisans and craftsmen, particularly in the first period, and, from the 17th century, the existence of a new Spanish-Mexican sensibility that gradually was to express itself with ever increasing strength and self confidence.

*The XVI. Century*
Soon after the Conquest the construction of monasteries for the religious orders began:

Cross, with head of Christ. Wood. 17th century. Cat. 869.

Cross of the Church of Atzacoalco. Rose basalt. 17th century. Cat. 870.

Saint Diego of Alcalá. Wood. Mid. 17th century. Cat. 867.

María Ignacia
a Sangre de Chr...
Hija Leg.ma del S.
tan. de Vribe y Sa...
al y de la S.ra D.a M.
fa Valcarcel y Ve...
o, Profesó en 1 de...
de 77, en el Reli...
ssimo Conv.to d S.t
ra de esta Cui.d
Mexico de
dad de 22 a.
y 3 Meses.

José Alcíbar: Sister María Ignacia of the Precious Blood. 18th century. Cat. 902.

Retable of the Ex-Convent of Tepotzotlán. 18th century. Cat. 871.

EL ECSMO SENOR CONDE DE GALVES.

Brother Pablo de Jesús: His Excellency the Count de Gálvez. 18th century. Cat. 901.

monumental churches, large atria, "posas", chapels or, permanent stations (for the procession of the Holy Sacrament) — a true innovation of religious architecture — gardens, aqueducts. The church — the house of God — always loomed over and dominated the convent — the house of men — even when the latter had two stories. Each of the religious orders had its own style. The Franciscan cloisters generally had wooden rafters and a flat roof, and their proportions and decorations were relatively modest. The Dominicans erected more massive buildings. The Augustins liked monumental proportions and grand frescoes, and their convents were the most sumptuous.

As a typical example of the Franciscan achitecture can be mentioned the monastery at Huejotzingo (the State of Puebla). Here we find the impressive arched entrances to the atrium. The exterior chapels (for the mass conversion of natives), the round arches, supported by bundles of columns with Gothic base and capital, the facades decorated with Romanesque-Gothic reliefs, flower-decorated crests, walls with crenellated tops of "mudejar" design, fronts where Renaissance and Medieval elements mix with elegance, white and black murals, vaults with Gothic ribs and complicated designs, and finally the monumental gilt retables in which sculpture, painting, and ornamentation combine.

The architecture of the Dominicans, who were animated by a more belligerent spirit than the Franciscans, offers examples like the monasteries of Tepotzlán (Morelos), Yanhuitlán and Santo Domingo (Oaxaca). They are vigourous constructions, suited to a tropical, a seismic climate, and they are impressive because of their proportions, their strategical situation, and the equilibrium and sobriety of their Romanesque style. The facade of the church of Tepotztlán, with its gigantic sumptuous and precise high relief, is remarkable.

In the constructions of the Augustins the indigenous characteristics appear for the first time. They are also the most sumptuously adorned. The church of Acolman has the most handsome "churrigueresque" (extreme baroque) facade of New Spain. The walls of the church of Actopan are completely covered with frescoes.

In the sculpture of the XVI. century there are clear reminiscences of Medieval, Romanesque and Gothic forms of expression. On the contrary the native tradition could not so easily be expressed. Still the aspersoriums, the choir seats, and particularly the retables differ in certain details from the imported Spanish art. The results are hybrid works that can be moving in all their indecision.

*Baroque art*
The baroque art took over, when the Medieval reminiscences had disappeared, leaving more scope for the "mudejar" (Moorish) influence and for the native spirit of the now christianized Indians. In Mexico the baroque style, that had been fairly moderated throughout the XVII century, reached its full development in the XVIII century. Be-

tween the tendencies towards "classical" art and the free play of forms, it finally found its original expression, and provided proof of a limitless imagination. The cathedrals in themselves give a complete panorama of the development of baroque art in New Spain, beginning with the one at Mérida (Yucatán), which is the oldest. The cathedral of Puebla still represents a severe architecture, reminiscent of the "Herreriano" style of El Escorial, but in the one in Mexico City, the erection of which lasted two hundred years, the baroque is flourishing: inside the altar of pardon and the retable of the Kings and Angels can be considered masterpieces of their kind. The baroque art reaches a peak in the facades of the Sagrario Metropolitano and of the cathedral of Zacatecas, the ornamentation of which is unequaled.

It is difficult to choose examples of baroque produced in New Spain, so vast, rich and original is the number of marvellous works. There was a moment, when it was impossible to recognize the classical order behind the ornamental proliferation, as the imported forms were definitively drowned by the local inspiration. Let us merely mention from Mexico the churches of Santa Teresa la Antigua, San Bernardo, San Lorenzo, la Enseñanza and Regina, from Guadalajara Santa Monica, from Oaxaca Santo Domingo, the interior splendor of which is worthy of an oriental temple, with its vault decorated with a polychrome and gilt high relief, representing the spiritual genealogy of the order. Not less remarkable is the Rosario dome in the Santo Domingo church at Puebla, a precursor of the capricious and exuberant ornamentation that was to reach its highest originality in Tonantzintla.

The masterpiece of the ultra-baroque still remains the church of Santa Maria Tonantzintla, at Puebla. Seen from the outside this church seems rather modest. But once you are inside, you are in a veritable forest created by man: in the midst of a luxurious vegetation you discover a whirling ballet of angels, cherubs, prophets, evangelists, saints, masks, and soldiers, who rise and climb on all sides to the ceiling, which they illuminate, with their large wide open eyes. It is a popular native version of the Rosario chapel at Puebla, a very Spanish work, designed by architects. Here we have a grotto with a pagan interpretation of christianity: we see, in effect, ears of maize, various fruits, etc. It is a masterpiece, not only of the baroque, but also of Mexican *popular art*.

In this period, sculpture had no autonomous existence. The same can be said of painting. The tendency of the baroque was to unite all the arts in a complete, extraordinary synthesis.

*Neo-classicism*

Neo-classicism, which was an official style, imported from Spain, and as a style — a reaction against the baroque — spoiled a large part of the baroque works, in particular the baroque retables, which were now considered simple accumulation of gilded wood. Neo-classicism is primarily a symbol of the rebellion against the past, inspired by the same ideas that contributed to establish the national independence. Two personalities dominated this period: the architect and sculptor Manuel Tolsá, and the universal artist Eduardo de Tresguerras, who was an architect, a painter, a sculptor, a composer, and a poet.

**867. Saint Diego of Alcalá***
Head of wood, carved and painted and with real eyelashes and teeth. 15³/4x15³/4″. 17th century. Coll.: Museo de Arte Religioso, Mexico.

**868. Saint Sebastian**
Carved in *tecali,* Mexican, transparent marble. 26³/4x11³/4″. 17th century. Coll.: Museo de Arte Religioso, Mexico.

**869. Cross***
With head of Christ, carved in one piece out of trunk and branches of a tree. Polychrome wood. 78³/4x61³/8″. 17th century. Coll.: Museo Regional del Estado de Michoacán, Morelia, Mich.

**870. Cross***
With the attributes of the Passion. Pink stone. 47¹/4x39³/8″. 17th century. (Church of Atzacoalco, Mex.). Coll.: Instituto Nacional de Belles Artes, Mexico.

**871. Retable from the chapel »Relicario de San José«***
In the center niche an image of Saint Joseph with the Child Jesus. In the side niches five sculptures. This retable is the smallest one of the ten at the Ex-Convent of Tepotzotlán. Wood, carved and completely gilded and painted. 210x142x31″. 18th century. Ex-Convent of Tepotzotlán, Mex.

**872-873. Two angels**
Carved wood, gilded and painted. 52³/8x39³/8″; 51¹/2x39³/8″. 18th century. Coll.: Private Chapel of the Old Monastery of Tepotzotlán, Mex.

**874. The Archangel Michael**
Carved and painted wood. 27¹/2x13³/4″. 18th century. Coll.: Museo Nacional de Historia, Mexico.

**875. The Archangel Michael**
Ivory figure, polychrome. 30⁷/8x13³/4″. 18th century. Coll.: Museo de Arte Religioso, Mexico.

**876. The Archangel Gabriel**
Stone. 102x39″. 18th century. Private collection, Querétaro, Qro.

**877-878. The Virgin Mary and saint Joseph**
Sculptures made out of carved, decorated, polychrome wood. Both 11⁵/8x8⁵/8″. 18th century. Coll.: Museo Nacional de Historia, Mexico.

**879. Saint John**
Carved and gilded wood. 51¹/8x31¹/2″. 18th century. Coll.: Museo de Arte Religioso, Mexico.

**880. The immaculate conception**
Wooden and gilded sculpture. 42⁷/8x15³/4″. 18th century. Coll.: Museo de Arte Religioso, Mexico.

**881. Lectern**
Mahogany with encrustations of mother-of-pearl. 13³/4x13³/4″. 18th century. Coll.: Museo de Arte Religioso, Mexico.

**882. »Fascistol«**
A kind of large music-stand for the choir. Carved wood. 63x43¹/4″. 18th century. Coll.: Museo de Arte Religioso, Mexico.

**883. Coffer**
Carved in wood with episcopal arms and pallium engraved on the lid. Wroughtiron mountings. 24³/₄x38¹/₄″. 18th century. Coll.: Museo Nacional de Historia, Mexico.

**884. Frame**
Carved wood, perforated and gilded. 68⁷/₈x 46¹/₂″. 18th century. Coll.: Museo de Arte Religioso, Mexico.

**884 A. Large frame with mirror**
Carved wood, perforated and gilded. 98x78″. 18th century. Coll.: Museo Nacional de Historia, Mexico.

**885. Platter**
Painted and lacquered wood in red and black. 25⁵/₈″ diam. Coll.: Museo Nacional de Historia, Mexico.

**886. Monstrance**
Chased, engraved and gilded silver. 27¹/₈x7⁷/₈″. 17th century. Coll.: Museo de Arte Religioso, Mexico.

**887. Chalice**
Chased, engraved and gilded silver. 10¹/₄x7¹/₈″. 17th century. Coll.: Museo de Arte Religioso, Mexico.

**888. Ewer**
Chased, engraved silver. 13³/₄x9⁷/₈″. 18th century. Coll.: Museo de Arte Religioso, Mexico.

**889. Piscina**
Chased, engraved silver. 14¹/₈x19⁵/₈″. 18th century. Coll.: Museo de Arte Religioso, Mexico.

**890. Candelabrum**
Chased, engraved silver. 15³/₈x5⁷/₈″. 18th century. Coll.: Museo de Arte Religioso, Mexico.

**891. Dish for alms**
Chased, engraved silver. 15″ diam. 18th century. Coll.: Museo de Arte Religioso, Mexico.

**892. Dish for alms**
Chased, engraved silver. 13³/₄″ diam. 18th century. Coll.: Museo de Arte Religioso, Mexico.

**893. Reliquary**
Engraved silver. 15³/₄x7⁷/₈″. 18th century. Coll.: Museo de Arte Religioso, Mexico.

**894. Small coffer for the holy oil**
Silver. 5¹/₈x9″. 18th century. Coll.: Museo de Arte Religioso, Mexico.

**895. Assumption of the holy virgin**
By Alfonzo López de Herrera. Oil on panel. 1622. 134x91″. Coll.: Galerías de San Carlos, Mexico.

**896. The immaculate conception**
By Baltasar de Echave Ibía. Oil on panel. 74x 46⁷/₈″. 1628. Coll.: Galerías de San Carlos, Mexico.

**897. Christ in the garden of olives**
By Luís Juárez. Oil on panel. 72⁷/₈x62⁵/₈″. First half of 17th century. Coll.: Galerías de San Carlos, Mexico.

**898. Portrait of Maria Josefa Aldaca as a child**
By Brother Miguel de Herrera. Oil on canvas. 70⁷/₈x52³/₈″. 1746. Coll.: Museo Nacional de Historia, Mexico.

**899. Portrait of Doña Juana Maria Romero**
By Ignacio María Barreda. Oil on canvas. 73⁵/₈x 52³/₈″. 1794. Coll.: Museo Nacional de Historia, Mexico.

**900. Portrait of Doña Manuela Esquivel y Serruto**
By Ignacio María Barreda. Oil on canvas. 30³/₄x 26″. 1794. Coll.: Museo Nacional de Historia, Mexico.

**901. His excellency the count de Galvez***
By Brother Pablo de Jesus. Calligraphed by Father San Geronimo. Galvez was the forty-ninth viceroy of New Spain who governed from 1785-1786. Oil on canvas. $87^3/8 \times 85^1/4''$. 1796. Coll.: Museo Nacional de Historia, Mexico.

**902. Sister Maria Ignacia of the precious blood***
By José Alcibar. Oil on canvas. $73^1/4 \times 43^3/4''$. 18th century. Coll.: Museo Nacional de Historia, Mexico.

**903. Portrait of a lady**
With fan, elaborate hairdo, and a rose branch.

Anonymous. Oil on canvas. $49^1/4 \times 43^3/4''$. 18th century. Coll.: Museo Nacional de Historia, Mexico.

**904. Portrait of a small girl**
Anonymous. Oil on canvas. $20^7/8 \times 16^1/2''$. 18th century. Coll.: Museo Nacional de Historia, Mexico.

**905. Fruit market**
Anonymous. Oil on canvas. $98^3/8 \times 76^3/4''$. 18th century. Coll.: Museo Nacional de Historia, Mexico.

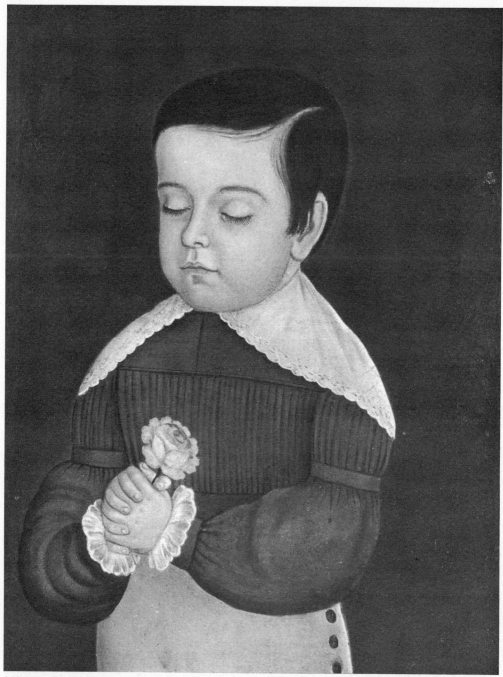

José María Estrada: Portrait of a dead child. Eustaquio Martínez Negrete. 19th century. Cat. 914.

José María Estrada: Portrait of a Lady in a green dress. 19th century. Cat. 911.

José Guadalupe Posada: "Calavera Catrina" (Vanitas Skull). 19th century. Cat. 930.

José Guadalupe Posada: "Calavera" (skeleton) of Don Quijote. 19th century. Cat. 927.

# 13. Modern Art

Neo-classicism was the dominant current in the official art of the 19th century. But parallel with this academic art there was another current, a popular and spontaneous style, that was centered in the provinces, particularly in Veracruz, Jalisco, Puebla, and Guanajuato. Much of this painting was anonymous. Among the known artists can be mentioned José María Estrada and Hermegildo Bustos. This ingenuous and poetic art will probably continue to attract modern artists.

The Mexican revolution is a historical event that changed the physiognomy of the country, as did the Conquest, but in the opposite direction. A new nation arose, or rather, the revolution revealed the true face of the people that had been hidden through several centuries, and was deformed by the long dictatorship of Porfirio Diaz at the end of the 19th century. The social movement of Mexico wanted not only to change the social and political structure of Mexico through agrarian reforms, ample scope for the workers' rights, nationalization of the resources of the subsoil, and of the railroads, oil, and electricity, a new politics aimed at economic independence and industrialization, etc. but also to renew culture. The tendency was a double one: on one hand to make the creative arts strike root, by rediscovering the popular pre-colombian tradition and express Mexican reality; on the other hand to break with the isolation and the academic tradition and open the doors to the universal currents of our time in art and philosophy. This corresponds to the typical features of the social movement: the common people's entrance on the stage, after having been passive subjects of history, and the simultaneous transformation of the country, brought about by modern technical methods.

The Mexican artists (painters, poets, novelist, composers, musicians and architects) turned their glance towards the Mexican tradition, which had survived in a very rich popular art. But they did not forget the great adventure of contemporary art. It was not a question of a merely aesthetic renewal, but of an artistic movement which was part of the historical change that comprised all of society. This explains the importance of mural painting, particularly in the first revolutionary period. By making his work part of official buildings, the artist expressed his will to escape private collections and museums and to take part in life. The mural was, particularly in this first period, a passionate impassioning expression, in which the artists and the spectators faced each other. It should be judged in this historical perspective, for its aesthetic experiments, its brilliant discoveries, and even its limitations are conditioned by the social movement that began in 1910.

Mexican painting has one great precursor: the engraver José Guadalupe Posada (1852-1913). His work, which was at the same time traditional and decisively new became a source of inspiration for the modern artists. Posada created an art destined for artisans, soldiers, peasants, who were the actual base of the people. The case of this artist is unique in the history of art: he possessed imagination, skill and work capacity far beyond the normal (his output is about 20.000 works), but he never pretended to be anything but an artisan engraver, and he never frequented artistic circles. He was an independent craftsman who took commissions from the print shops, papers and periodicals, for whom he made illustrations, vignettes or book jackets. Face to face with the people, Posada created a language that made this, largely analphabetic mass of people with its insatiable hunger for news and information, tremble, cry, laugh — and think. Soaked in the manners and myths of the people, he celebrated its deeds, honored its traditions, despised or glorified what it despised or glorified. Still nothing is more remote from mere illustration or journalistic realism than this concentrated and fantastic, direct and imaginative art. It was intended for the consumption of the moment, but has survived thanks to its vitality, but primarily thanks to what may be called poetic ferocity. Posada's art which is a satire and a chronicle of a society in a state of crisis, reaches, at its most sensitive moments, the contradictory and explosive domain of the "black humor", as André Breton has pointed out. Posada has observed the world without emotional, aesthetic or ideological prejudices. Instead of limiting himself to reflections on this world, he transformed it into a carnival, where daily life does not differ from the marvellous.

This article does not pretend to offer a panorama, however synthetic, of the Mexican art of our time, but it will be necessary to mention some of the most representative contemporary painters.

There is first and foremost José Clemente Orozco (1883-1949): dramatic violence, monstrous deformities, economy of elements, a vision of a torn and sombre world. In his drawings, engravings, easel- and mural paintings, we meet the prostitute, the woman soldier, the Conquest, the Independence, mysticism, dictatorship, the left and the right, the church, the trenches, the banquet, the classes of society, man, entire and absolute. His work is the great historic complaint, rising from rebellion and from the frustrations of a people. His aesthetic tendency is towards the baroque, since movement and contrast are essential in his work. His drawings suggest color in every line. At the same time his work is reminiscent of European expressionism in more ways than one, both in subject matter and in pictorial language. His production is very comprehensive. The murals he has done, partly in Mexico, partly in the United States, are his most important works. The mural of Cópula del Hospicio Cabañas (Guadalajara) is undoubtly his master piece. It is a grandiose composition, whose center is man aflame, a glorification of the transfiguration of life. It should be mentioned that Orozco's work has had considerable influence in the United States.

Diego Rivera (1886-1957) participated actively in the modern movement in painting. In the beginning he was influenced by Post-Impressionism, by Cézanne, fauvism and cubism. At the same time he studied, during his fourteen years stay in Europe, the art of the past. This study, combined with the assimilation of the great Mexican forms and tradition which he discovered with amazement on his return to Mexico, made him consider neo-classicism as a synthesis of all the art forms of the past that had validity as expressions of the present. He painted in fresco and distemper, and being an indefatigable worker, his works are subtle and delicate. The first important mural of this century was painted by Rivera, in encaustic, in the amphitheater Bolivar of Mexico University, in 1922. But his important mural work is only part of his immense production. Among his easel-paintings should be mentioned all of his cubistic period and numerous portraits, and female figures to say nothing of the smaller canvasses, particularly those of children and flowers that represented his vision of the life of the people. Rivera's main work is the decoration of the Solemnity Hall of the National Agricultural School at Chapingo, where he has painted a hymn to life.

Of David Alfaro Siqueiros (born in 1898) it might be said, as of Orozco, that he is predominantly a baroque artist, since his essential interest is movement. However, he shows affinity to the futurists, rather than to the expressionists, particularly in his first period, not only by his love of dynamic form, but also by his interest in machines and technical matters. Siqueiros who was the champion of an ideological realism, was already in 1930 preoccupied with the use of new materials and the possibilities of modern technology. In this capacity he has exercised a great influence not only on Mexican painters, but also, like Orozco, on the pioneers of abstract expressionism and "action painting", like Jackson Pollock. Apart from his great production of easel-paintings, Siqueiros has created numerous murals in official buildings, both in Mexico and abroad. His latest, unfinished "mural" is in the National Museum of History, in Mexico (1960).

A group of painters, who constitute another chapter of Mexican painting, follow different paths: Rufino Tamayo, Carlos Mérida, Frida Khalo, Augustín Lazo, Julio Castellanos, Carlos Orozco Romero, Manuel Rodríguez Lozano, Jésus Guerrero Galván, and many others.

Rufino Tamayo (born in 1899) has undertaken an aesthetic venture of great rigor. His work is based on the popular art, as well as on the conquests of modern painting. His colors are rich, refined, strong and logical, his forms firm and fantastic, he is himself, at the same time spontaneous and reflective, and his modernism is nourished by ancient art. Tamayo has not reached pre-Hispanic art through ideology or artistic theory, but by a more secret path, by virtue of an affinity we may call congenital. His vision of reality is that of a great poet. It is in this, rather than in his conscious conception of form and volume, or his skill in using color, we must see his connection with the pre-

Hispanic past. But his vision is as fresh as that of the popular artist. Maybe it is this very mixture of traditions in a spirit that is modern and native at the same time, that is his greatness. Tamayo has also painted murals, in Mexico, as well as in Paris (Unesco), and in other cities abroad.

Tamayo's, and to a less extent, Carlos Mérida's, aesthetic attitude, has contributed to the formation of a new group of artists, among which Ricardo Martínez, Juan Soriano, and Pedro Coronel stand out as strong personalities. Some, like the draughtsman José Luís Cuevas, continue the expressionistic line of Orozco. Others, like José Chavez Morado, Gonzáles Camarena, Alfredo Zalce, Raúl Anguiano continue the realistic school. Isolated, very talented, artists are Gunther Guerzo, Jesús Reyes, Alvar Carrillo Gil. It is not possible to mention everybody, but it would not be fair not to mention, in passing, the many foreign artists who have participated in the recent developments in painting, and whose works have become part of the heritage of their country by adoption: Jean Charlot, Wolfgang Paalen, Pablo O'Higgins, Leonora Carrington, Alice Rahon, Remedios Varo.

The contemporary graphics are rich and varied. Almost all the Mexican artists, from the masters to the youngest, have shown a predilection for this form of art. The group "Taller de Gráfica Popular", which consists of socially conscious artists, deserves mention. This "workshop", which is organized as a collective, produces illustrations, almanacs, posters, engravings, and other graphical works, that are commentaries on the national and international situation, in accordance with the political opinions of the group. Among the graphic artists of this group, Leopoldo Méndez stands out by virtue of his artistic personality. His very comprehensive production, which has roots in the tradition of Posada, shows his great originality of mind.

Mexico has a very great tradition of sculpture, that has been kept very much alive in folk art. This subterranean tradition has now and then broken through to the surface, as in the case of the naive artist Mardonio Magaña, who lived as a janitor in an art academy. To-day sculptors like Zuñiga, Bracho, and Monasterio, seek inspiration in this heritage, often successfully. Others, particularly in the younger generation, seek other paths.

Unfortunately considerations of space have made it impossible to show here work by all the painters, sculptors, and graphic artists, we have mentioned in this list, that does not claim to be complete. We have neither wanted to, nor been able to give more than a very general survey of modern Mexican art. Perhaps it will be sufficient after this to emphasize merely, that it is a question of a reality in movement — a reality in which highly different, and sometimes contradictory tendencies of modern painting are represented. This is no doubt a sign of Vitality. In recent years a new generation of painters has emerged. Some of them have already had shows in Paris and other places in

Europe. It would be premature to judge the works of these young artists. Let it suffice to say that they have begun a critical revision of their immediate past. And is this not the very destiny of art: to recommence the creation of the world, over and over again?

## Modern art

JOSÉ MARIA ESTRADA, painter (1800-1860). Born and died in Guadalajara, Jal.

**906. Portrait of a man in a white jacket***
Oil on canvas. 1830. 33⁷/₈x23⁵/₈". Coll.: Museo Regional de Guadalajara, Jal.

**907. Portrait of Doña Tranquilina Vidrios**
Oil on canvas. 1852. 76x46¹/₂". Coll.: Museo Regional de Guadalajara, Jal.

**908. Portrait of Sr. Ruiz Esparza**
Oil on canvas. 33⁵/₈x24⁵/₈". Coll.: Museo Regional de Guadalajara, Jal.

**909. Portrait of a man**
Oil on canvas. 9⁵/₈x7". Coll.: Instituto Nacional de Bellas Artes, Mexico.

**910. Portrait of Don Filomeno Vazquez**
Oil on metal. 13³/₄x9¹/₂". Coll.: Instituto Nacional de Bellas Artes, Mexico.

**911. Portrait of a lady in green dress***
Oil on canvas. 9⁵/₈x12³/₈". Coll.: Instituto Nacional de Bellas Artes, Mexico.

**912. Portrait of Don Segundino Gonzalez**
Oil on metal. 16¹/₂x13". Coll.: Instituto Nacional de Bellas Artes, Mexico.

**913. Portrait of Doña Jesusa Suarez de Garay**
Oil on canvas. 17⁷/₈x14". Coll.: Instituto Nacional de Bellas Artes, Mexico.

**914. Portrait of the young Eustaquio Martinez Negrete (The dead child)***
Oil on canvas. 16x20¹/₄". Coll.: Instituto Nacional de Bellas Artes, Mexico.

**915. The family Madroño (The agony)**
Oil on canvas. 57x65³/₄". Coll.: Instituto Nacional de Bellas Artes, Mexico.

HERMENEGILDO BUSTOS, painter (1832-1907). Born and died in San Francisco del Rincón, Guanajuato.

**916. Portrait of Maximiliano Cruz**
Oil on metal. 7¹/₈x5¹/₈". Coll.: Instituto Nacional de Bellas Artes, Mexico.

**917. Portrait of Don Eduviges Ruvalcaba**
Oil on metal. 5¹/₈x7¹/₂". Coll.: Instituto Nacional de Bellas Artes, Mexico.

**918. Portrait of Dionisia de la Trinidad Bustos**
Oil on metal. 4⁷/₈x3¹/₂". Coll.: Instituto Nacional de Bellas Artes, Mexico.

**919. Portrait of Doña Vicenta de la Rosa Reyes**
Oil on metal. 5¹/₈x3¹/₂". Coll.: Instituto Nacional de Bellas Artes, Mexico.

FRANCISCO DE P. MENDOSA, painter. Born 1867 at Saltillo (Coahuila), died 1937 in Mexico City.

**920. Battle of Silao**
Oil on canvas. 1861. 30⁷/₈x41³/₈". Coll.: Museo Regional de Guadalajara, Jal.

**921. The attack on Guadalajara**
Oil on canvas. 33¹/₈x44⁷/₈". Coll.: Museo Regional de Guadalajara, Jal.

HUESCA, painter. Born in Jalisco.

### 922. Still life with cat
Oil on canvas. $31^7/8\times24''$. Coll.: D. de la Borbolla, Mexico.

### 923. Still life with chicken
Oil on canvas. $31^7/8\times24''$. Coll.: D. de la Borbolla, Mexico.

ÁGUSTIN ARRIETA, painter. Born in Tlaxcala, died in Puebla.

### 924. Two peasants having breakfast
Oil on canvas. $46^1/2\times64^1/2''$. Coll.: M. G. Pérez Salazar, Mexico.

ANONYMOUS

### 925. Portrait of a little girl
Oil on metal. $12^5/8\times9^1/2''$. Coll.: Instituto Nacional de Bellas Artes, Mexico.

### 926. Portrait of the little Lugarda Hernandez
Oil on canvas. $23^3/4\times18^1/8''$. Coll.: Instituto Nacional de Bellas Artes, Mexico.

JOSÉ GUADALUPE POSADA, engraver. Born 1851 at Aguascalientes, died 1913, in Mexico City.

### 927. »Calavera of Don Quixote«*
(*Calavera:* humorous representation of Death, used to render concrete and abstract themes of life). Zincograph. $5^7/8\times10^5/8''$. Coll.: A. Carrillo Gil, Mexico.

### 928. Calavera of the 20th century
Zincograph. $5^7/8\times10^1/4''$. Coll.: A. Carrillo Gil, Mexico.

### 929. Calavera of news-sellers
Zincograph. $5^7/8\times9''$. Coll.: A. Carrillo Gil, Mexico.

### 930. Calavera Catrina (Vanitas)*
Zincograph. $4^3/4\times6^1/4''$. Coll.: A. Carrillo Gil, Mexico.

### 931. Calavera killer
Lead engraving. $5^3/4\times10^1/4''$. Coll.: A. Carrillo Gil, Mexico.

### 932. Calavera of Jarabe beyond the tomb
(Jarabe is a folk dance). Lead engraving. $5^1/2\times7^7/8''$. Coll.: A. Carrillo Gil, Mexico.

### 933. Calavera Huertista
(General Huerta, a Mexican dictator). Lead engraving. 1911. $8^5/8\times8^5/8''$. Coll.: Museo Nacional de Arte Moderno, Mexico.

### 934. The capital sins
Lead engraving. $3^7/8\times6^1/4''$. Coll.: A. Carrillo Gil, Mexico.

### 935. Execution
Lead engraving. $5^7/8\times9^1/2''$. Coll.: A. Carrillo Gil, Mexico.

### 936. The comet
Zincograph. $3^1/2\times5^1/2''$. Coll.: A. Carrillo Gil, Mexico.

### 937. Don Chepito is amused
Zincograph. $3^7/8\times3^1/2''$. Coll.: A. Carrillo Gil, Mexico.

### 938. Don Chepito as Bullfighter
Zincograph. $3^7/8\times6^1/4''$. Coll.: A. Carrillo Gil, Mexico.

### 939. The jealous one
Zincograph. $3^1/2\times5^3/8''$. Coll.: A. Carrillo Gil, Mexico.

### 940. The martyr
Lead engraving. $6^3/4\times5^7/8''$. Coll.: A. Carrillo Gil, Mexico.

**941. Son killing his mother**
Lead engraving. 5¹/₂×7⁷/₈″. Coll.: A. Carrillo Gil, Mexico.

**942. The entry of madero**
Zincograph. 4³/₈×5⁷/₈″. Coll.: A. Carrillo Gil, Mexico.

**943. Calavera maderista**
Zincograph. 6¹/₄×3¹/₈″. Coll.: A. Carrillo Gil, Mexico.

**944. The rope**
Zincograph. 3¹/₈×4⁷/₈″. Coll.: A. Carrillo Gil, Mexico.

**Contemporary art**

JOSÉ CLEMENTE OROZCO, painter, muralist, lithographer. Born 1883 at Zapotlán, Jalisco, died 1949, in Mexico City.

**945. Maguey plant**
Oil on canvas. 1930. 28×22″. Coll.: Margarita Valladares de Orozco, Mexico.

**946. The caudillo zapata**
Oil on canvas. 1930. 71¹/₄×47¹/₄″. Coll.: The Art Institute of Chicago, USA.

**947. Death**
Distemper on masonite. 1943. 48×38¹/₄″. Coll.: Margarita Valladares de Orozco, Mexico.

**948. Man pierced by a lance**
Proxeline on masonite. 1947. 48×81¹/₂″. Coll.: Margarita Valladares de Orozco, Mexico.

**949. The blue skin**
Proxeline on masonite. 1947. 67³/₄×48″. Coll.: Margarita Valladares de Orozco, Mexico.

**950. The drowned**
Proxeline on masonite. 1947. 48×68¹/₈″. Coll.: Margarita Valladares de Orozco, Mexico.

**951. Dismembered***
Proxeline on masonite. 1947. 63×48″. Coll.: Lucrecia O. Herrera, Mexico.

**952. The slave***
Proxeline on masonite. 1948. 82¹/₄×48³/₈″. Coll.: Margarita Valladares de Orozco, Mexico.

**953. Portrait of Annette Nancarrow**
Distemper on canvas. 1948. 29¹/₈×24³/₈″. Coll.: Annette Nancarrow, Mexico.

**954. Hand**
Duco on panel. 1948. 84¹/₄×48″. Coll.: Lucrecia O. Herrera, Mexico.

**955. Fight of symbols**
Duco on masonite. 1948. 28×22″. Coll.: Margarita Valladares de Orozco, Mexico.

**956. The truth**
Ink drawing from the series called "The Truth". 1948. 11³/₄×15³/₄″. Coll.: Margarita Valladares de Orozco, Mexico.

**957. The truth**
Ink drawing from the series called "The Truth". 1948. 11³/₄×15³/₄″. Coll.: Margarita Valladares de Orozco, Mexico.

DIEGO RIVERA, painter, muralist, lithographer. Born 1886 in Guanajuato, the State of Guanajuato, died 1957 in Mexico City.

**958. Zapata landscape**
Oil on canvas. 1915. 57×48³/₈″. Coll.: Marte R. Gómez, Mexico.

**959. Man with fountain pen**
Oil on canvas. 1916. 34×28″. Coll.: Dolores Olmedo de Olvera, Mexico.

**960. Flower festival**
Oil on canvas. 1925. 58³/₄×47⁵/₈″. Coll.: Los Angeles County Museum of Art, California, USA.

**961. Little girl with coral necklace**
Oil on canvas, 1926. 37³/₈×27¹/₈″. Coll.: San Francisco Museum of Art, California, USA.

**962. Woman grinding maize**
Wax on canvas. 1926. 35³/₈×46″. Coll.: E. Portes Gil, Mexico.

**963. A poor family**
Oil on canvas. 1934. 21¹/₄×26³/₄″. Coll.: Dolores Olmedo de Olvera, Mexico.

**964. Flower vendor**
Oil on canvas. 1935. 52×52″. Coll.: San Francisco Museum of Art, California, USA.

**965. Woman selling pinole (ground maize)**
Aquarelle on canvas. 1936. 32×23⁷/₈″. Coll.: Instituto Nacional de Bellas Artes, Mexico.

**966. Seated girl**
Oil on canvas, 1938. 35³/₈×23⁵/₈″. Coll.: Miguel Alemán Valdés, Mexico.

**967. Dance of the earth**
Oil on canvas. 1939. 51¹/₈×71⁵/₈″. Coll.: Dolores Olmedo de Olvera, Mexico.

**968. Dance to the sun**
Oil on masonite. 1942. 79⁷/₈×51¹/₈″. Coll.: Dolores Olmedo de Olvera, Mexico.

**969. Flower sellers***
Oil on canvas. 1943. 58¹/₄×47¹/₄″. Coll.: Miguel Alemán Valdés, Mexico.

**970. The night of the radishes**
Oil on canvas. 1947. 39×43¹/₄″. Coll.: José María Dávila, Mexico.

**971 Portrait of a tehuana**
Oil on canvas. 1950. 82¹/₄×63³/₄″. Coll.: Dolores Olmedo de Olvera, Mexico.

**972. Destroying the ice**
Oil on canvas. 1956. 55¹/₈×43¹/₄″. Coll.: Ministry of Finance, Mexico.

**973. Cityscape**
Oil on canvas. 1956. 57¹/₈×43¹/₄″. Coll.: Ministry of Finance, Mexico.

DAVID ALFARO SIQUIEROS, painter, muralist, lithographer. Born 1898 in Chihuahua, the State of Chihuahua.

**974. Peasant mother***
Oil on jute. 1929. 88⁵/₈×70¹/₂″. Coll.: Instituto Nacional de Bellas Artes, Mexico.

**975. Self-portrait**
Proxeline on masonite. 1939. 19³/₄×29¹/₂″. Coll.: John Coolidge, Cambridge.

**976. Ethnography**
Duco on masonite. 1939. 47¹/₄×31⁷/₈″. Coll.: Museum of Modern Art, New York, N.Y., USA.

**977. Victims of war**
Duco on cellotex. 1944. 146×96⁷/₈″. Coll.: Instituto Nacional de Bellas Artes, Mexico.

**978. Landscape**
Polyesther on masonite. 1956. 35⁷/₈×26″. Coll.: Gerónimo Bertrán Cusine, Mexico.

**979. Still life with fish**
Polyesther on masonite. 1958. 39³/₄×48″. Coll.: Mr. and Mrs. Juan Sordo Magdaleno, Mexico.

**980. The partisan***
Polyesther on canvas. 1958. 122×86⁵/₈″. Private collection, Mexico.

**981. Revolution gives us culture back**
Polyesther on canvas. 1959. 59×61″. Private collection, Mexico.

RUFINO TAMAYO, painter, muralist, lithographer. Born 1899 in Oaxaca, the State of Oaxaca.

**982. Yellow chair**
Oil on canvas. 1929. 28³/₄×25″. Coll.: Mr. and Mrs. R. Tamayo, Mexico.

**983. Advertisement for corsetry**
Oil on canvas. 1934. 17³/₈×29¹/₂″. Coll.: Mr. and Mrs. R. Tamayo, Mexico.

**984. Portrait of Olga in green**
Oil on canvas. 1934. 39×29¹/₂″. Coll.: Mr. and Mrs. R. Tamayo, Mexico.

**985. Woman with a birdcage**
Oil on canvas, 1941. 41×33″. Coll.: The Art Institute of Chicago, USA.

**986. Animals**
Oil on canvas. 1941. 29¹/₂×39³/₈″. Coll.: The Museum of Modern Art, New York, N.Y., USA.

**987. Native woman**
Oil on canvas. 1942. 45¹/₄×36⁵/₈″. Coll.: Mr. and Mrs. Selwyn S. Schwartz, Chicago, USA.

**988. Mad dog**
Oil on canvas. 1947. 44¹/₂×33⁷/₈″. Coll.: Philadelphia Museum of Art, Pa., USA.

**989. The tormented**
Oil on canvas. 1950. 39³/₈×31¹/₂″. Coll.: Marte R. Gómez, Mexico.

**990. Sleeping musicians***
Oil on canvas. 1950. 51¹/₈×76³/₈″. Coll.: Instituto Nacional de Bellas Artes, Mexico.

**991. Nude in white***
Oil on canvas. 1950. 78³/₄×59″. Coll.: Mr. and Mrs. R. Tamayo, Mexico.

**992. Watermelons**
Oil on canvas. 1950. 39³/₈×33⁷/₈″. Coll.: The Museum of Modern Art, N.Y., USA. (Gift from Mrs. Sam A. Lewisohn).

**993. Cry in the night**
Oil on canvas. 1953. 18⁷/₈×17³/₄″. Coll.: Nicholas Murray, N.Y., USA.

**994. Supersonic plane**
Oil on canvas. 1954. 24×29⁷/₈″. Coll.: Mr. and Mrs. Henry C. Rogers, Beverly Hills, Hollywood, California, USA.

**995. Man**
Oil on canvas. 1962. 39³/₈×31¹/₂″. Coll.: Mr. and Mrs. R. Tamayo, Mexico.

MANUEL RODRÍGUEZ LOZANO, painter, muralist. Born 1896, in Mexico City.

**996. Woman in white**
Oil on canvas. 1942. 37⁵/₈×27¹/₂″. Coll.: Alicia de Morillo Safa, Mexico.

CARLOS OROZCO ROMERO, painter, engraver. Born 1898, in Guadalajara, Jal.

**997. The threads**
Oil on canvas, 1939. 27¹/₈×22¹/₂″. Coll.: Instituto Nacional de Bellas Artes, Mexico.

JUAN O'GORMAN, painter, muralist, architect. Born 1905, in Coyoacán, Mexico.

**998. Mexico city**
Distemper on masonite. 1949. 26×48″. Coll.: Instituto Nacional de Bellas Artes, Mexico.

**999. Selfportrait**
Distemper on masonite. 1950. $27^1/8 \times 20^7/8''$.
Coll.: Instituto Nacional de Bellas Artes, Mexico.

FRIDA KHALO, painter. Born 1905 in Coyoacán, Mexico, died 1957.

**1000. My nurse and I**
Oil on tin. 1937. $11^3/4 \times 13^3/4''$. Coll.: Museo Frida Khalo, Mexico.

**1001. Roots**
Oil on metal. 1943. $11^3/4 \times 19^5/8''$. Coll.: Museo Frida Khalo, Mexico.

**1002. The broken column**
Oil on masonite. 1944. $15^3/4 \times 33^1/2''$. Coll.: Museo Frida Khalo, Mexico.

**1003. Portrait of Mrs Rosita Morillo**
Oil on masonite. 1944. $29^7/8 \times 23^7/8''$. Coll.: Museo Frida Khalo, Mexico.

**1004. Self portrait with monkey, dog and idol**
Oil on masonite. 1945. $22 \times 16^1/8''$. Coll.: Museo Frida Khalo, Mexico.

ALFREDO ZALCE, painter, muralist, engraver. Born 1908, in Pátzeuaro, the State of Michoacán.

**1005. Woman selling ducks**
Oil on masonite. 1958. $35^7/8 \times 47^1/4''$. Owned by the artist, Mexico.

RAUL ANGUIANO, painter, muralist, engraver. Born 1915, in Guadalajara, the State of Jalisco.

**1006. Red tiger**
Oil on canvas. 1956. $39^3/8 \times 66^7/8''$. Owned by the artist, Mexico.

RICARDO MARTÍNEZ, painter. Born 1918, in Mexico City.

**1007. Childbirth***
Oil on canvas. 1959. $65 \times 78^3/4''$. Coll.: The Contemporary Arts Gallery, N.Y., USA.

**1008. Maternity**
Oil on canvas. 1960. $65 \times 59''$. Owned by the artist, Mexico.

CARLOS BRACHO, sculptor. Born 1898, in Jalapa, the State of Veracruz.

**1009. Head of Indian woman***
Sculpture in green onyx. 1935. $15^3/4 \times 11^3/4''$. Coll.: Emma Sohlther de Bracho, Mexico.

FRANCISCO ZÚNIGA, sculptor. Born 1915, in San José, Costa Rica.

**1010. Woman in hammock**
Sculpture in stone. 1957. $39^3/8 \times 73^1/4''$. Private collection, Mexico.

**1011. Mexico in transformation and still inalterable**
Brown onyx. 1959. $39^3/8 \times 47^1/4''$. Private collection, Mexico.

José Clemente Orozco: Magueyplant. Cat. 1077.

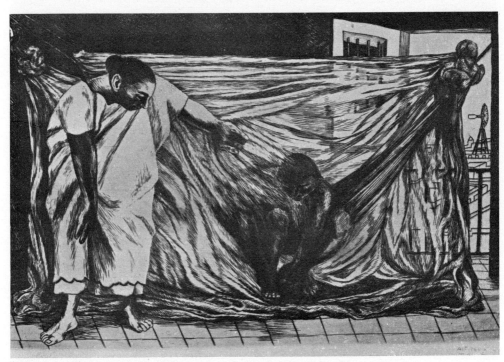

Alfredo Zalce: The Hammock. Cat. 1116.

Leopoldo Méndez: The Merry-Go-Round. Cat. 1050.

Leopoldo Méndez: Shot. Cat. 1046.

David Alfaro Siqueiros: Woman bathing. Cat. 1106.

Diego Rivera: Dream of the Poor. Cat. 1099.

Diego Rivera: Flower sellers. Cat. 969.

José Clemente Orozco: Slave. Cat. 952.

José Clemente Orozco: Dismembered. Cat. 951.

David Alfaro Siqueiros: Peasant Mother. Cat. 974.

David Alfaro Siqueiros: The Partisan. Cat. 980.

Rufino Tamayo: Nude in White. Cat. 991.

Rufino Tamayo: Sleeping Musicians. Cat. 990.

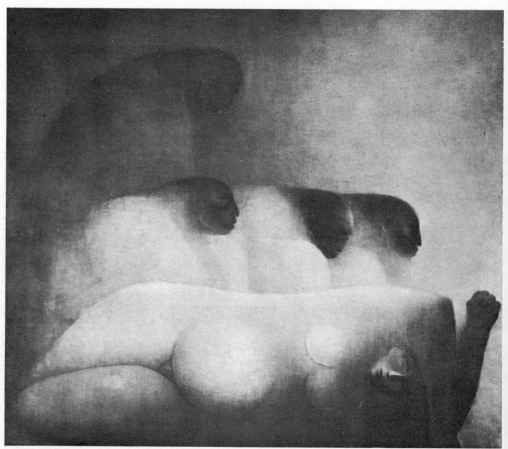

Ricardo Martínez: Childbirth. Cat. 1007.

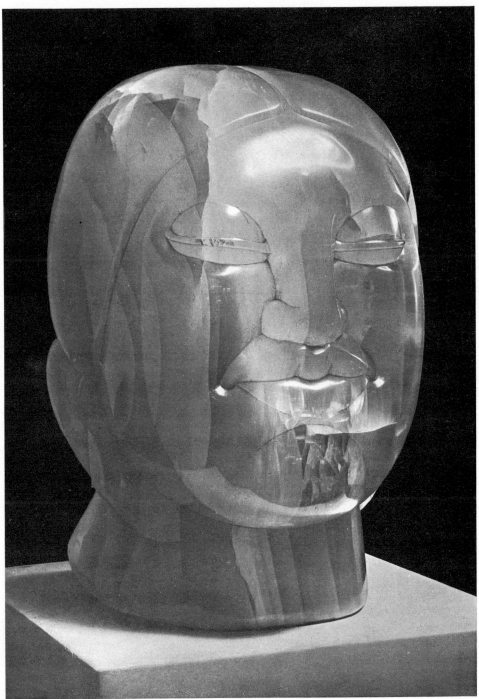

Carlos Bracho: Head of Indian woman. Cat. 1009.

# 14. Graphic Works

IGNACIO AGUIRRE, b. 1902 Guadalajara, Jal.

**1012. Women soldiers**
Lino-cut. 12⅝x16½". Coll. MNAM.

CARLOS ALVARO LANG b. 1905 Piedad, Mich., d. 1959.

**1013. Interior**
Steel engraving, 7⅞x5⅞". Coll. MNAM.

LUIS ARENAL, b. 1909 Mexico City.

**1014. Woman's head**
Lithograph. 11x13⅜". Coll. MNAM.

ALBERTO BELTRAN, b. 1923 Mexico City.

**1015. The agricultural laborer**
Wood. 7½x12". Coll. MNAM.

**1016. Scorpion with human face**
Lead engraving. 3⅛x2⅞". Coll. MNAM.

**1017. Scorpion with human body**
Lead engraving. 3⅛x2½". Coll. MNAM.

**1018. Victoriano Huerta's attempt to liquidate zapatism**
Lino-cut. 11¾x8½". Coll. MNAM.

**1019. The earth**
Lino-cut. 9x7¼". Coll. MNAM.

**1020. Parade**
Lino-cut. 7⅛x5⅛". Coll. MNAM.

**1021. Scorpion-man**
Lead engraving. 2x3". Coll. MNAM.

ANGEL BRACHO, b. 1911 Durango.

**1022. The palm tree**
Color lithograph. 11⅜x15". Coll. MNAM.

**1023. Transport of a thatched roof**
Lino-cut. 5⅛x7½". Coll. MNAM.

**1024. Zapata**
Lino-cut. 11⅝x8¼". Coll. MNAM.

FEDERICO CANTU, b. 1908 Cadereyta, Nuevo León.

**1025. Moses**
Steel engraving. 9¼x11½". Coll. MNAM.

**1026. Christ taken away by the angels.**
Steel engraving. 8x6⅛". Coll. MNAM.

**1027. François Villon**
Steel engraving. 8⅛x5¾". Coll. MNAM.

FERNANDO CASTRO PACHECO, b. 1918 Mérida, Yuc.

**1028. The victim**
Lino-cut. 8½x15½". Coll. MNAM.

**1029. Women of the mezquital**
Lino-cut. 10¼x13". Coll. MNAM.

**1030. Mother**
Wood. 14¾x12⅜". Coll. MNAM.

**1031. Sisal**
Lino-cut. 13¾x11⅜". Coll. MNAM.

**1032. Peasant revolutionaries**
Lino-cut. 7⅝x5½". Coll. MNAM.

JEAN CHARLOT, b. 1898 Paris.

**1033. Mexican cooking**
Lithograph. 13⅜x9⅝". Coll. MNAM.

**1034. The first steps**
Lithograph. 14x9⅞". Coll. MNAM.

JOSÉ CHAVEZ MORADO, b. 1909 Silao, Gto.

**1035. The revolutionary thrust against the feudal regime**
Lino-cut. 10¹/₄x16¹/₂″. Coll. MNAM.

**1036. The hammock**
Lithograph. 17³/₈x22⁷/₈″. Coll. MNAM.

**1037. The "Judas"**
Lithograph. 12⁵/₈x7⁷/₈″. Coll. MNAM.

**1038. "Alteños"**
Lithograph. 9x6¹/₂″. Coll. MNAM.

FRANCISCO DOSAMANTES, b. 1911 Mexico City.

**1039. Peasant from Yalala**
Lithograph. 17³/₄x14⁵/₈″. Coll. MNAM.

**1040. Landscape**
Lithograph. 18¹/₂x20¹/₈″. Coll. MNAM.

JOSÉ ESCOBEDO, b. 1918 El Oro, Mex.

**1041. Peasants in captivity**
Lino-cut. 8¹/₄x11³/₄″. Coll. MNAM.

**1042. The basket seller**
Lithograph. 11³/₄x9¹/₂″. Coll. MNAM.

**1043. Head**
Lino-cut. 7¹/₂x6¹/₄″. Coll. MNAM.

ARTURO GARCIA BUSTOS, b. 1926 Mexico City.

**1044. Bread-market**
Lino-cut. 13³/₄x18⁷/₈″. Coll. MNAM.

ANDREA GOMEZ, b. 1926 Mexico City.

**1045. Head of a peasant**
Lino-cut. 5³/₄x7⁷/₈″. Coll. MNAM.

LEOPOLDO MENDEZ, b. 1903 Mexico City.

**1046. Execution***
Wood. 11³/₄x16¹/₈″. Coll. TGP.

**1047. House of Chamula peasants**
Wood. 11³/₄x16¹/₈″. Coll. TGP.

**1048. Mexican peasants before 1910**
Wood. 8⁵/₈x6³/₄″. Coll. TGP.

**1049. Cuauhtemoc**
Lino-cut. 22¹/₂x18⁷/₈″. Coll. TGP.

**1050. Merry-go-round***
Wood. 12¹/₄x16¹/₈″. Coll. TGP.

**1051. Thirst**
Wood. 11³/₄x16¹/₈″. Coll. TGP.

**1052. Ambush**
Wood. 12¹/₄x16¹/₈″. Coll. TGP.

**1053. Hidalgo**
Lino-cut. 12¹/₄x16¹/₈″. Coll. TGP.

**1054. Solitude**
Lino-cut. 12¹/₄x16¹/₈″. Coll. TGP.

**1055. Pilgrims**
Lino-cut. 12¹/₄x16¹/₈″. Coll. TGP.

**1056. Juarez**
Lino-cut. 12¹/₄x16¹/₈″. Coll. TGP.

**1057. The flight**
Lino-cut. 12¹/₄x16¹/₈″. Coll. TGP.

**1058. Pay-office**
Lino-cut. 12¹/₄x16¹/₈″. Coll. TGP.

**1059. National defence**
Lino-cut. 12¹/₄x16¹/₈″. Coll. TGP.

**1060. Shot**
Lino-cut. 12¹/₄x16¹/₈″. Coll. TGP.

**1061. The little car**
Lino-cut. $12^{1}/4 \times 16^{1}/8''$. Coll. TGP.

**1062. The harvest**
Lino-cut. $12^{1}/4 \times 16^{1}/8''$. Coll. TGP.

**1063. The sowing**
Lino-cut. $12^{1}/4 \times 16^{1}/8''$. Coll. TGP.

**1064. Fight on horseback**
Lino-cut. $12^{1}/4 \times 16^{1}/8''$. Coll. TGP.

**1065. The heritage of Juarez**
Lino-cut. $12^{1}/4 \times 16^{1}/8''$. Coll. TGP.

**1066. Indian head**
Lino-cut. $12^{1}/4 \times 16^{1}/8''$. Coll. TGP.

ADOLFO MEXIAC, b. 1928 Mexico City.

**1067. Indian prayer**
Lino-cut. $12^{5}/8 \times 16^{7}/8''$. Coll. MNAM.

**1068. Cemetery**
Lino-cut. $16^{7}/8 \times 12^{5}/8''$. Coll. TGP.

SUSANA NEVE, b. 1928 Mexico City.

**1069. Landscape**
Dry point. $9^{1}/4 \times 11^{3}/4''$. Coll. MNAM.

ISIDORO O'CAMPO, b. 1902 Veracruz.

**1070. The seller of "Judas"-figures**
$15^{3}/4 \times 11^{3}/4''$. Coll. MNAM.

PABLO O'HIGGINS, b. 1904 Salt Lake City, USA.

**1071. Workers having breakfast**
Lithograph. $13^{3}/4 \times 17^{3}/8''$. Coll. MNAM.

**1072. Football players**
Lithograph. $10^{5}/8 \times 13^{3}/4''$. Coll. MNAM.

**1073. Sack-maker**
Lithograph. $12^{1}/4 \times 16^{1}/8''$. Coll. MNAM.

**1074. Man of the twentieth century**
Lithograph. $18^{1}/2 \times 10^{3}/8''$. Coll. MNAM.

JOSÉ CLEMENTE OROZCO, b. 1883 Zapotlán, Jal., d. 1949 Mexico City.

**1075. The wounded man**
Lithograph. 1931. $11 \times 18^{1}/8''$. Coll.: Margarita Valladares de Orozco, Mexico.

**1076. The widow**
Lithograph. 1932. $15^{3}/4 \times 9^{7}/8''$. Coll.: A. Carrillo Gil, Mexico.

**1077. Maguey***
Lithograph. 1932. $9^{7}/8 \times 15''$. Coll.: Margarita Valladares de Orozco, Mexico.

**1078. The flag**
Lithograph. 1932. $9^{7}/8 \times 15''$. Coll.: Margarita Valladares de Orozco, Mexico.

**1079. Mexican village**
Lithograph. 1932. $9^{7}/8 \times 11''$. Coll.: Margarita Valladares de Orozco, Mexico.

**1080. Peace.**
Lithograph. 1932. $10^{3}/8 \times 14^{1}/8''$. Coll.: Margarita Valladares de Orozco, Mexico.

**1081. Woman profile**
Etching. 1953.. $6^{7}/8 \times 5^{1}/8''$. Coll.: A. Carrillo Gil, Mexico.

**1082. Woman's head**
Etching. 1935. $6^{7}/8 \times 5^{7}/8''$. Coll.: A. Carrillo Gil, Mexico.

**1083. Acrobats**
Etching. 1935. $8^{7}/8 \times 10^{3}/8''$. Coll.: A. Carrillo Gil, Mexico.

**1084. Clown**
Etching. 1935. 10$^{1}$/4x6$^{3}$/4". Coll.: A. Carrillo Gil, Mexico.

**1085. Two men**
Lithograph. 1935. Coll.: A. Carrillo Gil, Mexico.

**1086. Vice**
Lithograph. 1935. 12$^{1}$/4x9$^{3}$/4". Coll.: A. Carrillo Gil, Mexico.

**1087. Fragment of catharsis**
Lithograph. 1935. 12$^{1}$/4x9$^{3}$/4". Coll.: A. Carrillo Gil, Mexico.

**1088. The broken bed**
Lithograph. 1935. 12$^{1}$/4x9$^{3}$/4". Coll.: A. Carrillo Gil, Mexico.

CARLOS OROZCO ROMERO, b. 1898 Guadalajara, Jal.

**1089. Woman**
Dry point. 6$^{1}$/8x4$^{1}$/4". Coll. MNAM.

**1090. Two women**
Dry point. 7$^{5}$/8x6$^{1}$/2". Coll. MNAM.

ANTONIO QUINTEROS, b. 1928 Mexico City.

**1091. The calvary**
Lino-cut. 12$^{5}$/8x17$^{3}$/4". Coll. MNAM.

**1092. The good catch**
Lino-cut. 12$^{1}$/4x20$^{1}$/8". Coll. MNAM.

**1093. Cooking gum**
Lino-cut. 17$^{3}$/4x12$^{5}$/8". Coll. MNAM.

**1094. The wait**
Lino-cut. 5$^{3}$/8x8$^{7}$/8". Coll. MNAM.

DIEGO RIVERA, b. 1886 Guanajuato, d. 1957 Mexico City.

**1095. Self-portrait**
Lithograph. 1930. 15$^{3}$/4x10$^{5}$/8". Coll.: A. Carrillo Gil, Mexico.

**1096. Naked**
Lithograph. 1930. 16$^{1}$/8x10$^{5}$/8". Coll.: A. Carrillo Gil, Mexico.

**1097. Flower market**
Lithograph. 1930. 10$^{5}$/8x15$^{3}$/8". Coll.: A. Carrillo Gil, Mexico.

**1098. Market**
Lithograph. 1930. 10$^{5}$/8x15$^{3}$/8". Coll.: A. Carrillo Gil, Mexico.

**1099. The dream of the poor ***
Lithograph. 1932. 16x11$^{3}$/4". Coll.: A. Carrillo Gil, Mexico.

**1100. The village schoolmistress**
Lithograph. 1932. 16$^{3}$/8x11$^{3}$/4". Coll.: A. Carrillo Gil, Mexico.

**1101. Emiliano Zapata**
Lithograph. 1932. 16x13$^{3}$/4". Coll.: A. Carrillo Gil, Mexico.

**1102. "Taco"**
(rolled maize "tortilla"). Lithograph. 1932. 16$^{1}$/8x11$^{3}$/4". Coll.: A. Carrillo Gil, Mexico.

**1103. Women**
Lithograph. 1934. 16x13$^{3}$/4". Coll.: A. Carrillo Gil, Mexico.

**1104. Nude**
Lithograph. 1934. 16x13$^{3}$/4". Coll.: A. Carrillo Gil, Mexico.

DAVID ALFARO SIQUEIROS, b. 1898 Chihuahua.

**1105. Zapata**
Lithograph. 1930. 19$^{5}$/8x15$^{3}$/8". Coll.: A. Carrillo Gil, Mexico.

**1106. Woman bathing ***
Lithograph. 1930. 13³/8×13³/4″. Coll.: A. Carrillo Gil, Mexico.

**1107. Portrait of Moises Saenz**
Lithograph. 1930. 19⁵/8×15³/8″. Coll.: A. Carrillo Gil, Mexico.

**1108. Nude**
Lithograph. 1930. 13×21¹/4″. Coll.: A. Carrillo Gil, Mexico.

**1109. Accident in the mine**
Lithograph. 1931. 11³/4×19¹/4″. Coll.: A. Carrillo Gil, Mexico.

**1110. Self-portrait**
Lithograph. 1933. 20¹/2×14⁵/8″. Coll.: A. Carrillo Gil, Mexico.

**1111. Portrait of a negress**
Lithograph. 1936. 19¹/4×13³/8″. Coll.: A. Carrillo Gil, Mexico.

**1112. The centaur of the conquest**
Lithograph. 1943. 20¹/2×16⁷/8″. Coll.: A. Carrillo Gil, Mexico.

**1113. Our present image**
Lithograph. 1947. 11³/8×9″. Coll.: A. Carrillo Gil, Mexico.

ALFREDO ZALCE, b. 1908 Pátzcuaro, Mish.

**1114. Woman peddler**
Lithograph. 13×11″. Coll. MNAM.

**1115. Wounded partisan**
Lead engraving. 6¹/4×5¹/8″. Coll. MNAM.

**1116. The hammock ***
Lead engraving. 7⁷/8×11³/4″. Coll. MNAM.

**1117. Mother and girl**
Print. 13×9″. Coll. MNAM.

**1118. Huerta dissolves parliament**
Lino-cut. 8¹/4×11⁵/8″. Coll. MNAM.

**1119. Laborers**
Lino-cut. 8¹/4×11⁵/8″. Coll. MNAM.

**1120. Woman and doves**
Lithograph. 3³/8×5¹/2″. Coll. MNAM.

**1121. Landscape of Cuautla**
Color print. 6³/8×11¹/2″. Coll. MNAM.

# 15. Folk Art

The folk art that each village produces for the market day, is one of the oldest forms of expression in Mexico. Its roots are native. Since the 16th century it has been enriched by influences from Europe and Asia.

Folk art and folk crafts are created, now as in the past, by artisans, peasants, and their families, who work to meet their own needs and those of their village. The richest and most varied folk art is to be found in central and southern Mexico.

The best expression of folk art is ceramics, jars, jugs, toys and decoration — which covers an inexhaustible variety of forms, from rudimentary glazed things to brilliant polychrome ceramics with complicated design. There are also examples of foreign influence. Apart from ceramics we find sculpture in wood, horn, wicker, paper, palm, carton, sugar, masks, textiles, baskets, laquer work, leather, religious offerings, silverware, and ornaments for personal wear.

## Ceramics

They are used generally in all Mexican homes. Numerous types of earthenware exist, varying according to region, technique, raw materials, the use for which the objects are intended, and traditions. The local character is often dominant, but in some cases a certain European or Asiatic influence is felt, e.g. in the so-called "talavera" ceramics from Puebla, or in the ceramics produced in Guanajuato, Aguescalientes, and Oaxaca. The folk ceramics are practically always made of clay. In rare cases the material is caoline. For kneading, mixing and preparing of the material, stone mortars are used, the so-called "metates", which resemble the pre-Hispanic ones. The Mexican potter has retained almost all of the old techniques: he models his ware by hand, or uses, for a potter's wheel, a rudimentary round instrument that he works with hands or feet. In some regions the artisans also use a mould, consisting of two smooth parts, on which decorative motifs are engraved or carved in relief. Most of the toys and the relatively large objects are modeled by hand.

In order to obtain a water proof surface, certain objects are polished while drying by help of a burnisher of agate or marble, with which the surface is rubbed till an absolutely matt or brilliant polish is obtained. This technique too is pre-Hispanic.

According to tradition or local style the decoration can be painted, engraved or applied. The painted ornamentation is done with great freedom, either in coarse brush-strokes or with great delicacy. The artisans try primarily to create a uniform simplicity, for which reason detail is always subservient to the general design. The ceramics are usually fired in open kilns. During the process the objects are separated by help of ceramic supports.

Traditionally all members of a family take part in the home ceramics industry. The work is divided among them, according to the technical demands, and to traditions. The man usually undertakes the hardest job: he digs out the clay and transports it to his home. He fills and empties the kiln, while his wife and children pound and wedge the clay, prepare the moulds or model the objects and execute the decoration. It can be maintained that large production of ceramics and its aesthetic tradition is the work of the wife and children of the artisan. In some regions it is, however, the man who does the whole job, only assisted by his family.

## Ceramics of predominantly indiginous character

Ceramics of predominantly indiginous character is still produced in many parts of the country, particularly in the East and the far South. Its technique, forms, and decorations have been preserved in relatively pure form. The ceramics of Amatenango (the State of Chiapas), which is shown here, is on ochre terracotta of varying forms. It is covered by orange or cream glaze, and the motifs, in orange or brown, represent flowers or abstract designs, often very austere, but at other times quite elaborate. Jars, vases and pots are of very simple lines, and the handles are the decorative element. The ceramics of Colimán (the State of Guerrero) are made of creamcolored clay, decorated with designs in red or dark brown. There is a large production of jars for the keeping of specially selected maize seeds, for the cooling of water; household dishes and vessels; candlesticks for the family altars; toys and figurines of men and women on horseback and many kinds of animals. Both shapes and decorations continue the native tradition. The artist often uses modern themes, when decorating a jar or jug, e.g. airplanes, steam engines or cars, but since he, like the majority of Mexican folk artists, has a rich imagination, he transposes the influences without ever betraying his own style. The same phenomenon occurs, when he is inspired by the pre-Hispanic art that is a profound influence which does not merely concern formal execution.

**1122-1125. Pitchers and pots**
Ochre terracotta, decorated with designs in orange and brown. (Amatenango, Chis.).

**1126-1128. Large jars**
Creamcolored terracotta with design in red and dark brown. (Tolimán, Gro.).

**1129-1132. Large pitchers**
Creamcolored terracotta, decorated with designs in red and dark brown. (Tolimán, Gro.).

**1133-1146. Small jars, round trays, dishes and candlesticks**
Creamcolored terracotta, with red and dark brown designs.

## Polished ceramics

This form of ceramics is produced in our time in the states of Puebla, Tlaxcala, Oaxaca, Michoacán, and Jalisco. The surface is completely smooth, glossy or matt.

The black, polished earthenware from Coyotepec (Oaxaca) has retained the pure form of the pre-Hispanic works.. The techniques and raw materials are the ones that were used for centuries, before the Spanish Conquest. The silhouettes of certain vessels can easily be taken for those from the first period of Monte Albán, when the dawning Zapotec culture was influenced by Olmec art. The black clay of Coyotepec can be modeled and polished by hand. It has a peculiar, almost metallic sound, which makes it suitable for bells. The craftsman shows a predilection for the shape of the mermaid, a mythological figure introduced by the Spaniards in the 16th century, and enthusiastically adopted by the Indians, who assosiated it with their religious traditions of anthropomorphic deities, and knew how to exploit its decorative possibilities.

The red, handpolished ceramics are common in various parts of Mexico. Though the "glaze" technique has replaced it in many places, it is still found in the States of Puebla, Tlaxcala, and Michoacán. Among the handsomest examples are the·ceramics from Patamban (the State of Michoacán). These are objects for ordinary household uses. The most common form is the pots and jugs for water. The color is deep red, and the very pure forms are decorated with designs of flowers and animals, painted in cream or white.

When the potters do work on commission, they draw the buyer's name on the objects, otherwise they decorate them with first names that are common in the region, in order to sell them better.

The braziers from Puebla, representing male heads with heavy moustaches and beards are reminiscent of pre-Hispanic ceramics (Mixteca-Puebla culture) in which braziers occur, shaped like gods' heads or fleshless skulls. These likenesses have doubtlessly been replaced by heads that look like the Spanish conquerors.

The handsomest polished ceramics in Mexico are those of Tonalá (the State of Jalisco) in the northern part of the country. Tonalá has for several centuries been a center of pottery, sharing its reputation with that of an other place in the region, San Pedro Tlaquepaque. Nowadays Tonalá has a population of about 8000 peasants, who are exclusively occupied by ceramics and agriculture. The entire population of this rural place is engaged in ceramic production, even the children. The polished, matt or glossy ceramics that are made here, are decorated with fantastic flowers and animals in exquisite execution. The shapes are very different from the traditional ones, but they are of great originality. The decoration is done with free brush work, and the potters of Tonalá pride themselves on inventing different decorations for each piece of ceramics. The clay they use is called "perfumed" (it is fragrant by nature), and it gives the water a pleasant taste. Half of the ceramics made at Tonalá are used for household purposes, the other half for decoration. The handsomest things are the large jars, the dishes and the water jugs, shaped like ducks.

In the colonial period Tonalá ceramics were heavily influenced particularly in the brush-work by Chinese art, which came to Mexico via Acapulco.

In the 19th century gold and silver colors were introduced in the decorations of these ceramics, under the influence of European porcelain. And finally, about 40 years ago, forms inspired by pre-Columbian art, such as the fret motifs and similar elements, were introduced — elements that were undoubtedly foreign to the local, native tradition. Still this "Mexican" influence, like the foreign ones (e.g. the Chinese designs in lacquer and on textiles, and those of European chinaware), were assimilated with such vigor, that neither one nor the other destroyed the local style. On the contrary: out of the mixture of all these elements, arose the "Mestizo" style, which is the most personal and characteristic contribution of Tonalá.

**1147-1148. Large jars**
Black, matt, polished terracotta, with glossy polished decorations. (Coyotepec, Oax.).

**1149-1178. Jars, vases, vessels, dishes and whistles\***
In the shapes of mermaids, horses, fish, lions and bells, shaped like angels. Black polished terracotta. (Coyotepec, Oax.).

**1179-1183. Pots**
Ochre polished terracotta, decorated with red and black. (Patamban, Mich.).

**1184-1186. Water jugs**
In the shape of ducks. Red, polished terracotta, with incised decorations. (Patamban, Mich.).

**1187-1188. Braziers**
In the shape of human heads. Red terracotta. (Puebla, Pue.).

**1189-1190. Pots**
Ochre, polished terracotta, decorated in red. (Oaxaca, Oax.).

**1191-1195. Small jars and bottles**
Red, glazed terracotta with white paint. (Tonalá, Jal.).

**1196-1215. Small and middle-sized jars and small bottles**
In the shape of calabashes, and bottles in the shape of ducks. So-called perfumed terracotta, polished and highly decorated. (Tonalá, Jal.).

**1216. Big lion\***
So-called perfumed terracotta, polished and highly decorated. (Tonalá, Jal.).

**1217-1221. Big and small cats\***
"Perfumed" terracotta, polished and highly decorated. (Tonalá, Jal.).

**1222-1249. Fish, horses, small dogs, doves, birds, toucans, bulls, frogs, turtles, rabbits, owls, and deer\***
Red "perfumed" terracotta, highly decorated. (Tonalá, Jal.).

**1250-1259. Decorative motifs**
Plates painted in distemper, ornamental models of ceramic objects, by the artisans Juan J. and S. Vázquez. (Tonalá, Jal.).

## Ordinary "glazed" ceramics

These ceramics are the kind most commonly used for domestic purposes, and they are found in all Mexican kitchens as jars, pots, jugs, and "cazuelas" (cooking pans of burned clay). They are produced in over 200 villages in various parts of the country. Shapes and decorations are of very old types. The big jars resemble the Aztec jars of the 15th century. They are intended for storing water, and "atole", a warm drink, made of maize flour, and "pulque", a fermented drink made of maguey-juice, and they have a special shape: round with very long necks and detachable handles. They are decorated with flowers and birds and almost all of them have some inscription or name, such as "For the beautiful Lupe", "Venture before you eat", "I serve my master", "Let us serve others".

For the "mole", the national dish, made of turkey and chicken, with a hot sauce, the basic elements of which are "chiles" (peppers), chocolate and spices, special pans are made up to 3 feet in diameter.

These ceramics are reddish, but may also be light or very dark brown, and the glaze is sufficiently strong to bear constant use. The most original objects are from Texcoco, Metepec, Tecomatepec (Mex.), Tonalá (Jal.), Puebla (Pue.), and San Miguel de Allende (Gto.).

The earthenware from Tonalá is handsomely decorated in an original technique, called "petatillo"; entwined, very fine geometrical designs, reminiscent of the patterns of the "petates", mats made of "tule", a flexible water plant.

There is a kind of black, glazed ceramic, used for offerings (foods, flowers, drinks) on All Souls' Day. It has preserved the old shapes, like that of the calabash; the jars, cups and candlesticks are reminiscent of the Aztec ceremonial braziers. These ceramics are made in the states of Michoacán, Mexico, Puebla, and Oaxaca. Another handsome and original kind of glazed ceramic is made at Patamban (Mich.), where the tradition is clearly respected. It is dark green, decorated with light green. The large water jugs in this style are famous. They are shaped like pineapples and decorated in the so-called pastillage technique.

The village Quiroga (Mich.) on the banks of the lake Pátzcuaro, produces a very original, black sort of ceramic, with flower motifs placed above each other, painted in oils, with bright colors and gilt spots.

A neighboring village, Tzintzuntzan, produces cream colored ceramics with white glaze and decorated with dark brown designs. These ceramics are distinguished by naive draw-

Cat of Tonalá (Jalisco). Cat. 1217-1221.

Fish of Tonalá (Jalisco). Cat. 1222-1249.

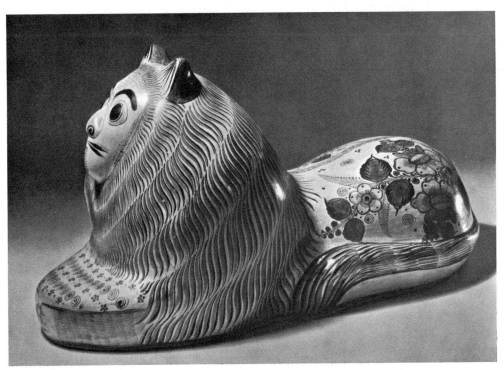

Lion of Tonalá (Jalisco) Cat. 1216.

Mermaid of Coyotepec (Oaxaca). Cat. 1149-1178.

Large candlestick, "Life Tree", Matamoros de Izúcar (Puebla). Cat. 1576-1585.

Crucifix in braided straw. Cat. 1876-1885.

Angel with trumpet, braided reed. Cat. 1866-1375.

Lion of Metepec (Mexico). Cat. 1526-1545.

ings, inspired by local themes: fishermen in boats, fish and ducks. No other Mexican ceramics compare to these as far as charm is concerned, particularly in the case of the virgins and other religious images.

The village of Atzompa (Oax.) is famous for its ceramics in reddish terracotta and green crockery, especially of zoömorphic objects. These figurines represent deer, goats, and sheep, and are intended for holding water. On the body of the animal are placed small seeds, called "chia", a sort of sage, that blooms in the humidity seeping through the clay. It is an announcer of spring, used as decoration on family altars and in village chapels.

**1260-1262. Jars for "pulque"**
Terracotta. (Texcoco, Mex.).

**1263-1268. Large and small jars, anthropomorphic jars and a large dish**
Ochre terracotta, painted and glazed. (Texcoco and Teotihuacán, Mex.).

**1269-1274. Jars for "atole", vases and pitcher**
Terracotta, painted. (Puebla, Pue.).

**1275-1278. Jars for "pulque" and cooking pot for rice**
Terracotta. (Metepec, Mex.).

**1279-1290. Jars, vases and animal figurines**
Red terracotta, decorated in pastillage technique. (Tonalá, Jal.).

**1291-1300. Candlesticks, funeral vessels and big receptacles**
Black, glazed terracotta, smooth with decorations applied to the surface. (Barrio de la Luz, Pue.).

**1301-1302. Vases**
Black, glazed terracotta. (Puebla, Pue.).

**1303-1306. Large dishes and large vessels**
Green, glazed terracotta. (Patamban, Mich.).

**1307-1310. Large and small vessels**
Green, glazed terracotta. (Patamban, Mich.).

**1311-1312. Cooking pots**
Terracotta. (Patamban, Mich.).

**1313-1315. Vessels**
Black, glazed terracotta, painted. (Quiroga, Mich.).

**1316-1325. Dogs, pigs, small bulls, small horses and small fish**
Black, glazed terracotta. (Quiroga, Mich.).

**1326-1327. Jars**
Terracotta, decorated in pastillage technique. (Santa Fe, Mich.).

**1328-1330. Small holy virgins**
Glazed terracotta. (Michoacán, Mich.).

**1331-1335. Jars and dishes**
Glazed terracotta. (Michoacán, Mich.).

**1336-1345. Jars, dishes and pitchers**
Light ochre terracotta, glazed and decorated in brown with fish and fishermen. (Tzintzuntzan, Mich.).

**1346-1355. Deer, goats and sheep**
Ochre terracotta and green crockery. (Atzompa, Oax.).

**1356-1365. Orchestra of frogs and deer, dish with frogs and swan figurines**
Glazed green terracotta. (Atzompa, Oax.).

**1366-1367. Flowers**
Glazed terracotta. (Atzompa, Oax.).

**1368-1371. Angels**
Glazed terracotta. (Atzompa, Oax.).

**1372-1373. Jars in the shape of swans**
Glazed terracotta. (Atzompa, Oax.).

**1374-1390. Jars, vases and dishes**
Glazed terracotta. (Oaxaca, Oax.).

**1391-1392. Mermaids, jars and dishes**
Glazed terracotta. (Oaxaca, Oax.).

## Glazed, painted and polished savings banks

An object often found in Mexican ceramics, and deserving a chapter to itself, is the savings bank. It appears in different shapes and different techniques, but the handsomest and most famous banks are made at Tonalá and San Pedro Tlaquepaque, in the State of Jalisco. The decorative motifs are usually animals and fruits. Their quality is so high that collectors don't hesitate to pay very high prices for them. Some of them are influenced by European and Asiatic, French and English works, but the Mexican craftsman re-creates the forms and the vigor of his own primitive mentality is brought to bear on them, and the result is ceramic, full of charm and personality. The most original ones represent smiling human faces and the most popular ones are shaped like "porkers", a symbol of saving.

**1393-1395. Savings banks**
Representing porkers. So-called perfumed ochre terracotta, polished. Flower decorations. (Tonalá, Jal.).

**1396-1403. Savings banks**
Female and male heads. So-called perfumed ochre terracotta, polished and richly decorated. (Tonalá, Jal.).

**1404-1420. Savings banks**
Dogs, carrying baskets in their mouths, lions, hyenas, cows, owls, cocks, horses, swans and bulls. Polychrome ochre terracotta, painted in oil and aquarel and polished. (Tonalá, Jal.).

**1421-1470. Savings banks**
In the shape of fruits. Ochre terracotta, painted in oil. (San Pedro Tlaquepaque, Jal.).

**1471-1480. Savings banks and whistles**
In the shape of lambs, dogs, and cocks. Ochre terracotta, painted in distemper and oil. (San Pedro Tlaquepaque, and Guadalajara, Jal.).

## Miniature sculpture in terracotta

San Pedro Tlaquepaque (the State of Jalisco), in the suburbs of Guadalajara, has long been one of the most important and popular earthenware centers in Mexico. Of the large production of the place the miniature figures in clay should be specially mentioned.

They are painted in oil or fresco and represent with great realism popular types, isolated or in groups.

The family of Panduro has ever since the 19th century, specialized in this form of miniature art. With their artistic quality, expressiveness, and the malicious spirit that inspires them, they recall the work of the engraver Guadalupe Posada. The miniatures of the Panduros particularly the satirical figures representing "catrines" (dandies), "charros" (peasants in riding outfit), "borrachos" (drunks), "vaciladores" (comical types), policemen, and particularly the "calaveras" (skeletons and skulls with satirical significance) remind us, by their spirit and artistic value of the engraver, who so well knew how to interpret the Mexican people's spirit. The descendants of Panduro, as well as others, imitate in that same spirit these figurines, which are for the most part modeled by hand, or started in a mould and finished by hand.

Tlaquepaque also produces sculptures for Christmas. They are rather unconventional reproductions that have certain features in common with the Provençal "santons" in France: apart from the Holy Child, the Virgin, Saint Joseph, the Magi, the angels, shepherds, and animals, they also introduce Adam and Eve, fantastic animals, and persons representing heroes from the War of Independence and from Mexican history — people like Hidalgo and Juárez — who, though they have no apparent connection with this religious celebration, still play a great role in the popular imagination, that incorporates the most varied elements in its world.

**1481-1490. Vendors of fruits, ceramics, vegetables, and flowers**
Also popular dancers and musicians. Miniatures in terracotta, painted in oil. (San Pedro Tlaquepaque, Jal.).

**1491-1515. Small sculptures**
Representing groups of "charros" on horseback, card players, and folk musicians. Terracotta, painted in oil. (San Pedro Tlaquepaque, Jal.).

## Ceramics painted with fresco

Ceramics with fresco painting builds on remote, pre-Hispanic traditions, and originated in the old cultures of Teotihuacán and Maya. It is still the same technique that is used: the clay is covered with a layer of lime and sand that is painted before drying. The painted layer adheres strongly to the surface, on account of the absorption of the material and the method of burning. This kind of earthenware is made mostly in the center of the country, in Acatlán and Huaquechula, Puebla and Metepec. Most of the works from Acatlán are modeled by hand, while the works from Metepec are started in moulds and finished by hand. The former have a white ground, on which is painted polychrome pictures in strong colors, particularly in blue and ochre. The most frequent motifs are doves, bunches of flowers and archangels, and the objects are used as candlesticks. The ceramics of Metepec are very varied in shape and their surface is covered entirely with strong colors, blue, purple, and yellow. Religious themes are preferred by the ceramists of Metepec: the earthly Paradise with Adam and Eve, the Magi, crucifixions, angels and virgins, but horses, lions and sirens are also found, universal motifs which the artists interpret in a highly native fashion. The most interesting and original things are the large fantastic candlesticks with very baroque shapes and rich ornamentation that recalls the pre-Hispanic urns. The "calavera", or skull, appears frequently, since this form of ceramic is used in connection with the cult of the dead.

Another very original type of candlestick is called "the tree of life". It is adorned with religious motifs, comprising angels, archangels, and virgins, sheep, birds, and often, unexpectedly, people in modern dress. They are made in Matamoros de Izúcar (the State of Puebla). These candlesticks are made according to the rules of the fresco technique, but are finished with oil paint. The incense burners, for offerings to the souls, made in Oaxaca as funeral ceramics, and painted in fresco technique, in white and blue, constitute another production that is interesting in its traditional flavor.

**1516-1525. Adam and Eve, crucifix, virgins, magi, a bishop, a shepherd, vendors, small churches and farmers with oxen**
Ochre terracotta, painted in fresco technique, in rose, blue, violet, and black, with applied gilding. (Metepec, Mex.).

**1526-1545. Horses, lions, crowns, young bulls, young cocks, doves, sirens***
Ochre terracotta, painted in fresco technique in various colors, and gilded. (Metepec, Mex.).

**1546-1560. "Trees of life", large and small candlesticks**
With archangels, angels, animals, and flowers. Terracotta, painted in fresco technique in different colors. (Metepec, Mex.).

**1561-1575. Candlesticks**
In the shape of bunches of flowers, bulls, doves, riders, and women with jars. Terracotta, painted in fresco, in blue, violet, and white. (Acatlán and Huaquechula, Pue.).

**1576-1585. "Trees of life", large candlesticks***
Adorned with religious figures, sheep, flowers and birds. Ochre terracotta, painted in fresco technique, and with oil paints. (Matamoros de Izúcar, Pue.).

**1586-1590. Censers**
Semi-spherical, with three supports, decorated with small figures, representing human souls in Purgatory. Terracotta, painted in fresco technique, in ultramarine blue. (Oaxaca, Oax.).

## Ceramics with European and Asiatic influences

The ceramic works, called "talavera", and others, which have been made since the 16th century in the cities of Puebla, Guanajuato, Aguascalientes, and Oaxaca, are the result of the encounter between Spanish and Asiatic ceramics. In their decorations pa-

Horse of Metepec (Mexico). Cat. 1526-1545.

Skeletons of cardboard, Barrio de Jamaica, (Mexico). Cat. 1945-1990.

"Judas". Cat. 1941-1944.

Large wooden box, Olinalá (Guerrero). Cat. 1751-1753.

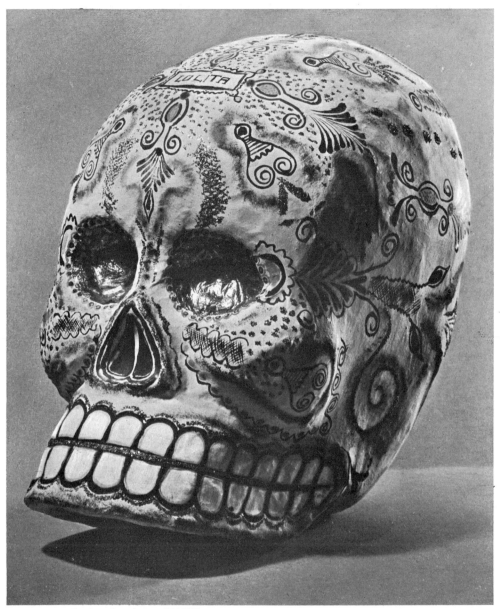

"Calavera" (skull) of cardboard. Cat. 1991-1995.

godas and Chinese birds mingle harmoniously with Moorish and native fret patterns. Cobalt blue, the Asiatic basis of the Mexican "talavera", has been an enduring influence, extending to all ceramics manufactured till to-day. The ceramics of Guanajuato have the polychrome pattern of the Spanish crocqueri that is stamped by Moorish influence. It is distinguished by a free expressiveness of the design and the richness of its colors. Yellows and greens combine with browns, reds and blues, making the resulting type entirely different from other glazed ceramics.

**1591-1600. Jars, dishes**
With profuse decorations of flowers and geometrical patterns. Ochre terracotta. (Guanajuato, Gto.).

**1601-1610. "Tibores" (vases) and flower vases**
Decorated with flowers and birds. Ochre terracotta, painted in cobalt blue. (Puebla, Pue.).

## Modern ceramics inspired by pre-Hispanic models

In recent years ceramics have been made which were inspired by old models, in places like Taxco (Gro.), and Texcoco (Mex.). They are not created by artisans, but by artists, who have gathered craftsmen around them to produce this form of ceramic that interprets old forms, adopting them to modern sensibilities. These works, which are technically very skillful, and have handsome colors, are enjoying an increasing appeal.

**1611-1627. Flower vases, salad bowls, ash trays, large and small dishes**
Polychrome terracotta, with matt or glossy surfaces. (Tissot, Taxco, Gro., and Texcoco, Mex.).

## Masks

Certain products of folk art, like ceramics and textiles, silverware and blown glass, are created by artisans with workshops, where they are occupied exclusively with this production. But others are made occasionally to meet the demands in connection with certain religious or secular celebrations.

The Mexican folk masks have several sources of inspiration: the pre-Hispanic, the European, and the Asiatic traditions. They are used in religious dances and pagan feasts, and as toys for the children. Though they cannot, of course, be compared to the pre-Hispanic masks, they have retained certain native features, particularly in the case of animal masks. The most common motifs are the devil, the peasant and — not least — the skull "calavera", which the Mexican craftsmen have endowed with great poetic force.

**1628-1640. Masks**
Representing men, women, old men, peasants, "calaveras" (skulls), heads of swans and other animals. Tin plate, lacquered wood, and poly-chrome cardboard. (Monterrey (the State of Nuevo León), Tlaxcala, Celaya, Guanajuato and Olinala (Gro.).

## Toys

One of the products of folk art that show the greatest abundance and artistic variety is the toy. The colors are strong and clear, the shapes graceful and imaginative. Some of the toys are inspired by European sources, like the clown, the circus people, the devil. But Mexican craftsmen have stamped them with their own tastes and character. The materials are highly varied: wood, palm leaves, clay, filligree, wire, maize leaves, cardboard, seeds, feathers, etc., and they are used with great inventiveness and ingenuity to create moving animals, miniature services, dancing puppets, religious processions of paper and beans, macabre toys, representing skeletons that get up from their biers, and many other things that are no less curious and exciting. The "tule"-dolls (made of a kind of woven cane or of maize leaves) are made, like the handmade dolls of earthenware, in the States of Jalisco, Michoacán, Querétaro, Mexico, Puebla, Oaxaca, Veracruz, Guerrero, Chiapas and Yucatán.

**1641-1650. Small male figures, goats and horses**
Ochre terracotta with white paint. (Yucatán).

**1651.-1655. Sheep**
Terracotta painted in fresco-technique. (Guanajuato, Gto.).

**1656-1660. Miniature doll's kitchens**
Wood, glass and terracotta. (Puebla, Pue.).

**1661-1680. Miniature guitars, boxes, furniture and chairs**
"Tejamanil", painted wood. (Paracho, Mich.).

**1681-1690. Clowns on horseback, partisans, small horses and dolls**
Painted cardboard. (Celaya, Gto.).

**1691-1695. Dancing Indians**
Terracotta and textiles. (Mexico).

**1696-1705. Monkeys playing musical instruments**
Wire and plush. (Mexico).

**1706-1730. Crocodiles and other animals**
Painted wood. (Guanajuato, Gto.).

**1731-1735. Goats**
Terracotta. (Tlaxcala, Tlax.).

**1736-1750. Doves**
Paper and cardboard. (Puebla, Pue.).

## Lacquer work

Lacquer work is a pre-Hispanic industry, many centuries old, primarily enriched by Asiatic influence, and later on by European influence, particularly in the way of rendering people and flowers. There are several methods of application: incrustation, which is very like the so-called "cloisonné": a layer of lacquer is applied, and then smoothed by hand, till it is dry, uniform and glossy, and on this base the decoration is projected. Then the carving starts, according to the colors and forms of the composition, and each section is filled with a color. It is rubbed and polished, and this process goes on till the decoration is finished.

Another technique, called "incised", consists in applying by hand colored layers, one on top of the other, and then carve them according to the sketch, letting the colors of the lower layers appear.

In the "paint-technique" the decoration is drawn with a very fine awl on a smooth monochrome surface, usually black. Then the parts of the composition that are to be gilded are painted. Finally the rest of the extremely delicate drawing is filled out in other nuances.

Lacquer work is used for chests, boxes, fruit bowls, "xicalpextles" (a sort of bowl made of big calabashes), "jícaras" (small bowls of wood or dried pumpkins). The peasants give them to their brides as brideal gifts.

**1751-1753. Large chests ***
Lacquered pine, incised technique. (Olinalá, Gro.).

**1754. Large chest**
Aloe-wood, painted lacquer. (Olinalá, Gro.).

**1755-1760. Small painted trays**
Lacquered pine, incised technique. (Olinalá, Gro.).

**1761-1770. Large trays**
Lacquered pine, incised technique. (Olinalá, Gro.).

**1771-1773. Small trays**
Lacquered aloe, incised technique. (Olinalá, Gro.).

**1774-1776. "Bateas"**
(Fruit trays). Lacquered pine, incised technique. (Olinalá, Gro.).

**1777-1779. Trays**
Pine, lacquer-encrusted. (Uruapan, Mich.).

**1780-1785. Fruit garlands**
Made of small calabashes, lacquered and painted. (Uruapan, Mich.).

**1786-1787. "Jícaras"**
Lacquered pine, encrustation technique. (Uruapan, Mich.).

**1788-1789. "Xicalpextles"**
Lacquered, painted technique. (Chapa de Corzo, Chis.).

**1790. Small box**
Lacquered white, painted technique. (Pátzcuaro, Mich.).

## Silverware

The gold and silversmiths' craft in Mexico goes back to pre-Hispanic times, but when the colonial period started, it was divided into several general types: religious, popular, jewellery, and household objects.

The production of silverware for religious use has always been abundant, and it has been inspired by European examples of Romanesque, Gothic, and baroque character. In the 17th century this production acquired a specifically Mexican character and flourished accordingly. Let us only mention the treasures of the cathedrals: altar fronts in chased and engraved gold or silver, monstrances, ciboria, missals, and candlesticks. Nowadays the Mexican gold and silversmiths produce handsome and richly decorated objects for religious use.

Among the different forms of popular silver work and jewellery the gold and silver filigree for earrings and necklaces hold a prominent place. The works in Moorish style, imported from Spain, were very well received by the rural population who recognized in it the techniques and types of pre-Hispanic gold and silver work.

Silverware for domestic use is, like the jewellery, strongly reminiscent of the styles of the old ceramics.

The most important centers of the craftsmanlike production of gold and silverware are: Taxco (Gro.), Mexico, Puebla, Morelia, and Guadalajara, and of these Taxco remains the principal one. In this city more than 800 workshops are primarily dedicated to the production of silver and jewellery. In colonial times Taxco was an important mining town. In the 19th century it declined abruptly, when its principal silver beds were unexpectedly exhausted. The artistic tradition was, however, so strong that the workers kept up production after the decline, making artefacts of tin. The present flourishing of Taxco began about 35 years ago, when the silversmiths, who had formed a new union, saw their products very well received, both in Mexico and abroad. The silverware of Taxco has developed according to its own forms and style, at first hesitantly and occasionally inspired, later on in a well defined style.

Apart from production of jewellery, the Taxco artisans practise other techniques such as assembling different metals, mosaics of silver and other metals, that are polished till they acquire a brilliant shine. Expensive woods, and semi-precious stones in lively colors are used as decorative complements. The pre-Hispanic art of mosaics, particularly with turquoise is currently reviving at Taxco, and the same is true of works in amethyst, obsidian, quartz, rock crystal, lapis lazuli, and other semi-precious stones, that are found in abundance in the Mexican soil.

**1791-1799. Trays, sugar bowls, spoons, brooch, and pendant of a necklace**
So-called "assembled metals" technique. (Workshop of Castillo Bros., Taxco, Gro.).

**1800-1815. Trays, boxes, cross, bracelets, necklaces, key-rings**
and jewellery. Gilded silver, silver inlaid with turquoise and lapis lazuli. (Castillo Bros., Taxco, Gro.).

**1816. Fish**
Silver work with engraved decorations. (Castillo Bros., Taxco, Gro.).

**1817-1821. Large and small jars, sugar bowl, milk jug**
Silver and rosewood. (Castillo Bros., Taxco, Gro.).

**1822-1858. Necklaces, bracelets, and pendants**
Silver with applied amethyst, obsidian, pearls and turquoise. (Pineda Bros., Taxco, Gro.).

## Basket-weaving and cane-weaving

The origins of basket-weaving go back to precolumbian antiquity. In the codices we find the floors of the dwellings covered with luxurious rugs woven of reeds and sedges. These raw materials are now used to make the "petates", which the poor use both as beds and as rugs.

Almost all regions of Mexico produce large quantities of works woven of osiers, palm, reeds or straw, comprising all types of basket-weaving or cane-weaving, such as baskets and purses and "sombreros", the famous and popular Mexican hats of palm fibres, of which more than thirty models exist, varying according to the climate and taste in the various regions.

The Mexican basket-weaving art is original by virtue of its forms, and is often enriched with lively, attractive colors. The peculiar figures of maize leaves, sedges and palm fibres, and the brooms with straw handles should be mentioned. The very inventive folk artists often find new themes and motifs.

The principal centers of this industry are Toluca and Lerma, in the State of Mexico, San Juán del Río, in the State of Querétaro, Oaxaca, Santa Ana Acatlán, the State of Jalisco, and Sahuayo. The State of Michoacán is specially known for its sombreros.

**1859-1865. Partisans and riders**
Sedge. (Lerma, Mex. and Oaxaca, Oax.).

**1866-1875. Angel musicians, stars and virgins ***
Sedge. (Lerma, Mex.).

**1876-1885. Christs and angels ***
Woven straw. (San Juán del Río, Que.).

**1886-1890. Angels, doves, cats, birds and poultry**
Osiers. (San Juán del Río, Que.).

**1891-1910. Large and small baskets**
Purses, glassholders, small roosters, and bunches of flowers. Polychrome and woven palm fibres. (Oaxaca, Oax., Puebla, Pue., and Toluca, Mex.).

**1911-1930. Figures**
Maize leaves and palm. (Santa Ana Acatlán, Jal.).

**1931-1935. Small brooms**
Polychrome straw. (Oaxaca, Oax.).

**1936-1940. Sombreros**
Palm. (Teocaltiche, Jal., and Cuernavaca, Mor.).

## Judas-figures

On Easter Saturday at ten o'clock in the morning the burning of "Judas" takes place
– one of the most important folk celebrations in Mexico. These "Judas" figures are
large dolls of sedges, covered with cardboard and paper ("papier maché") in strong
colors, and with attachments for fire crackers, which are made to explode in the streets
and squares of the towns and villages with much merriment. Afterwards the children
collect the sweets that are put inside the dolls.

One of the first contributions to the conversion of the natives to Christianity made
by the "conquistadores", was to establish the custom of burning paper effigies of the
traitor Judas. The Mexican population adopted this custom, but in time it acquired a
new meaning, so that by burning the "judas", they symbolically project vengeful feelings on national or international figures who are odious to the people. It should be added that they also occasionally burn in effigy legendary or real persons whom they like,
e.g. movie stars or popular actors.

In the week before Easter "Judases" of every size are seen in the streets. Taxi-drivers,
bus conductors, and bicyclists buy the figures, with which they adorn their vehicles, re-
moving them only when the celebration is over.

**1941-1944. "Judases" ***
Representing a clown, a "charro", a devil and a
skeleton. Large dolls of a kind of reed and

covered with several layers of cardboard and
painted paper. 13x5 feet. (Barrio de Jamaica,
Mex.).

## "Calaveras" (Death's heads)

In Mexico the 2nd of November (All Souls Day) is the Day of the Dead, which is in
no way a day of gloom or sadness. Mexican humor has transformed the symbol of
death into cakes and sweets, and objects of fun and farce. On this day the bakers sell
a special kind of bread with icing called bread of the dead, and in the markets skeletons of sugar and cardboard in the form of toys, are sold by the hundreds of vendors. The "calaveras" large and small ones made of cardboard, or of sugar are adorned with tin foil in brilliant colors and have the most common Mexican first names in-
scribed on their foreheads. None of these skulls suggest a melancholy mood: The buy-
ers take them quietly home and keep them a few days. From an artistic point of wiev
the skulls are sometimes as beautiful as the ones made several centuries ago of rock
crystal, obsidian, or other stones, covered with mosaics.

The Day of the Dead is essentially a pagan celebration, in spite of the lugubrious sound
of churchbells and the tomb monuments in the churches. Catholicism has not been able

to destroy the cult of the dead that has survived from Aztec times, and which continues to inspire these celebrations. In our time the Mexican "calaveras" that so surprise foreigners, are mainly a means to comment upon the customs of the living by help of the dead. Manuel Manilla and Guadalupe Posada, the Mexican graphic artists of the 19th century, who were precursors of contemporary painting, first used the "calaveras" as an element in their satire and social criticism. This form of artistic expression caught the imagination of the people, and since then the artisans also made "calaveras" of sugar and all kinds of malicious toys. In the market stalls the "calaveras" die with laughter, i.e. laugh with open jaws, and the skeletons of wood, wire and cardboard play their musical instruments and dance there — "jarabe", "rumba", etc.

**1945-1990. Big and little skeletons ***
Representing humorous figures, mostly musicians. Cardboard painted in distemper. (Barrio de Jamaica, Mex.).

**1991-1995. "Calaveras"**
Large skulls of painted cardboard, with applied tinfoil and proper names on their foreheads. (Barrio de Jamaica, Mex.).

**1996-2010. Skeletons**
Representing various people, playing musical instruments and dancing. Clay, wire and paper. (Mexico).

**2011-2013. Large skeletons**
Terracotta with white paint. (Mexico).

## Copper, tin and tinfoil

The city of Santa Clara del Cobre (the State of Michoacán) is a center dedicated to the production of objects of laminated and hammered copper for domestic uses. They are made in handsome, simple shapes, and although they are inspired by Spanish sources, they have their own personal, attractive character in the designs and engravings that adorn them (mostly flower and bird motifs). The old Tarascan population of Michoacán knew metallurgy long before the arrival of the Spaniards, and used metals, particularly copper and silver. Their priests wore on their chests a decoration in the shape of thongs of copper or silver, as an emblem of their clerical status.

The objects of tin were a popular imitation of the silversmiths' works, and they were carefully laminated and polished. Contemporary artisans make handsome candlesticks of tin plate for the village churches, carefully elaborated altar niches, star shaped lamps, chandeliers, mirror frames, and numerous objects shaped like flowers, animals, or abstract forms, as well as very expressive masks.

These artisans also produce a large selection of flowers in tin plate. These are mixed with flowers of brilliantly colored tinfoil, and used as decorations for house altars or small churches. The most important centers for works in tin, laminated or engraved copper and metal flowers, are Mexico, Taxco, Santa Clara del Cobre, Puebla, Oaxaca, and Guadalajara.

**2014-2021. Large dishes, flower vases, fruit bowls, water jugs, and trays**
Hammered copper, decorated with engraved patterns of flowers and birds. (Santa Clara, Mich.).

**2022-2024. Glass case with miniature objects**
Tin, mirror and glass. (Mexico).

**2025-2045. Small palms, candlesticks, sideboards, roosters, pineapples, and flower garland**
Painted tin plate. (Taxco, Gro.).

**2046-2049. Flower garlands**
Tin foil. (Oaxaca, Oax.).

## Blown glass

Though the traditions have changed through the centuries, and though the Mexican artisan has often been inspired by foreign models, he has never submitted to servile imitation, and his work is still stamped by his strong imagination. One of the most striking examples of this is Mexican glass blowing.

The first works in blown glass, after the method introduced by the Spaniards, were from La Granja. Later on others followed, imitating Venetian glass. But the Mexican craftsman quickly changed the character of his production, not only changing forms and colors, but also adapting his sources and motifs to his sensibility.

The Mexican production of glass and blown glass is highly varied: bottles in the shape of virgins or famous people, vases, flasks, flower vases, often of very picturesque shapes, are often seen in popular restaurants and cafés. Many objects for domestic use and many toys and ornaments are also made of blown glass. These things are popular because of their handsome shapes and colors: blue, wine red, violet, and dark yellow. The glass industry flourishes particularly in Mexico, Texcoco (Mex.), Guadalajara and Oaxaca.

**2050-2090. Large and small vases, bottles, flasks, colored balls, liqueur bottles**
Blown glass, handmade. (Barrio de Carretones, Mex., and Guadalajara, Jal.).

**2091-2093. Spiralshaped vases, descanters, "catrinas" (dandies)**
Glass. (Texcoco, Mex.).

**2094-2143. Fruit bowls, small and large animals**
Blown glass, handmade. (Mexico and Oaxaca, Oax.).

## The "charro" costume

The Mexican "charro" costume derives from Zamora in Spain. It is the costume of horseback riders and cattle herders. It consists of a round felt hat with narrow brim, a short jacket, and a pair of pants that are tightfitting around the waist, and widen down the sides. When it was adopted in Mexico as a luxury costume, both in towns and in the country, it was changed in several ways: a large sombrero with a wide brim in different colors, and decorated with embroideries in gold or silver thread. The short jacket was not changed, but the pants were made tightfitting all the way down and the whole costume was trimmed with silver buttons. It was usually made of chamois leather and wool. The work costume is of the same cut, but made of tightly woven woolen cloth, and without decorations. The felt hat was replaced by a palm hat.

This costume was completed by the equipment necessitated by work in the fields: deerskin gloves to protect the hands, when cattle are to be caught with lasso, spurs and "sarape".

**2144-2155. Large charro hats**

**2156-2161. Complete costume of chamois leather with silver decorations**
"Machete" spurs, lassoes, and saddle. (Mexico, Oaxaca, San Juán del Río, Gro., and Amozoc, Pue.).

## "Sarapes" and "rebozos"

The sarape is a very common garment in Mexico. It derives from Jerez in Spain, but underwent a radical change in Mexico. It is always rectangular, but the length and the way it is worn vary. The "sarape" proper is worn, rolled around the body. The "jorongo" has an opening for the head in the middle. The "gabán" is like the "jorongo", only smaller. All types have fringes along the edge.

The Mexican sarapes are of fine or ordinary wool. They are all handwoven on small looms. The ones from Saltillo and San Miguel are decorated with flowers and patterns. In the beginning, and particularly in the last century, these designs were orientally inspired. In the 19th century the ornamentation of the sarapes from Saltillo changed and it is now limited to ordinary fringes, or tassels, in strong colors, that merge and mix.

The "sarapes" from Tlaxcala, Oaxaca and Michoacán are the most indigenous ones, because of their strong colors and sober decoration. Some are adorned with silhouets of bulls, doves, flowers, geometrical patterns and fret motifs. There are also fringes, reminiscent of the motifs of "pintaderas" (a kind of native seal, used for painting of the body and for decoration of woven materials). In many "sarapes" from our time we also find the sun, a traditional native element.

The production of "sarapes" is very important nowadays. Because of their decorative value they are used as bedspreads and rugs, as well as garments.

Another fundamental part of the Mexican costume, is the "rebozo" that is mostly worn by women. It is rectangular, and lengthened by fringes. Women can wrap themselves in it, and carry their packages and children in them, while being covered themselves. It is safe to say that every Mexican woman, regardless of social position, owns at least one "rebozo".

Some "rebozos" are refined and expensive, others more modest, but no less handsome. They are made of real or artificial silk or cotton and in many colors. In some of them gold and silverthreads have been woven, and they are most often handwoven. The most famous ones the so-called "bolita", are made of a very fine cotton yarn. They are so flexible, that they can easily be drawn through a ring. The interesting thing about them, artistically, is the fringe, which sometimes is up to 20 inches long. "Rebozos" are primarily made at Santa Maria (San Luís Potosí), Pátzcuaro (Mich.), Moroleón (Gto.), Tenancingo (Mex.), and Oaxaca.

### 2162-2170. "Sarapes"
Wool, woven with threads of different colors in patterns, representing doves, jaguars, flowers, fret motifs, red sun and black sun, white and black lines, rectangles, mosaics, and blue and white diamond shapes. (Saltillo, Coah.; San Miguel, Allende, Gto.; Ocotitlán, Oax.; Teotitlán del Camino, Oax.; Tlaxcala, Tlax.; and Tlahuac, Mex.).

### 2171-2175. "Jorongos"
Woven wool, with threads of different colors, representing silhouets of bulls, small doves and mosaics. (Nahuantzen, Mich., Ocatepec, Harinas, Mex.).

### 2176-2198. "Rebozos"
Real and artificial silk, cotton. Gold thread, colored threads, various patterns. (Pátzcuaro, Mich.; Santa María, S.L.P.; Puebla, Pue.; Moroleón, Gto., and Tenancingo, Mex.).

### 2199-2200. Shawls
White and red, black and violet cotton, decorated with embroidered flowers. (Tlatlauiqui, Pue., and Tenancingo, Mex.).

# Bibliography

*Cultural and historical background*

Caso, Alfonso: El Pueblo del Sol. México, 1953.

Centro de Investigaciones Antropológicas de México: Esplendor del México Antiguo. 2 Tomes. México, D.F., 1959.

Danzel, Theodor Wilhelm: Mexiko. Band I-II. Hagen in Westfalen, 1922.

Diaz del Castillo, Bernal: Historia Verdadera de la Conquista de Nueva Espana. Ediciones Mexicanas. México, 1950.

Disselhof, Hans Dieter: Geschichte der Altamerikanischen Kulturen. München, 1953.

Duyvis, Guda E. G. Van Giffen: De Azteken. Amsterdam, 1957.

Garibay, K. Angel María: Historia de la Literatura Nahuatl. Editorial Porrua. México, 1953.

Gerbrands, Dr. A. A.: Dertig Eeuwen Mexicaanse Kunst – De Culturele Achtergronden. s-Gravenhage, 1959.

Guzman, Eulalia: Caracteres Esenciales del Arte Antiguo Mexicano, su Sentido Fundamental. Universidad Nal. Aut. T.V. Números 27-30. México, 1933.

Hoppenot, Hélène: Mexique Magie Maya. Lausanne, 1954.

Krickeberg, Walter: Märchen der Azteken und Inkaperuaner, Maya und Muisca. Jena, 1928.

Krickeberg, Walter: Altmexikanische Kulturen. Berlin.

Lehmann, Walter: Aus den Pyramidenstädten in Alt-Mexiko. Berlin, 1933.

Morley, Sylvanus Griswold: The Ancient Maya. Third Edition. Revised by George W. Brainerd. Stanford, Cal. 1956.

Portilla, Miguel León: La Visión de los Vencidos. Universidad Nal. Aut. de México. México, 1960.

Prescott, William H.: Die Eroberung von Mexiko. Herausgegeben von Gerdt Kutscher. Berlin-Grunewald, 1956.

Preuss, Konrad Theodor: Mexikanische Religion. Bilderatlas zur Religionsgeschichte: 16. Leipzig. 1930.

Rivet, Paul: Cités Maya. Paris, 1954.

Sahagun, Fray Bernardino de: Historia General de las Cosas de Nueva Espana. Editorial Nueva Espana. México, 1946.

Séjourné, Laurette: Pensamiento y Religión en México Antiguo. Fondo de Cultura Económica. México, 1957.

Seler, Eduard: Gesammelte Abhandlungen zur Amerikanischen Sprach- und Altertumskunde. Band I-V. Berlin, 1902-1923.

Soustelle, Jacques: La Vie Quotidienne des Aztèques à la Veille de la Conquête Espagnole. Hachette, Paris, 1955.

Spinden, Herbert Joseph: Maya Art and Civilization. Indian Hills, Colorado, 1957.

Termer, Franz: Die Mayaforschung (Nova Acta Leopoldina. N.F. Band 15, Nr. 105). Leipzig, 1952.

Thompson, John Eric S.: The Rise and Fall of Maya Civilization. Norman, Oklahoma, 1954.

Vaillant, George C.: Aztecs of Mexico. Origin, Rise and Fall of the Aztec Nation. Garden City, 1948.


*Pre-Columbian*

Bernal, Ignacio: Compendio de Arte Mesoamericano (Enciclopedia Mexicana del Arte: 7). México, 1950.

Burland, Cottie A.: Art and Life in Ancient Mexico. Oxford, 1948.

Covarrubias, Miguel: Indian Art of Mexico and Central America. New York, 1957.

Disselhoff, H. D. y.s. Linne: Amérique Précolombienne. Édition Albin Michel. Paris, 1961.

Fernández, Justino: Coatlicue. Estética del Arte Indígena Antiguo. México, 1954.

Groth Kimball, Irmgard y Franz Feuchtwanger: Kunst im alten Mexiko. Freiburg in Brsg., 1953.

Joce, Thomas Athol: Maya and Mexican Art. London, 1927.

Kelemen, Pal: Medieval American Art. Vol. 1-2. New York, 1946.

Krickeberg, Walter: Die Kunst der Altamerikanischen Kulturvölker. Stuttgart, 1957.

Lehmann, Walter: Altmexikanische Kunstgeschichte. Ein Entwurf in Umrissen (Orbis Pictus-Weltkunst-Bücherei: 8). Berlin o.J., 1922.

Linne, Sigvald: Treasures of Mexican Art. 2.000 Years of Art and Art Handicraft. Stockholm, 1956.

Lothrop, S. K., W. F. Foshag y Joy Mahler: Pre-Columbian Art. Robert Woods Bliss Collection. London, 1957.

Medioni, Gilbert: Art Maya du Mexique et du Guatémala. Ancien Empire. Paris, 1950.

Pijoan, José: Arte Precolombino Mexicano y Maya (Summa Artis. Historia General del Arte: X). Madrid, 1946.

Rivet, Paul: Alt-Mexiko. Aufnahmen von Gisèle Freund. München, 1954.

Spinden, Herbert Joseph: A Study of Maya Art. Its Subject Matter and Historical Development (Memoirs of the Peabody Museum of American Archaeology and Ethnology, Harvard University: VI). Cambridge, 1913.

Toscano, Salvador: Arte Precolombino de México y de la América Central (2 ed.). México, 1952.

Vaillant, George C.: Artists and Craftsmen in Ancient Central America (The American Museum of Natural History. Science Guide: 88). New York, 1945.

Westheim, Paul: Arte Antiguo de México. México-Buenos Aires, 1950.

Westheim, Paul: Ideas Fundamentales del Arte Prehispánico en México. México-Buenos Aires, 1957.

Instituto Nacional de Antropología e Historia: Pre-Spanish Art of México. México, 1946.

Aguilar P., Carlos H.: La Orfebrería en el México Precortesiano (Acta Antropologica II:2). México, 1946.

Ashton, Dore et Lee Boltin: Abstract Art before Columbus. New York, 1957.

Bernal, Ignacio: Mexiko. Präkolumbianische Wandmalereien. Vorwort von Jacques Soustelle. UNESCO-Sammlung der Weltkunst. München, 1958.

Caso, Alfonso: Las Estelas Zapotecas. México, 1928.

Caso, Alfonso et Ignacio Bernal: Urnas de Oaxaca (Memorias del Instituto Nacional de Antropología e Historia: II). México, 1952.

Covarrubias, Miguel: Mezcala. Ancient Mexican Sculpture. New York, 1956.

Enciso, Jorge: Design Motifs of Ancient Mexico. New York, 1953.

Holmes, William H.: Archaeological Studies among the Old Cites of Mexico. Vols. I-II. (Field Museum of Natural History Publications, Anthropological Series: 1, 1.). Chicago, 1895 y 1897.

Linne, Sigvald: Archaeological Researches at Teotihuacan, Mexico (The Ethnographical Museum of Sweden, N.S.: 1). Stockholm, 1934.

Linne, Sigvald: Zapotecan Antiquities and the Paulson Collection in the Ethnographical Museum of Sweden. Stockholm, 1938.

Lothrop, Samuel Kirkland: Pottery of Costa Rica and Nicaragua. (Vols. I-II). (Contributions from the Museum of the American Indian, Heye Foundation: VIII). New York, 1926.

Marquina, Ignacio: Arquitectura Prehispánica (Memorias del Instituto Nacional de Antropología e Historia: I). México, 1951.

Medioni, Gilbert: L'Art Tarasque du Mexique Occidental. Paris 1952.

Medioni, Gilbert et Marie Thérèse Pinto: Art in Ancient Mexico. New York, 1941.

Proskouriakoff, Tatjana: An Album of Maya Architecture (Carnegie Institution of Washington, Publ. N° 558). Washington, 1946.

Proskouriakoff, Tatjana: A study of Classic Maya Sculpture (Carnegie Institution of Washington, Publ. N° 593). Washington, 1950.

Saville, Marshall H.: The Goldsmith's Art in Ancient Mexico (Museum of the American Indian, Heye Foundation. Indian Notes and Monographs). New York, 1920.

Saville, Marshall H.: Turquoise Mosaic Art in Ancient Mexico (Contributions from the Museum of the American Indian, Heye Foundation: VI). New York, 1922.

Saville, Marshall H.: The Woodcarver's Art in Ancient Mexico (Contributions from the Museum of the American Indian, Heye Foundation: IX). New York, 1925.

Solier, Wilfredo du: La Plástica en las Cabecitas Arcáicas del Valle de México y la Huaxteca (Enciclopedia Mexicana de Arte: 2). México, 1950.

Stirling, Matthew W.: Stone Monuments of Southern México (Bureau of American Ethnology, Bulletin 138). Washington, 1943.

Villagra Caleti. Agustin: Bonampak, La Ciudad de los Muros Pintados (Instituto Nacional de Antropología e Historia). México, 1949.

Westheim, Paul: La Escultura del México Antiguo (Universidad Nal. Aut. de México. Colección de Arte: 1). Mexico, 1956.

*Art of the New Spain*

Atl, Benitez, Toussaint: Iglesias de México. Secretaría de Hacienda y Crédito Público, 6 vols. México, 1924-1927.

Baxter, Silvestre: Arquitectura Hispano-Colonial en México. (Traducción de la edición en inglés de 1901). México, 1934. Introducción y notas de Manuel Toussaint.

Diez Barroso, Francisco: El Arte en Nueva Espana. México, 1921.

Fernández, Justino: El Retablo de los Reyes. Estética del Arte de la Nueva Espana. Instituto de Investigaciones Estéticas. Universidad Nal. Aut. de México. México, 1959.

Gante, Pablo C. de: La Arquitectura de México en el Siglo XVI. Editorial Porrúa, S.A. México, 1954.

Keleman, Pál.: Baroque and Rococo in Latin America. The Mac Millan Co. New York, 1951.

Kubler, George: Mexican Architecture of the Sixteenth Century. Yale University Press. New Haven, 1948.

Mac Gregor, Luís: El Plateresco en México. Editorial Porrúa, S.A. México, 1954.

Ricard, Robert: La Conquista Espiritual de México. Editorial Polis, Mexico, 1947.

Rojas, Pedro: Tonantzintla. Colección Arte 2. Dirección General de Publicaciones. Universidad Nal. Aut. de México. México 1956.

Toussaint, Manuel: Arte Colonial en México. Instituto de Investigaciones Estéticas. Universidad Nal. Aut. de México. México, 1956.

La Catedral de México y el Sagrario Metropolitano. México, 1948.

Paseos Coloniales. Imprenta Universitaria, México, 1939.

Taxco. Publicaciones de la Secretaría de Hacienda y Crédito Público. México, 1931.

Pátzcuaro. Instituto de Investigaciones Estéticas y Escuela de Arquitectura. Universidad Nal. Aut. de México. México, 1942.

Arte Mudéjar en América. Editorial Porrúa, S.A. México, 1954.

Planos de la Ciudad de México. Siglos XVI y XVII. En colaboración con Federico Gómez

Orozco y Justino Fernández. Instituto de Investigaciones Estéticas. Universidad Nal. Aut. de México. México, 1938.

Velázquez Chávez, Agustín: Tres Siglos de Pintura Colonial. Editorial Polis. México, 1939.

Villegas, Victor Manuel: El Gran Signo Formal del Barroco. Instituto de Investigaciones Estéticas. Universidad Nal. Aut. de México. México, 1956.

Maza, Francisco de la: Los Retablos Dorados de Nueva Espana. Enciclopedia Mexicana de Arte N° 9. México, 1950.

Wilder Weismann, Elizabeth: Escultura Mexicana. 1521-1821. Editorial Atlante. México, 1950.

*Modern and Mexican Art*

Calderón de la Barca, Mme: Life in Mexico. London 1843. Everyman's Library N° 664. London 1954. Introduction by Manuel Romero de Terreros (New edition). La Vida en México. Traducción y notas de Felipe Teixidor. Biblioteca Porrúa, México, 1958.

Encina, Juan de la: El Paisajista José María Velasco. El Colegio de México. México, 1943.

Fernández, Justino: El Grabado en Lámina en la Academia de San Carlos durante el Siglo XIX. Prólogo de Manuel Toussaint. Reimpresión de 24 láminas por Carlos Alvarado Lang. Instituto de Investigaciones Estéticas. Universidad Nal. Aut. de México. México, 1938.

Gamboa, Fernando: Posada, Printmaker to the Mexican People. The Art Institute of Chicago. Chicago, 1944.

Linati, Claudio: Trajes Civiles, Militares e Religiosos de México. (1828). Estudio y traducción de Justino Fernández. Prólogo de Manuel Toussaint, Reproducción facsimilar de la obra original. Instituto de Investigaciones Estéticas. Universidad Nal. Aut. de México. México, 1956.

Montenegro, Roberto: Pintura Mexicana. 1830-1860. México, 1933.

Gardoza y Aragón, Luís: La Nube y el Reloj. Ediciones de la Universidad Nal. Aut. de México. México, 1940.

Pinturas Murales de la Universidad de Guadalajara, 1937.

Pintura Mexicana Contemporánea. Imprenta Universitaria. México, 1953.

Orozco: Estudios y Fuentes del Arte en México. Instituto de Investigaciones Estéticas. Universidad Nal. Aut. de México. México, 1959.

Fernández, Justino: Prometeo. Ensayo sobre Pintura Contemporánea. Editorial Porrúa, S.A. México, 1945.

Litografos y Grabadores Mexicanos Contemporáneos. Editorial Delfin, 1944. Forma e Idea. Editorial Porrúa, S.A. México, 1956.

Obras de José Clemente Orozco en la Colección Carrillo Gil. Catálogo y notas de J. Fernández. México 1949. Complemento y notas del Dr. Alvar Carrillo Gil. México, 1953. (2 vols.).

Textos de Orozco. Con un estudio y apéndice de J. Fernández. Estudios y Fuentes del Arte en México N° 4. Instituto de Investigaciones Estéticas. Universidad Nal. Aut. de México. México, 1955.

Arte Mexicano de sus Orígines a Nuestros Días. Editorial Porrúa, S.A. México, 1958.

Arte Moderno y Contemporáneo de México. Instituto de Investigaciones Estéticas. Universidad Nal. Aut. de México. México, 1952.

Documentos para la Historia de la Litografía en México. Recopilados por Edmundo O'Gorman. Imprenta Universidad. México, 1955.

Goldwater, Robert: Rufino Tamayo. The Quadrangle Press. New York, 1947.

Helm, Mac Kinley: Modern Mexican Painters. Harper Bros. New York & London, 1941.

Man of Fire: Orozco. The Institute of Contemporary Art, Boston. Harcourt, Brace & Co. New York, 1958.

Myers, Bernard S.: Mexican Painting in our Time. Oxford University Press. New York, 1956.

Myers, I. E.: Mexico's Modern Architecture. Introduction by Richard Neutra. Architectural Book Publishing Co. New York, 1952.

Orozco, Jose Clemente: Autobiografía. (1942). Ediciones Occidente. México, 1945.

Paz, Octavio: Tamayo. Colección Arte 6. Dirección General de Publicaciones. Universidad Nal. Aut. de México. México, 1958.

Portrait of Latin America as seen by her Printmakers. Editor: Anne Lyon Haight. Preface; Monroe Wheeler. Introduction: Jean Charlot. Hastings House Publishers. New York, 1946.

Ramos, Samuel: Diego Rivera. Colección Arte 4. Dirección General de Publicaciones. Universidad Nal. Aut. de México. México, 1958.

Reed, Alma: Orozco. Fondo de Cultura Económica. México, 1955.

Diego Rivera: Cincuenta Anos de su Labor Artística. Instituto Nacional de Bellas Artes. México, 1951.

Schmeckebier, Laurence E.: Modern Mexican Art. The University of Minnesota Press. Minneapolis, 1939.

Siqueiros, David Alfaro. No hay más Ruta que la Nuestra. México, 1945.

Monografía de la obra de Siqueiros. Instituto Nacional de Bellas Artes. México, 1951.

Tibel, Raquel: Siqueiros, Introductor de Realidades. Universidad Nal. Aut. de México. México, 1961.

Westheim, Paul: Hamayo. Ediciones Artes de México. México, 1957.

Wolfe, Bertram D.: Diego Rivera. His Life and Times. Alfred A. Knopf. New York, London, 1939.

*Mexican folk art*

Anderson, Laurence: El Arte de la Platería en México. Editorial Porrúa, S.A. México, 1956.

Atl, Dr.: Las Artes Populares en México. Editorial Cultura. (2 vols.). México, 1921.

Toor, Frances: A Treasury of Mexican Folkways. Crown Publishers. New York, 1947.

Maroto, Gabriel García: La Arquitectura Popular de México. Instituto Nacional de Bellas Artes. México, 1954.